MANUAL FOR SHORT-TERM PSYCHOANALYTIC CHILD THERAPY (PaCT)

MANUAL FOR SHORT-TERM PSYCHOANALYTIC CHILD THERAPY (PaCT)

*Tanja Göttken and
Kai von Klitzing*

Routledge
Taylor & Francis Group

LONDON AND NEW YORK

First published 2014 by Karnac Books Ltd.

Published 2018 by Routledge
2 Park Square, Milton Park, Abingdon, Oxon OX14 4RN
711 Third Avenue, New York, NY 10017, USA

Routledge is an imprint of the Taylor & Francis Group, an informa business

British Library Cataloguing in Publication Data

A C.I.P. for this book is available from the British Library

ISBN 9781780490366 (pbk)

Edited, designed and produced by The Studio Publishing Services Ltd
www.publishingservicesuk.co.uk
e-mail: studio@publishingservicesuk.co.uk

CONTENTS

ACKNOWLEDGEMENTS

Writing this book has been a long process in which many people gave us their encouraging support. Now, we can present the result of this intense engagement with this *Manual for Short-term Psychoanalytic Child Therapy (PaCT)* and it is a pleasurable task to write the acknowledgments for this book.

We would like to start by thanking the psychologists and medical doctors in training who work at the Department of Child and Adolescent Psychiatry, Psychotherapy and Psychosomatics, at the University of Leipzig, Germany. We want to thank them for their enthusiasm in piloting the PaCT manual and their openness in discussing systematic, theoretical, and technical problems with us when treating children and parents with the PaCT manual. The work with them in regular focal conferences has been very fruitful for the process of developing this book.

Early versions of the ideas presented in this book were presented across Europe and even at the conference of the World Association of Infant Mental Health in Cape Town, South Africa. We would like to thank our collegues in Stockholm, Sweden, Majlis Winberg Salomonsson and Björn Salomonsson, for encouraging us and for providing us with opportunities for stimulating exchange.

We would also like to thank the International Psychoanalytic Association for sponsoring our research training programme as well as the faculties of the 14th IPA research training programme in London, 2008, in particular Peter Fonagy, as well as Rolf Sandell, Doris Peham, and John Clarkin, for always encouraging us and for providing us with so much excellent scientific support in developing the research design for evaluating the outcome of this new treatment manual.

In Leipzig, Germany, we would like to thank the Psychoanalytic Institute SPP, Therese Benedek, for being open-minded towards our conceptual and scientific approaches. Furthermore, Tanja Göttken would like to thank in particular Hildgund Schwarz-Köhler for giving her the opportunity to learn so much from her about psychoanalytic understanding.

In Leipzig, we would like to continue by thanking Annette Klein and Lars White for the constructive discussions as well as for helping to conduct the resource- and time-intensive PaCT evaluation project. We also want to thank our translators, Jackie Leach Scully and Monica Buckland, for being always co-operative and flexible within the creative process of translating our book. Furthermore, we would like to thank Lars White for correcting the translation of the manual.

We are very grateful to the children and families whom we met at the Department of Child and Adolescent Psychiatry, Psychotherapy and Psychosomatics, at the University of Leipzig, for giving us an insight into their individual and familial problems, and the opportunity to find words to communicate, and ways to test, the relevance and efficacy of our ideas.

Especially, we would like to thank Heidehof Foundation GmbH for funding the process of the manual's development and evaluation.

Finally, we would like to end by thanking our families. Tanja Göttken would like to thank her parents for giving her so much love and parental support. Particularly, she would like to thank her husband, Jan Klaas Müller, for encouraging and supporting her in her time-intensive research during the past years.

Tanja Göttken and Kai von Klitzing
Leipzig

Tanja Göttken, MSc, is a psychologist, psychoanalyst, research associate, and head of the local psychotherapy section at the Department of Child and Adolescent Psychiatry, University of Leipzig, Germany, a member of the German Psychoanalytical Association/IPA, and member of the editorial advisory board of the journal *Kinderanalyse*. Her research activities include psychotherapy research, emotional disorders in children and adolescents, early triadic relationships, and operationalised psychodynamic diagnostic for children and adolescents (OPD-KJ). Her PhD thesis studies the outcome and underlying fine mechanics of psychodynamic child psychotherapy.

Kai von Klitzing, MD, is Professor of Child and Adolescent Psychiatry, University of Leipzig, Germany, a psychoanalyst for adults, adolescents, and children, a member of the Swiss Psychoanalytical Society and German Psychoanalytical Association/IPA, a training analyst, Editor of the journal *Kinderanalyse*, Associate Editor of the *Infant Mental Health Journal*, President Elect of the World Association for Infant Mental Health (WAIMH). His scientific interests include developmental psychopathology, early triadic relationships, children's narratives, psychotherapy research, and neurobiology. He has published books on the subjects of attachment disorder, immigrant children, psychotherapy in early childhood, and psychoanalysis in childhood and adolescence.

Introduction

In the Western world, childhood depression and anxiety derail child development at much higher rates than is acceptable for a modern-day society. In fact, we know so little about these disorders at this stage that it remains questionable if depression and anxiety should even be considered as separate entities. Thus, depression in childhood often co-occurs with anxiety disorders up to adolescence (Sterba, Egger, & Angold, 2007). This gap in our knowledge has also led to an exasperating lack in the range of age-appropriate interventions on offer, especially in the psychodynamic domain. In this book, we present an innovative guide to brief psychoanalytic child therapy (PaCT) for the treatment of children aged 4–10 with anxiety disorders and depression, illustrating the principles with a number of case studies.

What is PaCT?

PaCT integrates the concepts of drive psychology, self psychology, object relations theory, and elements of French psychoanalysis, and links them up with the conflict-centred procedure of focal therapy (Klüwer, 2005; Malan, 1963). PaCT adheres to the interventional guidelines that have recently been published as practice parameters of the American Academy of Child and Adolescent Psychiatry (AACAP, 2012). Consisting of 20–25 psychotherapy sessions, PaCT is held in a variety of settings (parent–child, child alone, parents alone), in which a relational theme that has led to the development of a symptom is uncovered and worked through. This relational theme constitutes the focus of treatment, in terms of a *psychodynamic hypothesis* of the current predominant conflict. We conceptualise this psychodynamic focus as a *triangle of psychodynamic constellations* (ToP, see Chapter Six, pp. 147–148, "The focus of PaCT: 'triangle of psychodynamic constellations'" (ToP), Figure 3, p. 149). PaCT is a development-orientated method of treatment that aims to assist the families and children in discovering new possibilities for themselves (Emde, 2011). We understand the child's symptoms as a precipitate of intrapsychic and interpersonal conflicts. Thus, as Anna Freud taught us, we shift the focus from the elimination of symptoms to the promotion of developmental capacities (Freud, 1945). Starting from psychoanalytical treatment concepts, we aim for two effects: first, the treatment seeks to alter the child's mental representations and, by extension, his or her cognitive–emotional style; in addition, regular psychoanalytically orientated parental work (every fourth session) attempts to improve the parents' own insight into the inner psychic states of their child: that is, the parents' mentalization concerning their offspring. Free play with the child is used as a means to understanding and processing the child's central conflict. Depending on the child's structural level, supplementary techniques to promote mentalization are applied (Verheugt-Pleiter, Zevalkink, & Schmeets, 2008). In our manual, we deal with both the potential and the challenges of psychoanalytic child therapy. Short-term therapy is usually provided due to economic constraints of day-to-day clinical care—in order to extend help to a larger number of children and parents—rather than to meet the individual needs of the patient (who would often benefit more from long-term treatment). Despite this state of affairs and the undeniable need for long-term interventions in severe cases, the effectiveness of PaCT has been substantiated in a recent waiting-list controlled clinical study, yielding strong effects across a range of psychological domains (Göttken, White, Klein, & von Klitzing, under review). The development of the manual and systematic evaluation was funded by Heidehof Foundation GmbH.

For whom is PaCT appropriate?

PaCT can be used to treat children with various symptoms (behavioural disorders, "hyperactivity", neurotic relationship disorders, disorders of performance, etc.), provided anxiety and/or depression play a key part in giving rise to these symptoms. Through the psychoanalytic stance and technique, the therapist can gain access to the feelings of helplessness and hopelessness that are often hidden behind the behavioural symptoms of children with emotional problems. As we have previously emphasised, "Children's subjective suffering, their emotions and conflict-ridden interior worlds associated with the disorder, are only rarely perceived" (von Klitzing, 2007, p. 285). A depressive pre-school child does not cause noticeable disturbance (the so-called "quiet symptoms"). Yet, children with attention deficit/hyperactivity disorders and "oppositional behaviour" are often suffering—as becomes clear on closer examination—because they cannot cope with the anxiety and depression they are experiencing. Unlike children who exclusively manifest internalising symptoms, children with ADHD or ODD often act out these anxious and depressive feelings hypomanically.

Who can practise PaCT?

PaCT is suitable for therapists who have successfully completed a basic training in a treatment method that includes psychodynamic psychotherapy (with training in psychoanalysis if possible) and its application in children. Given that analysis of one's own psychic resonances and countertransferences plays an important role in PaCT, it is essential that the training has encompassed adequate first-hand psychoanalytic experience (if possible a training analysis). Psychotherapists who are in psychoanalytic training can also use PaCT, provided they have already undergone enough training analysis of their own, and are formally permitted to carry out their own, supervised, treatment of children. For therapists in training, we suggest supervision in focal conferences (Klüwer, 2005). In these focal conferences, one therapist will present his or her case, and the psychodynamic focus identified by the therapist can be evaluated as part of the supervision and modified if necessary. One much neglected prerequisite in the history of child psychotherapy is that the therapist should be in a position to enter into reciprocal, triadic relationships with the family members, and not intervene exclusively by way of the relationship to the child. Therefore, we emphasise that child therapists should develop triadic capacity, and that this is particularly vital to the training as a psychotherapist for children and adolescents.

Psychoanalytically orientated short-term interventions are based on the paradoxical need rapidly to establish an understanding that normally develops over a much longer period. Through only a small number of initial sessions, therapists must sense the burgeoning transference between parents, child, and themselves, while at the same time sustaining a dialogue with the parents, reflecting on the emerging countertransference, and absorbing and understanding the child's disclosures. Emanuel describes this process as "a slow unfolding, but at double speed" (Emanuel, 2011, p. 218). Short-term therapy presents the therapist with the particular challenge of accelerating the diagnostic process, without impairing his or her capacity for "reverie" (Bion, 1962, p. 36) by adopting this tempo. At the same time, he or she must carry out afocal psychoanalytic work, so that unconscious conflicts can be made evident, and, by drawing on focal technique, bring together this afocal material relatively quickly through the formulation of a focus that serves as a psychodynamic hypothesis.[1]

Aims of the PaCT manual

1. The systematic illustration of psychoanalytic short-term therapy aimed at treating children aged four to ten years with emotional disorders, based on classical child-analytical and focal therapy concepts.
2. Support for the systematic training of therapists.
3. The laying down of principles for a targeted scientific evaluation of the efficacy of short-term therapeutic interventions.

Note on the structure of this book

In Part I of this book, we examine the central psychological and psychoanalytic concepts on which the PaCT treatment approach is based.

First, we outline the current state of empirical research on depressive and anxiety disorders in childhood. Besides epidemiology and phenomenology, the developmentally sensitive diagnosis of affective disorders and anxiety disorders plays an important role. As well as presenting the symptoms descriptively, we shall also collate recent findings on the nosological categories of disorders. In addition to the descriptive models of disorders, however, we shall also examine the psychodynamic diagnoses that are based more strongly on the idea of intrapsychic conflicts. The term "comorbidity" will play an important role here, since a "purely" depressive disorder, or a "pure" anxiety disorder, is rare in childhood. This part of the manual will also present emotional symptoms such as depression, anxiety, and behavioural problems in childhood in terms of the psychoanalytic models of their aetiological origin. Our psychodynamic considerations of depression and anxiety in childhood assume that some children display their internal and interpersonal conflicts overtly in the form of emotional symptoms such as depression and anxiety, while other children (often boys) defend against depressive experience hypomanically through behaviour that presents as problems of aggression and hyperactivity. As children often hide their depressive interior world, or even ward it off with temper tantrums and behavioural problems, childhood depression often remains unrecognised and untreated.

In our engagement with the psychoanalytic models that have influenced PaCT, we present various theories of psychoanalytic development that still exert a substantial impact on the therapeutic treatment of children and their parents.

We combine psychoanalytic drive theory with object-relations theory and an intersubjective perspective on human psychic development. Classic Freudian drive psychology and the theory of the dynamic unconscious serves as a foundation for our considerations of theory and treatment. Classic child analysis, as handed down to us by Anna Freud, together with her crucial reflections on the defence mechanisms of the ego, are of central importance to our thinking. In addition, Melanie Klein's ideas benefit child psychotherapists both diagnostically and as part of the therapy process. Donald Winnicott further enriched psychoanalytic thinking about the significance of the real other and through his considerations of transitional phenomena and spaces in child development and in the therapeutic relationship.

Furthermore, we also address the theoretical concept of mentalization (Fonagy, Gergely, Jurist, & Target, 2004) in order to better understand the structural differences between children in the same age group. We describe the concept of mentalization, with its implications for the diagnostic assessment of the capacity for self-object differentiation, for control of affect, and for reflection of the child's own inner psychic states, as well as the states of others.

We use findings from developmental psychology within the framework of the therapeutic interventions to help the child who cannot sufficiently symbolise his inner states through the process of mentalization. On the other hand, the neurotic child who is already capable of forming mental representations will benefit from our verbalisation of his inner conflicts and interpretation of his unconscious desires, fears, aggressive impulses, and defences. It is noteworthy that these are usually mixed forms of structural and neurotic impairment.

In Part II, we present our treatment manual. The use of short-term psychoanalytic child therapy (PaCT) to treat emotional disorders in childhood will be described in detail and illustrated with numerous case examples. After an initial phase of (implicit) focus formulation in discussion with the parents, as well as in a parent–child setting, there follows the psychotherapeutic treatment of the child. In the course of play, verbal interventions and explanations help to convey to the child that there are meanings underlying the symptom. Interpretations serve to make intrapsychic and interpersonal conflicts conscious, and aim to establish a link between symptom (behaviour) and internal conflicted experience. In this part of the book, fundamental considerations concerning the choice of treatment are also raised, such as the children and parents for whom treatment with PaCT is feasible, and which families would find other therapies more effective. As Anna Freud emphasises, it is important not just to examine the level of neurotic symptoms, but also to assess them in relation to their significance for an undisturbed developmental capacity (A. Freud, 1945).

The foundational concept of therapy is aligned with focal therapy (Klüwer, 2005; Malan, 1963), in particular its further development in terms of the parent–child intervention, and the concept of mentalization (Fonagy, Gergely, Jurist, & Target, 2004). We take a close look at the integration of the case history into a psychodynamic treatment focus, the triangle of psychodynamic constellations (ToP), which is formulated after the first five sessions. A central question for the therapist is: how can the different pieces of information and "scenes" be integrated into a treatment focus? This places particular significance on the question of how the theme of transgenerational conflict, which creates a link between the child's symptom and the parents' conflicts, can be formulated as a treatment focus. Here, we assume that the core conflict (Luborsky, Popp, Luborsky, & Mark, 1994) precipitates the emerging transference relationship between therapist–child–parents. We devote a section of Chapter Three to the special features of transference in treatment with PaCT, contrasting it with transference in adult analysis or in classic long-term child therapy.

One section in Chapter Six deals with the central therapeutic component of work with the parents, which is undertaken every fourth session. We do not consider the work with parents to be supplementary to the work with the child, but, rather, as complementary to it: that is, it has the clear aim of promoting the parents' mentalization about their child. Essentially, this is done in order to improve the parents' understanding of the inner states, motivations, and conflicts that are at the root of their child's behaviour, by using episodes that the parents relate about their interaction with the child.

Part II of this book also describes the different phases of the therapy with the particular challenges they present to the therapist's attitude and technique. We give concrete guidelines for specific treatment phases. Case vignettes serve to explain specific therapeutic constellations in these phases.

In Part III, we explain psychotherapeutic work using detailed case studies. Reading these case studies, it should become clear how oscillation between the immersion in the transference and deliberately stepping back in order to take a triadic perspective can succeed in practical interaction with the child in the therapy process.

PART I
THEORETICAL BACKGROUND

Emotional symptoms and affective disorders in childhood: epidemiology, aetiopathogenesis, diagnosis, and indications

Current state of research

Diagnosis

D epression and anxiety are the "common cold" (Seligman, 1975) of psychological disorder in adulthood (Bramesfeld & Stoppe, 2006; Ihle, Esser, Schmidt, & Blanz, 2000). In both paediatric medicine and psychiatry, there is currently a lack of systematic knowledge about the early manifestations of affective disorders. Although emotional symptoms in mentally ill adolescents, such as depressed mood, anxiety, dysphoria, shyness, or a tendency towards somatisation, can often be traced back to the preschool period, such symptoms at this age are often not taken seriously enough by parents and specialists. Furthermore, diagnostic uncertainties arise from the limited applicability of the *DSM-IV / ICD-10* criteria for children under six. The prevalence of depressive illness is on the increase, especially in younger age groups (Alonso et al., 2004; Birmaher et al., 1996; Wittchen, Kessler, Pfister, & Lieb, 2000). Retrospective reports from those affected indicate that emotional symptoms (anxiety, dysphoria, shyness) were often experienced in childhood, sometimes as early as preschool or primary school age. On a larger scale, we note that adult psychiatric illnesses have their roots in behavioural problems that are already apparent in childhood or adolescence (e.g., Kim-Cohen et al., 2003). Accordingly, it is important to find out more about the appearance of emotional problems and affective disorders at preschool age, to enable both early recognition and intervention. The relevant diagnostic criteria of *DSM-IV* need to be modified and "translated" in terms of developmental psychology (Luby et al., 2002).

In addition to the classical core symptoms of depression such as low mood, a feeling of hopelessness, and sadness, depression in childhood may also be expressed through symptoms that are not normally associated with depression.

These symptoms include:

- persistent sense of sadness and hopelessness;
- irritability;
- social withdrawal;
- heightened sensitivity;
- decreased or increased appetite;
- sleep disturbances (problems falling or staying asleep, or excessive sleeping);
- temper tantrums or excessive crying;
- loss of energy and drive;
- feelings of worthlessness or guilt;
- lack of playfulness;
- reduced creativity;
- impaired concentration;
- thoughts of suicide or death.

Not all children display all symptoms, and most symptoms vary with time and situation.

Common anxiety disorders in children, according to *DSM-IV* (American Psychiatric Association, 2000) are: social phobia, specific phobia, separation anxiety disorder, generalised anxiety disorder. At preschool age, we use the Preschool Age Psychiatric Assessment (PAPA (Egger, Ascher, & Angold, 2004)), and at school age, the Child and Adolescent Psychiatric Assessment (CAPA (Angold & Costello, 2000)) to assess these disorders.

Definition

Research criteria

There is a lack of expert consensus on the diagnostic criteria for affective disorders in children of preschool age. The criteria from *DSM-IV* and *ICD-10* have not been appropriately operationalised for this age group, which compromises the comparability of the available data. For example, there are significant differences between the USA and Europe in the frequency of diagnosis of major depression (McArdle, Prosser, & Kolvin, 2004; McDonnell & Glod, 2003). Since 2003, the research criteria of the American Association for Child and Adolescent Psychiatry (AACAP) have provided guidance on the categorisation and evaluation of disorders at preschool age (Research Diagnostic Criteria—Preschool Age; RDC-PA). These criteria are based on the instrument we use for the categorical assessment of psychological disturbances in preschool age children (Preschool Age Psychiatric Assessment, PAPA; Egger & Angold, 2004; Egger, Ascher, & Angold, 2004).

In the age group that we treat, there is a very marked variation in child development, which makes diagnostic classification a particular professional challenge (Wiefel et al., 2007). When diagnosing emotional disorders, it is of fundamental importance to differentiate the dimensional from the categorical approach. Thus, we speak in the dimensional sense of *emotional symptoms*, if the number and severity of observable or otherwise ascertainable phenomena such as anxiety or depression exceed a particular level, so that the phenomena can be described as symptoms. Anxiety and depression play a role in normal development and become pathological only above a particular intensity. Typical survey procedures used to record symptoms include questionnaires or rating scales; the standardisation of these instruments enables the distribution pattern of these phenomena in the population to be shown. This provides a basis for determining the cut-off point at which we start referring to "abnormality" or "(borderline) abnormality". In contrast, we refer to an *emotional disorder* in the *categorical* sense, if, in addition to the quantitative level of symptoms, there are qualitative characteristics that indicate a pathological disorder is present. Typical criteria for these evaluations are the child's or the parents' subjective feeling of stress, or the issue of whether the symptoms have a significant impact on development and social integration (e.g., impairment of learning at school, of family life, of peer group relationships, or of play). Typical survey procedures used to record affective disorders are (standardised) diagnostic interviews, which record both the severity, duration, and intensity and the effects of the symptoms and allow them to be precisely allocated to defined categories of disorders. In dimensional characterisation, the outcome is proportional to the symptoms. The result of the categorical identification, however, is an either/or classification: that is, the statement that the pathological disorder is either present or is not. If symptoms are present, but with a low level of impairment, intensity, and duration that does not justify the categorical diagnosis of an affective disorder, we refer to a *subclinical disorder*. In the research context, childhood problems should always be determined in terms of both dimension and category, if possible.

In the commonly used diagnostic classification systems for psychiatric disorders in childhood and adolescence (cf. *DSM-IV*, Multiaxiales Klassifikationssystem für das Kindes- and Jugendalter nach *ICD-10*) as well as in the literature, the terms associated with emotional symptoms and affective disorders are used very inconsistently. Therefore, we start by giving the following definitions:

Emotional symptoms

Depressed mood, anxiety, dsyphoric mood, shyness, and somatising tendency are characterised as emotional symptoms. These symptoms occur either in isolation, or combined with oppositional, aggressive, or disruptive behavioural symptoms or hyperactivity ("comorbidity").

Emotional disorders

In our manual, we use this as an umbrella term for a group of clinical disorders, for all of which affective dysregulation plays a significant role in the disorder: mood disorders (*DSM-IV*) (including major depressive disorders, dysthymic disorders), anxiety disorders (*DSM-IV*), somatisation disorders, and post traumatic stress disorders, if these clearly show attendant affective depressive and anxious symptoms, in addition to the emotional disorders of childhood specifically listed in *ICD-10*, including disorders of social conduct and emotions

(F92: mixed disorders of conduct and emotions; F92.0: depressive conduct disorder). We do not recommend PaCT for monopolar manic disorders because of their strong diagnostic uncertainty in early childhood. As a reference system, we use the research criteria of the Preschool Age Psychiatric Assessment (PAPA (Egger & Angold, 2004).

Clinical relevance

Depressive and anxiety disorders are well-characterised conditions with the status of a disease. Emotional symptoms show different levels of severity. According to the dimensional cut-offs of the Strengths and Difficulties Questionnaire, SDQ (Goodman, 2001) or the *Child Behaviour Checklist, CBCL* (Achenbach, 1991), children are categorised as "clinical", "borderline", and "normal".

Internalisation vs. externalisation

The affective disorders and emotional symptoms described above are often referred to in the scientific literature (particularly in studies based on the Child Behavior Checklist) as disorders of internalisation, because the symptoms are directed more inwardly and less outwardly than in externalisation disorders, or disorders with behavioural difficulties.

At this point, we show how criteria for emotional disorders may be adapted to the context of early and middle childhood, using major depression according to the *DSM-IV* as an example.

Major depression

Luby and colleagues (2002) modified the well-known diagnostic criteria of *DSM-IV* for major depressive disorder (MDD) to be more appropriate for the particular features of preschool developmental psychology. This included confronting the fluctuations in affect typical of this age by lowering the two-week time criterion. They also reduced the number of symptoms required from five out of nine to four. Luby and colleagues (2002) recruited a clinical sample of $n = 136$ children aged between 3.0 and 5.6. $N = 101$ of these children were recruited from a community sample and $n = 35$ from a clinical sample. Using the unmodified criteria, only twelve of 136 preschool children were diagnosed with major depression. However, on the basis of the modified criteria, Luby and colleagues were able to classify forty-nine cases. The modifications made by the authors to the classification of *DSM-IV* (American Psychiatric Association, 2000) for MDD are presented below (given in italics).

Diagnostic classification according to Diagnostic Criteria for Preschool Major Depressive Disorder, P-DC-MDD (Luby et al., 2002):

Major Depression

A. Five (or more) of the following symptoms have been present *but not necessarily persistently* over a 2-week period and represent a change from previous functioning; at least one of the symptoms is either (1) depressed mood or (2) loss of interest or pleasure *in activities or play. If both (1) and (2) are present a total of only four symtoms are needed.*

(1) Depressed mood *for a portion of the day for several days, as observed (or reported) in behaviour. Note. May be irritable mood.*

(2) Markedly diminished interest or pleasure in all, or almost all, activities *or play for a portion of the day for several days (as indicated by either subjective account or observation made by others).*

(3) Significant weight loss when not dieting or weight gain or decrease or increase in appetite nearly every day.

(4) Insomnia or hypersomnia nearly every day.

(5) Psychomotor agitation or retardation nearly every day (observable by others, not merely subjective feelings of restlessness or being slowed down).

(6) Fatigue or loss of energy nearly every day.

(7) Feelings of worthlessness or excessive or inappropriate guilt (which may be delusional) *that may be evident in play-themes* nearly every day (not merely self-reproach or guilt about being sick).

(8) Diminished ability to think or concentrate, or indecisiveness, *for* several days (either by subjective account or as observed by others).

(9) Recurrent thoughts of death (not just fear of dying), recurrent suicidal ideation without a specific plan, or a suicide attempt or a specific plan for committing suicide. *Suicidal or self-destructive themes are persistently evident in play only.* (Luby et al., 2002, p. 931)

At this point, we should emphasise that the symptom descriptions and diagnoses presented are purely phenomenologically descriptive categories or descriptions. In the sense of the diagnostic classification systems *DSM* and *ICD*, they are not entities with uniform aetiologies. In our treatment approach, additional psychodynamic-orientated operationalisations are important, which should be differentiated from the descriptive diagnostic categories of *DSM-IV* and *ICD-10*. We shall address the psychodynamic aspects of emotional symptoms and affective disorders later, especially in Chapter Three, in sections titled "Psychoanalytical models of the genesis of depression", pp. 80–83 and "Affective disorders and emotional symptoms in the light of psychoanalytical concepts of structural integration: the OPD–KJ axis 'structure'", pp. 101–102.

Clinical diagnosis

In addition to standardised diagnostic interviews, procedures such as the MacArthur Story Stem Battery, MSSB (Bretherton & Oppenheim, 2003), should be employed. These use children's narratives to provide information about the child's defence mechanisms and his or her way of dealing with interpersonal conflicts (e.g., interpersonal solutions, avoidance or raw aggression). The child's mental representations or mentalization disorders can be identified using performative elements and elements of the content of these narratives. Operationalised psychodynamic diagnosis (Arbeitskreis OPD-KJ, 2007) is an indispensable diagnostic instrument in this context. Within psychoanalytic child therapy (PaCT), we limit our assessment of suitable intervention strategies to the "structural" axis (see Chapter Three, p. 101).

Prevalence and course of emotional symptoms and emotional disorders from preschool to school age

Epidemiological studies show that psychiatric disorders occur in 15–22% of schoolchildren in Western European and North American countries (Esser, Schmidt, & Woerner, 1990; Ravens-Sieberer, Wille, Bettge, & Erhart, 2007; Rutter, 1989; Steinhausen, Metzke, Meier, & Kannenberg, 1998). Numerous prospective studies investigate psychopathological developmental pathways (e.g. Breton et al., 1999;

Costello et al., 1996; Costello, Mustillo, Erkanli, Keeler, & Angold, 2003; Rutter, 1989), but only a few start with preschool age (Esser, Schmidt, & Woerner, 1990; Fuchs, Klein, Otto, & von Klitzing, 2013; Klein, Otto, Fuchs, Zenger, & von Klitzing, 2012; Lavigne et al., 1998a,b; Meltzer, Gatward, Goodman, & Ford, 2003; Offord, Boyle, Racine, & Fleming, 1992; Richman, Stevenson, & Graham, 1982). Studies of emotional problems and internalising symptoms (e.g., depression and anxiety) are significantly underrepresented compared to the investigation of behavioural problems and externalising symptoms (e.g., oppositional, aggressive, or disruptive behaviour).

Internalising disorders as a risk to development

In childhood the point prevalence of depressive disorders is approximately 1–3% (Fleming & Offord, 1990). In adolescence, these rates double (Lewinsohn, Rohde, & Seeley, 1998). Anxiety is a common disorder in childhood and adolescence. Epidemiological studies vary substantially in the prevalence rates that they report. The minimum rates of "any anxiety disorder" reported was 2.4% (Costello, Mustillo, Erkanli, Keeler, & Angold, 2003), the maximum 41.2% (Cartwright-Hatton, McNicol, & Doubleday, 2006); separation anxiety appears to be most common in preschoolers. The statements made by five- to six-year-old children about depressive or anxious symptoms have predictive power for later psychopathological developments (Ialongo, Edelsohn, & Kellam, 2001; Ialongo, Edelsohn, Werthamer-Larsson, Crockett, & Kellam, 1995).

Gender differences

Previous research results show that there are gender differences in the prevalence rates of internalising and externalising symptoms, and that these differences vary within developmental stages (Ihle, Esser, Schmidt, & Blanz, 2000; Lahey et al., 2000). At both preschool and primary school age, boys are considered to be particularly vulnerable (Beyer & Furniss, 2007); their developmental pathways are more complex and have a higher predictive power (Mesman, Bongers, & Koot, 2001). The pattern of risk factors does not differ between boys and girls in childhood and adolescence, but adolescent girls show more, and more stable, anxiety symptoms (Bosquet & Egeland, 2006).

Phenomenology

At preschool and school age, depressive disorders are characterised by lack of play, a sudden drop in performance at school, reduced creativity and patience, lack of fantasy, as well as psychosomatic symptoms and observable behaviours (von Klitzing, 2008). Depressive symptoms frequently show a strong association with anxiety disorders, up to adolescence (Sterba, Egger, & Angold, 2007; Wittchen, Kessler, Pfister, & Lieb, 2000). Anxiety disorders such as social anxiety, specific anxiety disorder, or general anxiety disorder often coincide with uncontrollable fear of specific situations which results in severe impairment of social–cognitive functions and distinct avoidance behaviour (Egger, Ascher, & Angold, 2004).

Co-morbidity and course of disease

If depressive disorders present in childhood and adolescence, there is a particularly high risk of progression to severe disease with frequent relapses (Dunn & Goodyer, 2006; Leverich et al., 2007; Mondimore et al., 2006). Co-morbidity of internalising and externalising disorders is a particular risk factor for later psychopathological developments (Hofstra, van der Ende, & Verhulst, 2002; Offord, Boyle, Racine, & Fleming, 1992).

Social, psychological, and biological risk factors

Factors of the social environment

A raised level of internalising problems in child development should be expected if there was depression in the parental and/or grandparental generation (Olino et al., 2008), or if the children experience rejection by their parents (Mun, Fitzgerald, Von Eye, Puttler, & Zucker, 2001).

Family adversity and life events

Child psychiatric disorders occur more frequently in families that are chronically burdened by psychological illness, crime and delinquency, low educational level, relationship problems, or limited parenting skills (Blanz, Schmidt, & Esser, 1991; Rutter & Quinton, 1984; Scheithauer, Mehren, & Petermann, 2003; Scheithauer & Petermann, 1999). The occurrence of various life events and living with a single parent also have predictive value for mood and anxiety disorders (Kroes et al., 2002). More recent studies have shown that the early experience of critical life events mediates the relationship between the family history of mood disorders and the severity of depression at preschool age (Luby, Belden, & Spitznagel, 2006). The greater the exposure of a child to stressful life events, the stronger the link between a familial burden of depressive disorders and the severity of depression at preschool age.

Quality of family relationships

Studies have shown a link between anxious, overprotective and over-controlling parental behaviour and emotional disorders at preschool age (Bayer, Sanson, & Hemphill, 2006; Hastings et al., 2008; Hudson & Rapee, 2000; Muris, Meesters, Merckelbach, & Hulsenbeck, 2000; Whaley, Pinto, & Sigman, 1999; Wood, McLeod, Sigman, Hwang, & Chu, 2003). Poor parental care and inconsistent or harsh discipline increase the probability of externalising behavioural problems in childhood (Beelmann, Stemmler, Losel, & Jaursch, 2007; Deater-Deckard, Dodge, Bates, & Pettit, 1998; Hahlweg, Heinrichs, Bertram, Kuschel, & Widdecke, 2008; Lucia & Breslau, 2006; Rothbaum & Weisz, 1994). The interaction between the family environment and features of childhood temperament is currently under discussion (Leve, Kim, & Pears, 2005).

Individual factors of the child

Cognitive-emotional styles

In addition to factors found in the social environment, there have been numerous studies of how children deal internally with relationship conflicts and themes (Baldwin, 1992; Bretherton, 1985; Rudolph, Hammen, & Burge, 1995). The evaluation of children's stories (e.g., through story stem completion) gives some access to the intrapsychic world of children (Bretherton, Rodrigues, & Cassidy, 1990; Buchsbaum & Emde, 1990). A few studies find evidence of connections between the content and structure of the children's stories and their emotional and behavioural symptoms (Overview: Emde, Wolf, & Oppenheim, 2003; Oppenheim, Emde, & Warren, 1997; von Klitzing, Kelsay, Emde, Robinson, & Schmitz, 2000). The study by von Klitzing and colleagues (2000) of more than 500 twins found gender differences as well: predictive associations between incoherent aggression in narratives and behavioural symptoms were present only in girls, but not in boys. Children with emotional symptoms are able to find coherent solutions for everyday difficulties to only a limited extent in their narratives (Stadelmann, Perren, von Wyl, & von Klitzing, 2007).

Social skills

The level of children's social skills is documented as a key factor influencing a child's healthy development (Alsaker & Gutzwiller-Helfenfinger, 2009; Deater-Deckard, 2001; Hay, Payne, & Chadwick, 2004; Perren, Groeben, Stadelmann, & von Klitzing, 2008). Both over and underdevelopment of prosocial behaviours can represent a risk of psychopathology. Lyons, Uziel-Miller, Reyes, and Stokol (2000) found that psychosocial strengths are negatively associated with symptoms. Behavioural symptoms are related to a low expression of prosocial behaviour (Eron & Huesman, 1984; Hastings, Zahn-Waxler, Robinson, Usher, & Bridges, 2000; Hay & Pawlby, 2003). Children with emotional symptoms, on the other hand, show higher markers of prosocial behaviour. Children who are very concerned about the wellbeing of others and are excessively friendly appear to have an increased risk of emotional symptoms (Bohlin, Bengtsgard, & Andersson, 2000; Gjerde & Block, 1991; Hay & Pawlby, 2003; Perren, Stadelmann, von Wyl, & von Klitzing, 2007).

Biological factors

Hypothalamic–pituitary–adrenal system

The hypothalamic–pituitary–adrenal (HPA) system has been extensively investigated in the context of biopsychosocial models of developmental psychopathology. The HPA axis enables the equilibrium of physical functions to be maintained even during heightened stress. An overproduction or dysregulation of hormones over a longer period has been shown to be significant for the occurrence of psychiatric illnesses (McEwen, 2002). Variations in basal activity and the stress reactions of the HPA system can be analysed by measuring cortisol concentrations in saliva.

Numerous studies in recent years have identified a change in the HPA axis of depressive patients.

The HPA-axis describes a hormone cascade: if a stressor occurs, corticotrophin-releasing hormone (CRH) is liberated by the hypothalamus into the arterial system of the pituitary gland. There, through binding to appropriate receptors, the CRH triggers the release of adrenocorticotropic hormone (ACTH). This is then disseminated via the blood vessels, and in the adrenal cortices it stimulates the production and secretion of glucocorticoids; in humans this is cortisol. The glucocorticoids bring about a comprehensive stress reaction in the body (including raised blood pressure, raised pulse). Glucocorticoids act not only on peripheral organs, but also feed back to the central nervous system. The glucocorticoids bind in the hypothalamus and in the pituitary gland at appropriate binding sites, the so-called glucocorticoid receptors (GR). This mechanism sets off a negative feedback process, which inhibits the further production and release of CRH and ACTH. This down-regulates the stress response and lowers the concentration of glucocorticoids in the blood. Numerous studies show that this negative feedback mechanism of the HPA axis is dysregulated in depressive patients.

Findings on HPA

50% of patients with depressive disorders show over-activity and altered responsiveness of the HPA axis, primarily in the form of raised cortisol concentrations (Holsboer, Lauer, Schreiber, & Krieg, 1995; Vreeburg et al., 2009). In the dexamethasone suppression test (DST), approximately 50% of acutely depressed patients showed an altered cortisol reaction in comparison with healthy subjects. In the DST, a small amount of dexamethasone (synthetically produced cortisol derivative) is administered orally or intravenously. This inhibits cortisol production, and, if applied for longer periods, it suppresses the release of ACTH. A significant drop in cortisol blood values can be shown in the healthy organism. It should, however, be mentioned that these observed abnormalities of the HPA axis have not yet led to the formation of a coherent concept, although previous investigations have indicated that there is a link between changes in the HPA axis and psychopathology in childhood (von Klitzing et al., 2012).

Externalising psychiatric disorders such as aggressiveness or adjustment disorders are generally associated with lower cortisol concentrations (Flinn & England, 1995; McBurnett, Lahey, Rathouz, & Loeber, 2000; Moss, Vanyukov, & Marti, 1995; Shoal, Giancola, & Kirillova, 2003), and internalising symptoms such as depression with raised cortisol concentrations (Granger, Weisz, McCracken, Ikeda, & Douglas, 1996; Schmidt et al., 1997; Zahn-Waxler, Klimes-Dougan, & Slattery, 2000). However, the findings have only limited comparability due to the variability in the methodology used (Jessop & Turner-Cobb, 2008).

Hatzinger and colleagues (2007) found that five-year-old girls show higher HPA axis activity than boys, both in the morning and under stress conditions. In boys, but not in girls, the raised cortisol concentrations in the morning were associated with emotional and hyperactivity symptoms.

Von Klitzing and colleagues (2012) showed that negative family relationships in children of preschool age predicted emotional symptoms if the children showed a higher level of cortisol secretion (measured in saliva) while telling a story (MacArthur Story Stems). In contrast, negative peer relationships predicted the occurrence of emotional symptoms if cortisol secretion was suppressed during the test.

The following neurobiological and genetic findings and theories, which cannot be presented in detail here, are currently under investigation in research.

Neuroanatomical findings

A reduction in the total volume of the hippocampus has been found in depressive adults. These neuro-degenerative processes are more marked the longer the depressive episode has lasted. Continuous stress, depression, and childhood trauma all appear to promote the release of glucocorticoids and may ultimately lead to cell death in the hippocampus, and, thus, a loss of memory (Jacobs, van Praag, & Gage, 2000).

Overall, the physiological explanations are very diverse and cannot yet provide a uniform, coherent model for the establishment and maintenance of depression. Rather, it should be concluded that numerous factors—psychosocial, neurobiological, and genetic—interact to generate a depressive syndrome.

Gene-environment interaction

Since there is considerable heterogeneity in reactions, even if the environmental conditions are very negative, the question arises of whether part of this heterogeneity is caused by genetic influences on susceptibility towards environmental conditions (Rutter, 2008). The theory of "differential susceptibility" (Belsky, Bakermans-Kranenburg, & van IJzendoorn, 2007; Ellis, Boyce, Belsky, Bakermans-Kranenburg, & van IJzendoorn, 2011), states that genetic factors mediate a variable responsivity to environmental influences (Uher & McGuffin, 2008). For example, Caspi and colleagues (2003) have shown that the 5-HTT genotype moderates the depressogenic effect of critical life events. In carriers of the s-alleles, negative life events were predictive of depression, but this was not the case for carriers of two l-alleles. This finding has been supported by Kaufmann and colleagues (2004), who showed that only those carriers of the s-alleles who were exposed to maltreatment developed childhood depression, especially if they were not socially supported.

Furthermore it has been shown that carriers of the s-alleles react more strongly with negative emotions to external events (neuroticism) (Lesch, Bengel, & Heils, 1996), and show a higher level of cortical activity in the limbic system in response to anxiety-causing stimuli (Hariri, Mattay, & Tessitore, 2002). The theory of "differential susceptibility" assumes that carriers of the s-alleles have a generally heightened sensitivity towards positive and negative environmental aspects. Thus, this 5-HTT genotype is associated with an increased vulnerability to adverse conditions. At the same time, there is also a higher sensitivity of carriers of the s-alleles to positive environmental conditions, which leads to a very positive developmental outcome (Uher & McGuffin, 2008). This probably involves many gene loci that have yet to be identified.

Epigenetics

Epigenetic mechanisms serve to regulate genetic activity at the molecular level, or represent heritable changes in gene expression that are not coded in the DNA sequence itself. An important epigenetic mechanism that is currently under a lot of discussion is DNA methylation. Animal experiments have investigated the impact of early environmental characteristics on the molecular memory, with long-term consequences for gene expression.

The offspring of female rats who showed a high degree of care behaviour (much licking and grooming) show moderate reactions when confronted by a stressor, compared to the animals whose mothers did not show much care behaviour (Liu, Diorio, Day, Francis, & Meaney, 2000; Weaver et al., 2004).

The researchers were able to show that expression of the glucocorticoid receptor gene is programmed by the environmental factor of maternal care. The DNA of the young rats who received little licking and grooming showed methylation blocking the expression of the glucocorticoid receptor gene, but the young rats who received significantly more maternal care did not show this blocking of the glucocorticoid receptor gene through methylation. In these animals, there was a higher level of expression of the glucocorticoid receptor gene, making the negative feedback mechanism more efficient.

These animal experiments appear to offer the first indications that maternal care behaviour, and not just genetic features, have a lasting effect on interindividual differences in behaviour and the HPA response to stress (Caldji, Diorio, & Meaney, 2003).

Conclusion for PaCT

Neurobiological research shows that memory has to be reactivated in order to modify synaptic connections and thus be encoded and stored anew (LeDoux, 1996). Experiences before the acquisition of language can also be restaged and understood in the transference relationship and thus be remembered. In children whose brain is not yet fully developed, the lifting of developmental inhibition takes on particular significance through a psychotherapeutic intervention. PaCT is intended to make the child's cognitive–emotional styles more flexible as part of new object-relationship experiences. Without psycho-analytic treatment, depressive processing mechanisms remain rigid, particularly because depressive object-relationship experiences later on in treatment are often restaged in the relationships to the objects, "whereby the depressive patient remains fixed to rigid forms of conflict management and information processing" (Leuzinger-Bohleber, 2010, p. 15, translated for this edition).

The theory of "differential susceptibility" (Belsky, Bakermans-Kranenburg, & van IJzendoorn, 2007; Ellis, Boyce, Belsky, Bakermans-Kranenburg, & van IJzendoorn, 2011) states that genetic factors mediate a variable responsivity to environmental influences. Carriers of the s-alleles of the 5 HTT genotype appear to be particularly sensitive to environmental factors. It is possible that these children will benefit from PaCT intervention particularly well, experiencing it as a supporting environmental factor.

CHAPTER TWO

Classical psychoanalytical concepts

In this chapter, we describe in detail the psychoanalytic theory on which our PaCT treatment approach is based. We link the psychoanalytic theory of drive psychology with an object-relations theoretical and intersubjective view of human psychic development. Thus, within our therapeutic approach, we understand the self in its subjectivity—and this significantly includes internal phantasies, desires, and subjective mental representations—as developing through intersubjective experiences.

One central assumption of our approach to the treatment of internalising disorders such as anxiety and depression in childhood is that in the course of their development, children with emotional symptoms will turn the aggressive impulses originally directed against the object towards the self. Intrapsychic conflicts that arise in the context of primary object relations are processed in the depressive mechanism in such a way that it is not the object that is accused, but the self, which leads to an impaired developmental capacity of the self. The early attempts by Karl Abraham, Sigmund Freud, and Sandor Radó to conceptualise the causes of depression emphasise the significance of loss, disappointment, and anger. In his "Mourning and melancholia" (Freud, 1917e), Freud described this connection between unconscious anger against the object and an impoverishment of the ego through depressive processing with the often-quoted words: "Thus the shadow of the object fell upon the ego, and the latter could henceforth be judged by a special agency, as though it were an object, the forsaken object" (Freud, 1917e, p. 248). More recent models also stress the significance of unconscious aggression in the aetiopathogenesis of depression. For example, Mentzos describes three processes that pertain to the development of depression: the "real or internal loss of the object", the "turning of aggression against the Self" and the "disruption of narcissistic regulation" (Mentzos, 2006).

The therapeutic work with the depressive and anxious child, however, does not aim at liberating the aggression or helping the child to direct it towards his or her relational objects, but focuses on familiarising the child with it in working together psychologically and on making it conscious. Thus, the child is increasingly able to access at a symbolic level the lack, loss, and disappointment that are at the basis of the aggression turned towards the self. We assume that the lack, loss, and disappointment with the object will also be expressed in the transference situation. The transference relationship allows the child to experience another person who does not react to his/her aggression with counter-attacks by breaking off contact, but who attempts to introduce a level of understanding that enables the aggression to be expressed at the symbolic level (through language, play, narrative, etc.). Following successful treatment, children are able to show more flexible defences, less self-reproach, and less inhibition of *joie de vivre*.

The drive psychology of Sigmund Freud

According to Freud, teaching psychoanalytic theory is no easy matter. Famously, he pointed out that psychoanalysis sets itself some challenges:

> Psycho-analysis is the name (1) of a procedure for the investigation of mental processes which are almost inaccessible in any other way, (2) of a method (based upon that investigation) for the treatment of neurotic disorders and (3) of a collection of psychological information obtained along those lines, which is gradually being accumulated into a new scientific discipline. (Freud, 1923a, p. 235)

In both his teaching on personality structure, the so-called structural model consisting of the id, the ego, and the superego, and in his teaching on psychosexual organisation, Freud refers to the significance of the early years of life for the construction of internal psychic structures as fundamental psychological regulation mechanisms. Early experiences gained in the course of instinctual drives and forms of gratification in the oral, anal, and phallic phases are at the root of every individual story of the libidinal (conflict) dynamic. This means that conflicts and failures in this early period of childhood experience have permanent effects on the development of the personality and its predominant defence mechanisms. The personality theory of Freud has three central aspects: one is dynamic, and concerns the development of the drives, their fate and satisfaction; one is structural, and is expressed in the so-called structural model of id, ego, and superego; a third is topographical, which differentiates between the unconscious, conscious, and preconscious states of an idea or drive representation. A person's intrapsychic life consists in the ongoing negotiation and conflict between the three instances of the id, ego, and superego and the topographical "states" of a psychic content such as a desire or an idea. At the same time, the psychological apparatus in the Freudian model must continually mediate between psychic and social reality. Ideally, both the needs of the instinctual world within the subject and the requirements of the outside world should reach an accommodation. The fact that this cannot always be achieved is the starting point for neurotic developments.

The id

The id forms a reservoir of the libido. It contains unconscious desires and drives, memories that come from the time before language acquisition and that, therefore, remain unconscious. The id strives primarily for direct drive satisfaction. It tolerates no postponement of drive satisfaction, and is geared towards the direct gratification of needs. The id, as a "cauldron" (Freud, 1933a, p. 73), lacks any form of ego function. It knows "no good and evil, no morality" (Freud, 1933a, p. 74). Since the primary processes represent the first mode of functioning of the psychic apparatus and the secondary processes act only after a delay and never gain full dominance over the psychic, a large part of the memory material remains unconscious. This buried store of memories forms the unconscious core of human life. From the point at which the superego establishes itself as the internal moral entity, the desires of the id are compelled to satisfy themselves in a distorted, disguised form. The id obeys only the pleasure principle. Since this core consists of visual memories that comprise only thing-representations (*Sachvorstellungen*) and not word-representations (*Wortvorstellungen*), their bringing to consciousness remains blocked. Bringing to consciousness is mediated via language as an important ego function. The id as a psychic entity represents the precipitation of unconscious desires and drives and the associated individually acquired desires and drive representations.

Freud described the relationship between the unconscious and the id as follows:

> You will not expect me to have much to tell you that is new about the id apart from its new name. It is the dark, inaccessible part of our personality; what little we know of it we have learnt from our study of the dream-work and of the construction of neurotic symptoms, and most of that is of a negative character and can be described only as a contrast to the ego. We approach the id with analogies: we call it a chaos, a cauldron full of seething excitations. We picture it as being open at its end to somatic influences . . . It is filled with energy reaching it from the instincts, but it has no organization, produces no collective will, but only a striving to bring about the satisfaction of the instinctual needs subject to the observance of the pleasure principle. The logical laws of thought do not apply in the id, and this is true above all of the law of contradiction. Contrary impulses exist side by side, without cancelling each other out or diminishing each other: at the most they may converge to form compromises under the dominating economic pressure towards the discharge of energy. There is nothing in the id that could be compared with negation; and we perceive with surprise an exception to the philosophical theorem that space and time are necessary forms of our mental acts. There is nothing in the id that corresponds to the idea of time; there is no recognition of the passage of time, and . . . no alteration in its mental processes is produced by the passage of time. (Freud, 1933a, p. 73)

The ego

The ego is both conscious and unconscious. The conscious part of the ego is a mediator of physical and social reality. It organises perception, action, control, and also defence. Through the influence of the ego, defence mechanisms can ensure that particular contents are not perceived and, thus, do not reach consciousness, resulting in gaps in, or distortions of, perception. To simplify matters, we could describe the ego as usually working consciously, according to the laws of the secondary process, and mediating between the individual, his drives and desires, his often inexpedient motivation, and the requirements of reality and the physical and real environment. While the id is governed by the laws of the pleasure principle, the ego works principally according to those of the reality principle. The ego represents the central place of conflict within the individual. Although it draws its energy from the id as the source of drive energy, it also represents the moral demands of the superego and the ideal ego, as well as the demands of the external world; hence, the ego is like the rope in a tug-of-war, which is pulled in more than one direction and which must be stable enough to prevent the trial of strength coming to a premature end in favour of one or the other opponent. In the words of Freud:

> The ego portion that has been expediently modified by the proximity of the external world with its threat of danger. From a dynamic point of view it is weak, it has borrowed its energies from the id . . . The ego's relation to the id might be compared with that of a rider to his horse. The horse supplies the locomotive energy, while the rider has the privilege of deciding on the goal and of guiding the powerful animal's movement. But only too often there arises between the ego and the id the not precisely ideal situation of the rider being obliged to guide the horse along the path by which it itself wants to go. (Freud, 1933a, p. 77)

If a conflict arises between the demands of the id and the ego's task of applying the reality principle, the ego expresses the conflict through anxiety. One central, mature form of defending against the id's instinctual drives is repression, but undoing, denial, or reaction formation are alternative defence mechanisms of the ego. Freud later formulates this conflict thus:

> We are warned by a proverb against serving two masters at the same time. The poor ego has things even worse: it serves three severe masters and does what it can to bring their claims and demands into harmony with one another. . . . Its three tyrannical masters are the external world, the super-ego and the id. (Freud, 1933a, p. 77)

The important ego functions include imagination, memory, cognition, synthesis, and integration, control of motility and perception, and the ability to anticipate. The central ego function is adaptation to the external and internal world.

The superego

The superego is an entity in the ego with both conscious and unconscious parts. Freud pointed out that there is a link between the strength of libidinal urges directed towards the parent desired in the Oedipus complex and the severity of the superego. In the Freudian concept, the superego is the direct precipitate of father-representation, which sanctions and punishes the oedipal erotic love towards the mother. The fear of being punished through castration by the father for the oedipal desire to possess the mother as an object of love leads, in the "decline of the Oedipus complex", to the child repressing the oedipal desires and installing the prohibition of incest and, thus, also the law of the father in his/her own ego. The superego, as a part of the ego, then keeps watch over the moral integrity of the child and later the adult, renouncing the turbulent phallic–narcissistic urges, placing the child in competition with the father and the mother, then leading the child into the latency phase, in which the drive is sublimated and satisfied. In latency, as the ego increasingly gains control over the physical impulses, epistemophilia and pleasure in intellectual achievement are great.

Psychosexual development

The publication of Freud's *Three Essays on the Theory of Sexuality* (1905d) was a milestone in the early days of psychoanalysis. In his drive theory, Freud starts from the following assumptions and observations: he recognised that drives (or instincts) lie at the root of the sexual desires and fantasies of both the child and the adult. Their diversity of expression, from normal sexuality to perversions, then became the object of further investigation. Freud's drive theory showed that so-called perverse urges are present in every person. Thus, he postulates, that the "neuroses are, so to say, the negative of perversions" (Freud, 1905d, p. 165). The drives are strongly countered and resisted only in the course of developing the ego, which goes hand in hand with an increasing repression of forms of drive satisfaction that are individually or culturally unacceptable. In the *Three Essays*, Freud links the conscious or unconscious perverse urges in adults with normal infantile sexuality.

Freud understood the libidinal phases in the light of a heightened libidinal cathexis of various erogenous zones. In the course of development from a relatively undifferentiated psychic state at birth to a complex psychic apparatus that works in a differentiated way, the basal bodily functions always have a corresponding psychic meaning in the interaction with the relationship object.

Oral phase (first year of life)

In the *oral phase*, which characterises the whole first year of life, the mouth and the lips, because of their role in food intake, are the principal sources of pleasure. Drives are satisfied through touching, sucking, chewing, and swallowing—in other words, through drinking and eating. In these oral forms of expression there is an active (oral–sadistic) and a passive mode. The oral–sadistic active mode emerges only with the arrival of teeth, which enable biting. Oral function modes, according to Freud, comprise biting, placing in the mouth, holding fast, spitting out, and closing. The shared activity of breastfeeding, involving sucking and biting as well as chewing, offers interpersonal meanings to both the mother and child. Meanings arise through which the object relationship is organised. The early libidinal relationship to the mother, for example, is marked by the meaning of eating and being eaten. Disorders in the mother–child relationship then manifest themselves on the level of oral food intake (e.g., in feeding disorders). Weaning also acquires a great significance: is it undertaken too quickly and abruptly, or is withdrawal of the breast managed slowly? The way oral needs are handled (for example, their excessive satisfaction or refusal) influences the development of drive fixations. Freud understands this as the precipitate of a conflictual organisation of the libidinal phase in question.

Anal phase (second and third year of life)

In the period from the second year to about the age of three and a half or four, the libidinal primacy of the *anal* zone is reflected in the pursuit of expelling and withholding faeces. In this libidinal phase, a multitude of childhood activities, which Freud recognises as the derivative of anal eroticism, are accompanied by pleasurable sensations. In a more or less direct or indirect way, the child creates relationships to his objects, which reflect his pursuit of and concern with defecation. The primary erogenous zone in the anal phase is the area around the anus. Thus, the child may gain pleasure from retaining faeces, which stimulates the anal mucosa. On this, Freud writes,

> Children who are making use of the susceptibility to erotogenic stimulation of the anal zone betray themselves by holding back their stool till its accumulation brings about violent muscular contractions and, as it passes through the anus, is able to produce powerful stimulation of the mucous membrane. (Freud, 1905d, p. 186)

Control over the expulsion or withholding of faeces gives the child a sense of control not only over the intestinal contents, but also over objects in his environment, aspects of which take on anal symbolic meaning (e.g., faeces = gift). In Freud's words:

> They [the intestinal contents] are clearly treated as a part of the infant's own body and represent his first 'gift': by producing them he can express his active compliance with his environment and, by withholding them, his disobedience. (Freud, 1905d, p. 186)

The elementary, pleasurable experience of defecation is antagonised by the demands of the environment: this requires defecation to be delayed and to occur to order and in a clean way. An unsatisfactory resolution of the conflict between environment (mother/parent/society's cleanliness rule) and child can, according to Freud, lead to anal fixations, or the so-called anal character. Either one of the poles of the conflict can be overemphasised: the conflict about holding back might, for example, bring with it exaggerated avarice and stinginess; while the aspect of defecation and giving in the anal mode might then show itself later in liberality, self-sacrifice, and generosity. Subsequently, the meaning of the stool shifts from a "gift" to a "child", which, according to one of the infantile theories of sexuality, is generated through eating and is then brought to birth via the gut.

Phallic–oedipal phase (third–sixth year of life)

In the phallic phase (from approximately three and a half to five years of age), boys and girls are intensely engaged with their genitals, according particular significance to the presence or absence of a penis. The boys are worried by the realisation that girls and women do not have a penis. The possibility that this organ, which is experienced with such pleasure, could be lost is terrifying.

The oedipal phase is a complex interplay of fantasies about one's own body and the bodies of others. Pleasurable autoerotic activity with the genitals, with associated object relationship fantasies, accompanies the Oedipus complex. Here, Freud formulates both a positive Oedipus and a negative Oedipus complex. The Oedipus complex describes the organised grouping of the child's loving and hostile desires in relation to both parents. In its so-called positive form, it presents itself, according to Freud, as we know it from the Oedipus myth: the boy's desire for the mother, leading to rivalry with, and the wish to kill, the father. The negative form of the Oedipus complex describes the desire for the parent of the same gender, with its associated rivalry and hate towards the parent of the opposite gender. From this, Freud postulates a person's constitutional bisexuality. Gender identity is something that is produced through a developmental process. The outcome of a heterosexual choice of object is not an obligatory end result of this development. According to Freud's conceptualisation, the boy's desire has the effect of containing his fear of castration. In girls, the relationships are somewhat different. Freud considered that a girl is so disappointed by her mother's failure to equip her with a penis, that she rejects the pre-oedipal ties to her mother and turns to her father with the wish that he gives her a child and, thus, symbolically, a penis. The girl's shift towards the positive Oedipus complex in that she desires her father is, in this classic Freudian conceptualisation, reparative rather than active. Thus, the girl turns from her pre-oedipal love object, the mother, and turns to the father in the hope of compensation. Since, in this theory, the girl already finds herself to be castrated, she also lacks any motivation to give up her oedipal rivalry and autoerotic phallic activity focused on her clitoris. In the boy, the fear that his father could punish him through castration for his competing oedipal wishes leads to the collapse of the Oedipus complex. According to Freud, the installation of the superego then brings this turbulent and conflictual period to a calmer close. In the phallic phase, the partial drives that previously coexisted in anarchic juxtaposition are bundled together. In the latency period, the child turns away from the competing eroticised fantasies, until they are reactivated in puberty.

Freud's theory of phallic monism and the parallels of male and female sexual development have been called into question by several authors (e.g., Deutsch, 1925; Horney, 1926; Jones, 1935). Modern concepts of female sexual development describe the development of a girl along a relationship matrix that is influenced not only by the fantasies of the girl herself, but also through the unconscious fantasies of the primary object (Ogden, 1987). Understood like this, the relationship constellation of the oedipal child is then only one of several conceivable variants of so-called "scenic triads" (Boothe, 1992; Boothe & Heigl-Evers, 1996).

The Oedipus complex and the structural model (id, ego, superego)

The Oedipus complex organises the infantile libido and leads to the construction of psychic instances. Thus it achieves a kind of "subsequent" integration of early life impressions, which are fixed as a psychic structure only at the moment when the Oedipus complex dissolves. This oedipal drama is accompanied by the child's fantasies about his body and the bodies of others. These fantasies accompany the libidinal setting and the child's wishes in relation to his parents— "coitus with the mother", "child from the father"—that in turn are stimulated by the fantasies from the "theories of infantile sexuality". They generate fantasies of lacking a penis or of castration, which lead to the destruction of the Oedipus complex in favour of the narcissistic, libidinal interest in one's own sex organ, accompanied by the development of anxiety. The precipitation of this conflictual confrontation with infantile incestuous desires and culturally installed (incest-) prohibition, which is accompanied by fantasies, is the setting up of a psychic structure that places these oedipal origins of the individual in the unconscious as things unavailable to consciousness, and keeps watch over their return. Thus, the subject becomes situated in time and simultaneously it installs the difference between before and after within itself, splitting itself into prohibited and prohibiting parts. In *The Ego and the Id* (Freud, 1923b), as well as in "The dissolution of the Oedipus complex" (Freud, 1924d), Freud described the "completed Oedipus complex", which consists in both boys and girls of erotic and jealous–hostile attitudes to both parents. The prohibition of these incestuous attitudes is achieved principally through the castration anxiety, as a fantasised loss of narcissistic integrity through identification with the prohibiting parent (who represents the cultural demands for recognition of the generational difference as a reminder of the repression of the incestuous drive) in the ego, where, as the superego or conscience, it critically observes the ego itself and thus constitutes the Subject. The stronger the child's libidinal desires in the oedipal constellation, the stricter is the construction of this instance of the superego, which brings about repression. The ego draws strength for this act of suppression from its identifications with the lost object of love, and in this identification Freud sees the possibility that the id withdraws its object cathexis: "Perhaps this identification is even the condition under which the id gives up its objects" (Freud, 1917). It appears to us to be more than plausible that this identification, which leads to the construction of a psychic structure, can only take place in the medium of fantasy.[2] What else should this identification be than the fantasised incorporation of the forbidden love object? Freud himself, in *Group Psychology and the Analysis of the Ego* (Freud, 1921c) points out the precursor of identification, the introjection from the oral phase of drive development, and the ambivalent undertone of each identification. "It [identification] behaves like a derivative of the first, oral phase of the organization of the libido, in which the object that we long for and prize is assimilated by eating and is in that way annihilated as such" (Freud, 1921c, p. 105).

In "Mourning and melancholia" (1917e), Freud referred to the mode of incorporation of a lost love object in order to circumvent this loss by maintaining it in fantasy in the ego itself.

> We have elsewhere shown that identification is a preliminary stage of object-choice, that it is the first way – and one that is expressed in an ambivalent fashion – in which the ego picks out an object. The ego wants to incorporate this object into itself, and, in accordance with the oral or cannibalistic phase of libidinal development in which it is, it wants to do so by devouring it. (Freud, 1917e, p. 249).

It is remarkable that regressive and progressive elements are transmitted together and create a new psychic structure: the superego. The old mode of introjection in the medium of fantasy can be understood as a regression to a level of earlier experience structuring. In progressive engagement with the demands of the (cultural) world outside, however, regression is limited to the mode of introjection, and progression to the identification and construction of the prohibiting but still loved instance in the creation of a new psychic structure. This permits a lost libido position to be conserved, and the object relationship to be continued phantasmatically in the ego, while protecting oneself through libidinal cathexis of the prohibiting instance against the return of the repressed. The prohibition, thus, penetrates into the interior of the desire; the sublime itself becomes a desire. Here, we find ourselves in the territory of the second drive theory, but it should be noted in passing that desire and fantasy in the human being always remain powerful, and that it is the human aim to extend the pleasure principle as far as possible into the comprehension of reality.

Only in the acceptance of the generational difference, and, thus, in the construction of guilt by setting up the superego, which is constituted out of the identification with the prohibition, or, rather, with the prohibiting love object, is self-reflexivity, that is, subjectivity, possible. The oedipal result consists in the subsequent attribution of guilt; the subject becomes guilty of his prohibited oedipal urges and fantasies only at the moment of his fixation through the construction of the prohibitive instance. The interplay of libido, desire, fantasy, and guilt thus becomes the necessary sphere of the constitution of subjectivity. The acknowledgement of the generational difference makes human beings into historical subjects by situating them in time. Subjectivity as a reflexive self-observation means here, in Freud, a socialisation of a person, who can only become a subject if he accepts the cultural norms, establishes them within himself, and, thus, installs them in himself, while at the same time—and this is what differentiates Freudian subject theory from many others—cathecting this ideal libidinally, so that out of the fulfilment of the ideal through suppression of desire, narcissistic gratification can be derived.

Primary process–secondary process

In his conception of an early state of inner life, Freud describes an infant who is subject to the illusion that what he desires right now—

a stream of warm milk from the mother's breast—is instantly fulfilled. The desire, thus, directly leads to the hallucinatory fulfilment of desire. However, this primary narcissistic infant of Freud's does not perceive that the reduction in the displeasure brought about by hunger in reality depends on care given by a helpful other. This inter-actional perspective is emphasised by modern infant research (see Chapter Three, under "The consequences of maternal depression on the early emotional development of the infant", pp. 88–93). In the Freudian conception of the early state of inner life, the infant initially denies his fundamental dependency on the outside world, as he fanta-sises that the external actually belongs to the internal. The infant fails to recognise reality; moreover, he adapts reality to his instinctual need. This is the first psychic way of functioning; the primary process will later dissipate, through the necessary withdrawal of satisfaction from the infant and its subsequent frustration, in favour of the secondary process. However, the subject again loses this more realis-tic secondary processual thinking (in a regression). In individuals with structural (early) disorders, the secondary processual thinking can be available only in a deficient way.

What consequences, then, does this structure of primitive desire described by Freud have for the genesis of the subject? In Freud's conception, the infant hallucinates the gratification of his desires and in this way fulfils his desires, but this is only possible for as long as the basic needs are met from outside by a carer. If this care fails to materialise, as repeatedly happens in the normal course of child development, this hallucinatory gratification cannot provide real grat-ification for the infant. According to Freud, this leads to the genera-tion of massive displeasure. The hallucination must be curbed. The arousal that results from the physical need gradually becomes attached to ideas, and is directed towards motility and no longer to the mere cathexis of memory. "A new principle of mental functioning was thus introduced; what was presented in the mind was no longer what was agreeable but what was real, even if it happened to be disagreeable" (Freud, 1911b, p. 219).

In his "Project for a scientific psychology" (Freud, 1950a[1895]), Freud describes the ego as a system of constant cathexis and, thus, as being in a position to curb the primary process, that is, the primary processual desiring and hallucinating. The possibility of delaying the removal of arousal is, thus, supplied by thought. Through the activity of thinking, the psychic apparatus is in a position to bear the build-up of tension during the delay of arousal up to the realistic action. Imagining what is real and not just what is desired becomes a performance of the secondary process.

Repression

Since the primary processes represent the first way in which the psychic apparatus works, and the secondary processes only take effect after a delay and never obtain full dominance over the psyche, a large part of this memory material remains unconscious. This treasure trove of memories, unavailable to consciousness, forms the unconscious core of the human being. In the metapsychology that Freud outlines in Chapter VII of *The Interpretation of Dreams* (Freud, 1900a), Freud indicates the appeal of this core of unconscious desires, which his later theory of primal repression, *Urverdrängung*, was to articulate more precisely. The key characteristic of primal repression, he said, is that it represents an unconscious core that constitutes itself at a point in time in the subject's development before the acquisition of language. Freud suggests that this never-conscious core holds a strong attraction to conscious thinking, which becomes possible through the secondary system:

> We have reason to assume that there is a primal repression, a first phase of repression, which consists in the psychical (ideational) representative of the instinct being denied entrance into the conscious. With this a fixation is established; the representative in question persists unaltered from then onwards and the instinct remains attached to it. (Freud, 1915d, p. 148)

The instinct is, from now on, fixated on one idea, and the possibility of becoming conscious is never given to this idea. This unconscious core, however, is now in a position to draw down into itself particular ideas or derivatives of these repressed ideational representatives, which are connected it only through associations. With the occurrence of the secondary function, some of the "indestructible and uninhibitable desires stemming from the infantile" (Freud, 1900a, p. 609) pose a contradiction to the demands of the outside world that constitute the ego. The influence of the objectives of secondary thinking is expressed, according to Freud, in the way that the fulfilment of such

CLASSICAL PSYCHOANALYTICAL CONCEPTS

forbidden, illegitimate desires causes displeasure instead of a sensa-
tion of pleasure. Such a transformation of affect represents the essence
of repression. A transformation of affect during child development is
seen, for example, in the emergence of previously absent sensations of
disgust (aversion, revulsion), which become possible through the
secondary system.

The preconscious has no influence on these unconscious desires
that form the core of the human being. The development of affect
comes about through the conflictual relationship of precisely these
unconscious desires with the social demands transmitted via the
secondary system. According to the pleasure principle, the displeasure that is felt causes the psychic apparatus to turn away from these
"thoughts of transference" (*Übertragungsgedanken*) to which the
unconscious desires have transferred the force of their desire.

Freud concludes

> that repression is not a defensive mechanism which is present from
> the very beginning, and that it cannot arise until a sharp cleavage has
> occurred between conscious and unconscious mental activity – that
> the essence of repression lies simply in turning something away, and
> keeping it at a distance, from the conscious. (Freud, 1915d, p. 147)

Later, in his writing on narcissism, he states that the person who
represses has constructed an ideal in himself. The repression takes
place to benefit the ego ideal. "For the ego the formation of an ideal
would be the conditioning factor of repression" (Freud, 1914c, p. 94).
Once a separation of conscious and unconscious operations of the
psychic apparatus is there, it is in accordance with the pleasure principle to block such thoughts of transference, on to which the unconscious desire has transferred its power, from becoming conscious, in
order to avoid massive displeasure (Freud, 1900a). Accordingly, it is
in the second phase of repression—repression proper—that the drive
representations that stand in associative connection to a (primally)
repressed representation are pressed into the unconscious.

> Repression proper, therefore, is actually an after-pressure. Moreover,
> it is a mistake to emphasize only the repulsion which operates from
> the direction of the conscious upon what is to be repressed; quite as
> important is the attraction exercised by what was primally repressed
> upon everything with which it can establish a connection. (Freud,
> 1915d, p. 148)

Freud describes the drama of repression that is constitutive of the person in terms of energy. Repression is about withdrawing the preconscious cathexis from a preconscious idea, but maintaining its unconscious (energy) cathexis. The transition of an idea from one system to the other is "not effected through the making of a new registration but through a change in its state, an alteration in its cathexis" (Freud, 1915e, p. 180). The conditions for repression are two economic processes: the first, as mentioned, the withdrawal into the preconscious of a cathexis that is tied to a displeasurable idea. However, since the unconscious cathexis of this idea continues, this energetic cathexis accordingly represents a force that empowers the unconscious idea to penetrate into the preconscious or return to it, if it once was conscious. Second, there must, according to Freud, be a mechanism that guarantees the constant repression. It is the countercathexis which uses the energy that results from the withdrawal of the preconscious cathexis, and, thus, cathects a preconscious idea, that prevents the unconscious repressed idea from becoming conscious. "The indestructability of unconscious desire is countered by the relitive rigidity of the ego's defensive structures, which require a permanent expenditure of energy", say Laplanche & Pontalis (1973, p. 37) in their indispensable *Language of Psychoanalysis*. Repression leads to an extraordinary impoverishment of the person, a constant wasting of energy; the significant task of psychoanalysis consists in reversing repression again.

> The anticathected element may be of several kinds. It may be simply a derivative of the unconscious idea (a substitutive formation, as in the case for example, of those animals which in phobia become the object of an unremitting awareness and of which the function is to keep the unconscious wish and its related phantasies repressed). Or it may be an element directly opposed to the unconscious idea (a reaction formation – for example the exaggerted concern of a mother for her children masking aggressive wishes, or a preoccupation cleanliness representing a struggle against anal tendencies). (Laplanche & Pontalis, 1973 pp. 36–37)

The unconscious

The dynamic unconscious in psychoanalytic theory should not be confused with the concept of the procedural unconscious, which describes memory contents that are able to control the actions of the subject (e.g., when driving a car) without the subject being conscious of them. By contrast, the content of the dynamic unconscious can become available to consciousness only in a distorted form, or after intensive working through of the patient's resistances to the repressed material becoming conscious, as part of a psychoanalytic process. The repressed ideas continue to exist in the unconscious, retaining their unconscious cathexis and constituting a realm in which psychic processes follow very different rules from those that govern the way in which the conscious and the preconscious work. In the unconscious, the primary process holds sway, characterised by "far greater mobility of cathexis intensities". The "nucleus of the Unconscious consists of instinctual representatives which seek to discharge their cathexis; that is to say, it consists of wishful impulses" (Freud, 1915e, p. 186). These desires, which exist in the unconscious and are indestructible and uninhibitable, constantly strive to become conscious and, thereby, pose a threat to the ego, but they also create a subversive space as a kind of refuge, inaccessible to the inhibitions of the secondary system and ignorant of hard external reality. These unconscious desires populate a timeless playground, striving for fulfilment. They are relatively autonomous, constituting an area of the psyche that is no longer derived from a need, but follows its own rules: those of the primary process. In Freud's theory, a desire is linked with the psychic primary process in such a way that it forms a foundation for the psyche prior to all cultural formation. Infantile desires that do not accord with the requirements made of the ego must be rejected and kept in repression.

Psychoanalytic study of neuroses

Psychodynamic intrapsychic conflicts are unconscious, internal collisions of contradictory unconscious desires, bundles of motivations, urges, or behavioural tendencies, for example, the basic desire for dependency and to be cared for by the object, and the basic desire to be autonomous. Long-lasting psychodynamic conflicts are shaped by an individual's patterns of experience, which lead to behavioural patterns being repeated in corresponding situations, without the person's being conscious of it.

For the processing of conflicts, Anna Freud's systematisation of defence mechanisms, *The Ego and Mechanisms of Defence* (1936), should be consulted.

Long-lasting intrapsychic conflicts contain antagonistic, unsuccessfully integrated perspectives of experience and action. They act to inhibit the child's development. Fundamentally, intrapsychic conflicts contain themes that are processed in every human being's development, but not in the development-inhibiting exclusivity meant here. Conflicts are determined by the level of structural integration on which they are based, and are formed in characteristic relationship episodes.

The classical *psychoanalytical study of neurosis* assumes that in the course of child development there are necessarily conflicts between the infantile urge towards pleasure (originally the pleasure principle = reduction of tension as the central motivation system) and the demands of the environment. Both massive denial of instinctual desires in the form of frustration and deprivation and reconciliation and compliance with the infantile urge towards pleasure can lead to fixations on particular conflict themes.

Regression

If, during the course of development, the child (or adolescent or adult) repeatedly experiences similar conflict themes for which he or she does not have adequate solutions readily available, there will be some regression to steps of libidinal development that have previously been achieved. Through this regression, which also serves as a means of avoiding fear, earlier forms of need satisfaction are brought into the present. However, this is perceived by the matured ego as a threat. What previously provided pleasure is now severely condemned by the ego under the influence of the moral instance of the ego ideal and later the superego, leading to anxiety. The ego now meets this anxiety by attempting to compromise between the demands of the id and the demands of reality (the moral demands of the environment represented by the ego ideal/superego). This compromise can only succeed through the expenditure of energy through counter-cathexis. A neurotic symptom is always a compromise between two antagonistic desires or strivings. These are the desires of the two different instances, the id and the superego, between which the ego is attempting to mediate through its defences. The effort of making this compromise can lead to the generation of disturbing rituals and apparently pointless behaviours and habits (symptoms).

After Freud's death, the so-called structural model served as a foundation for the classical psychoanalytic approach of the ego-psychological school based around Anna Freud, Hartmann, Kris, and Loewenstein, and even today can be used as an important conceptualisation of the sometimes conflicting parts of a person's ego. The more severe the pathology, the more unbalanced and conflicted is the relationship of the structural instances (ego, id, superego) to each other.

Conclusion for PaCT

Freud's notion that human development takes place in psychosexual phases, in which drives form the constitution of the subject, is of central importance for PaCT. The development of the psychic internal space is modelled on the first experiences of one's own body (the erogenous zones) and subsequently on experiences of the external object. We take a genuinely Freudian perspective by understanding the child's symptoms against the backdrop of his or her conflicts within their psychosexual development. Thus, a child, through fear induced by the developmental steps that bring new psychosexual phases, may regress to developmental phases that are no longer age-appropriate, or even remain fixated on one mode of drive satisfaction, failing to reach the next stage.

Case illustration

Pete, eight years old

Although Pete's general cognitive performance was clearly above average, he failed at various school tasks. He found reading and writing particularly difficult, as well as having problems handling numbers, to the extent that he failed at school and his mother and teacher became concerned. Pete said that he "forgot everything", and "just couldn't remember it". The therapist was surprised that this boy's interactions were so appropriate to his age, and in symbolic play he was markedly concerned with his masculinity: he was particularly interested in phallic symbols such as cannons and guns. His failure at school can consequently be understood as a neurotic symptom, a compromise between unconscious desires to be strong and manly, and fear of being punished by his father. Both the anal ability to hold something in (including knowledge) and the genital curiosity sublimated in the thirst for knowledge were abandoned in favour of early infantile passivity and dependency. Another factor that made the situation more complicated was that his mother had had traumatic experiences in her early relationship with her father and brother, so that expressions of male sexuality caused her great anxiety. By regressing to an age-inappropriate "helplessness", the boy tried unconsciously to secure his link to his mother, without exposing himself to the risk of incest, of shocking his mother, or of entering into competition with his father. Thus, there remained for Pete only the neurotic solution, through which his development was stymied by a fundamental inhibition: without being able to read or write, he could never become like the male objects he admired with their daggers and cannons, but, at the same time, while remaining like this he did not need to fear his mother's shock if he were to become as strong as a man.

Anna Freud on the issue of diagnosis and meaning of neurosis in childhood

Anna Freud addressed the question of diagnosis, that is, the differentiation between severe and mild neurosis (A. Freud, 1945). She observed that children who need psychotherapy are often kept away from analytic treatment because their parents are afraid that family secrets and taboos will become public. Rivalry or jealousy towards the analyst are also common reasons why parents do not send their children to therapy. The degree of suffering—which in adults is a diagnostic indication for treatment—is unsuited to assessing the indication for child analysis (A. Freud, 1945, p. 133). Adults suffer from their symptoms more than children do, and make independent decisions to enter therapy. The child, on the other hand, generally does not suffer directly from the neurotic symptoms; it is usually the parents who experience the symptoms as disturbing. Parents often bring their children to psychoanalytic treatment because they think that particular developmental functions of the child are impaired.

Thus, Anna Freud claimed that, for example, neurotic eating disorders are the expression of negative feelings in the relationship with the mother, and can arise through defending against oral and anal sadistic unconscious fantasies. With bedwetting, night terrors, temper tantrums, and so on, it is again usually the parents who suffer and not the child. "Acute neurotic suffering is felt by the child in all states of anxiety before a consistent defence against it has become established" (A. Freud, 1945, p. 134). Thus, she concludes that it tends to be the children whose symptoms disturb the parents or teachers who receive treatment, rather than the children who are less disruptive. Disorders with invisible symptoms are often particularly severe, such as inhibited, compulsive disorders, but children with these disorders are often not brought to therapy.

In adults, a so-called "functional disorder", that is, a disorder of the ability to love or work, has been an indication for psychoanalytic treatment since the time of Sigmund Freud. Anna Freud claimed that it is extremely difficult to recognise when a child is sexually disordered, particularly in relation to the criterion of the ability to love. The child's sexuality is not goal-orientated, has no climax, and is divided up into partial drives that coexist alongside each other, with no single drive assuming primacy over another. The child's ability to love can best be assessed according to the relationship of narcissistic and object libido: "Normally after the first year of life object-love should outweigh narcissism; satisfaction derived from objects should become increasingly greater than autoerotic gratification. An infantile neurosis can seriously interfere with these proportions" (p. 135). Too strong a degree of self-centredness and disinterest in shared play with others can thus indicate childhood neurosis (see case study, Elisabeth, Chapter Fourteen).

The analogy between the adult's inability to work as a treatment criterion and the child's inability to play/fantasise is also incomplete. However, problems in a child's ability to play are an indicator for neurotic disorders. If play behaviour, for example, is compulsive and monotonous, or if it starts to inhibit every other activity, then it betrays its nature as an inhibition: that is, "it is a sign that the child is fixated at a certain point of his libidinal development" (p. 136). The difficulty in finding analogies between the treatment indications for adults and children shows—as Anna Freud emphasises—that alternative or new criteria are required in order to assess the severity of a childhood neurosis, and whether it needs treatment. But these criteria are difficult to find, since "Childhood is a process sui generis" (p. 136). Anna Freud taught us:

> There is only one factor in childhood of such central importance that its impairment through a neurosis calls for immediate action; namely, the child's ability to develop, not to remain fixated at some stage of development before the maturation process has been concluded. (p. 136)

The child's inability to grow further psychically is a criterion for assessing the severity of a child's neurotic disorder. It is important, she stresses, not to view the level of symptoms alone (as children can quickly grow out of symptoms), or suffering, or the current degree of disruption to the child's life (including interpersonal conflicts caused by the symptom). Childhood neurosis should be assessed, "according to the degree to which it prevents the child from developing further" (p. 136).

Libido development and its disorders

In order to assess the age-appropriateness or any disturbance of a child's libido development, defects in intelligence or organic damage must first be excluded. A neurotic inhibition or disorder is diagnosed "where the developmental phases are chaotic, or where the child remains fixed at a particular stage" (p. 142). Anna Freud also pointed out, "Gross disturbance in the order of events, or a child's failure to progress from any of these transitory stages when he is neither organically nor mentally deficient, points to serious neurotic interference" (p. 136). This is, however, not as simple as it seems, because the libidinal phases are not sharply delineated, but, rather, merge into one another. For example, there are oral elements in the middle of the anal–sadistic phase: "It would, for instance, be erroneous to conclude from a persistence of oral or anal forms of autoerotic gratification into the fourth or fifth year, that the child has failed to reach the phallic level" (p. 137). According to Anna Freud, it is normal for the libido never to cathect the final developmental stage to its full extent. Parts of the libido remain bound to the forms of gratification characteristic of earlier stages: "To ensure normality it is sufficient if the major proportion of the libido reaches the organisation appropriate to the age of the child" (p. 137). Thus, it dominates over the other partial drives.

Anna Freud stressed how important it is to gain a comprehensive picture of a child's libido development: that is, to follow the paths taken by the individual partial drives. A severe neurotic disorder occurs where a child manifestly has "no indication of one or another partial drive" (p. 243). She also remarks, "We would not expect any of the component instincts to be completely absent from the clinical picture . . . except as a sign of severe neurotic disturbance" (p. 137). However, note should be taken of constitutional differences in the dominance of the individual partial drives: "Neurosis in an adult damages the intactness of the sex organisation; an infantile neurosis also interferes directly with the forward movement of the libido" (p. 138).

Anna Freud described the development of a childhood neurosis as follows:

> In the beginning stage of a neurotic conflict the libido flows backward (regression), and attaches itself once more to earlier libidinal wishes (fixation point), in order to avoid anxiety that has arisen on a higher level of sex organisation. (p. 138)

However, since the ego has rejected these primitive early forms of gratification in the course of its development, the child's regression generates an intrapsychic conflict. The ego of the child protects himself/herself from the risk presented by the drive with the help of various defence mechanisms (repressions, reaction formation, displacements, etc.), but, as Anna Freud wrote, ". . . if such defence is unsuccessful, neurotic symptoms arise which represent the gratification of the wish, distorted in its form by the action of the repressive forces" (p. 138). These symptoms incur all the drive energy, and thus become first the carriers of the child's sexual life. In childhood eating disorders, the process takes place as follows: the drive remains fixated at the oral stage; this fixation inhibits further libido development (e.g., phallicity, in the form of a drive for knowledge or curiosity, is impaired, and cannot experience its full developmental potential):

eating, or refusing to eat, instead of moving exploratively in the world; here the child remains fixated in oral or anal–sadistic forms of drive satisfaction (see case study Max, Chapter Six, under "Explanation using case studies", pp. 155–161).

With the regression from the phallic to the anal–sadistic stage, there are noticeable changes in the child's personality, particularly the loss of attitudes and abilities that depend on a higher libido organisation. Regression from the phallic to the anal–sadistic stage "destroys the hardly acquired attributes of generosity, manliness and protectiveness, and substitutes for them the domineering possessiveness that belongs to the earlier libidinal level" (p. 138). Anna Freud stresses that childhood neurosis often spontaneously resolves, probably as a consequence of passage through biological developmental phases: "This possibility is greatest at times when the biological urges are of especial strength, as they are at the onset of the phallic phase (four to five years) and of puberty" (p. 140) and is based on real changes in the libido economy. By contrast, there are no spontaneous recoveries from adult neurosis. The neurotic symptom, as a compromise between repressed and repressing impulses, must remain unchanged as long as drive, ego, and superego do not change significantly.

Ego development and its disorders

Neurotic children, especially children with internalising symptoms, often show a high degree of psychosocial adjustment and, on first impression, appear to be very mature. Nevertheless, their development-inhibiting symptom results in a stagnation of their development process. Thus, Anna Freud questioned whether the precocious ego that can be observed in neurotic children is the cause or the consequence of a neurosis, and in connection with diagnosis the following questions must be asked.

- Does the infantile neurosis disturb or promote ego development?
- What points of contact are there between ego development and the process of neurosis formation?
- Can possible damage to the ego due to the neurosis be evaluated as an additional diagnostic criterion?

According to Anna Freud, ego strength

refers to the relative efficiency of the ego with regard to the contents of the id (instinctual drives) and to the forces of the environment with which the ego has to deal. . . . In the beginning of life the instinctual drives are of overwhelming strength and the first crystallizations of an ego are completely under their domination and at their service. The child's growing awareness of the outside world, the beginnings of his ability to retain and connect memory traces, to foresee events, to draw conclusions from them, etc., are used exclusively for the purpose of instinct gratification. (A. Freud, 1945, pp. 141–142)

As her father, Sigmund Freud, had stated, the more strongly the child cathects his objects with libido, the more strongly he will identify with the parents' demands to suppress drive, and the more he will identify through the development of the ego ideal with the wishes and demands of the parents, even if they directly conflict with his own desires (Freud, 1914c). The child appropriates these "hostile attitudes towards his instinctual demands" (A. Freud, 1945, p. 142) through identification and makes increasing efforts to master the demands placed on him by managing the instinctual life. Pre-oedipally, the ego is not yet strong enough to be able to deploy defence mechanisms such as repression consistently. There is still a predominance of the pleasure principle and primary processes in the psychic functioning of the child. It is the oedipal disappointments that lead to a predominance of the ego over the anarchic coexistence of the partial drives. With the construction of the superego, the ego's efforts are more strongly directed towards the id, and, thus, fulfil the demands to suppress drive and acknowledge the generational difference. In latency, the ego functions are extended further and, thus, increasingly determine the actions of the child. Only with the arrival of the drives of puberty do the pregenital and then the genital libido gain strength. Here begin the endless battles between ego and id that are characteristic of puberty. "Throughout adolescence ego forces and id forces struggle with each other for the upper hand, a combat that is responsible for many of the conflicting and abnormal manifestations of that period" (p. 142). For personality development it is important, according to Anna Freud, "that this part of character formation . . . should not be terminated too early" (p. 142). An uninhibited development of the drive in one or another direction is important for healthy development (A. Freud, 1968).

A neurosis paralyses the natural developmental process. "Every neurotic symptom represents an attempt to establish an artificial balance between an instinctual wish and the repressive forces of the ego" (A. Freud, 1945, p. 143). Every further development of the relationship between the instances is undermined if the balance between drive satisfaction and drive inhibition sets too quickly. A neurosis always leads to a drive regression.

> Libidinal regression is always accompanied by a certain amount of ego regression . . . that a child who regresses from the genital to the oral level simultaneously regresses from ego strength to ego weakness. Or, to put it differently, regression from the genital to the oral level implies regression from the reality principle to the pleasure principle. (p. 143)

Thus, neurotic children lack ego strength, but their ego is precociously exposed to solidification. Because he/she is putting effort into maintaining neurotic compromise and symptom formation, such a child can no longer freely develop his psychic functions and his developmental ability is consequently inhibited (see case study Sophie, Chapter Eleven).

The child's ego develops from the first months of life from a primitive starting point of basic valences of pleasure and displeasure, into a precise mental apparatus that receives, orders, interprets, and evaluates arriving stimuli.

The superego, as a special entity in the ego, evaluates motives and thought contents from the standpoint of morality. Ego development is a process that makes many demands on the child and is not without displeasure. Testing by the superego reveals the presence of dangerous drives within the child himself, and signifies a downgrading of the child's sense of self. Testing by reality means that it is not only pleasurable things that are perceived, or that are imagined as belonging to the ego. Neither is the memory as pleasurable as before, and the reign of the ego over motility is also unpleasant, as it now prevents the child from directly releasing tensions. "Each one of the new functions has its disagreeable consequences" (A. Freud, 1945, p. 144), as displeasure arises from it. The child therefore attempts to dismantle developing ego functions. Diverse defence mechanisms such as denial, reaction formation, projection, flight from reality into fantasy, the introjection of desired parts of the exterior world into the self, accompany these attempts to ward off displeasurable feelings. This serves to keep the child free of fear. "A certain retrograde movement in the development of the ego achievements is, therefore, the rule" (p. 145). Only after entry into latency can the ego functions gain strength, as anxiety declines through instinctual pressure. However, if, in pre-oedipal or oedipal development, severe neurotic conflicts dominate (e.g., where oedipal jealousy causes belief in the parents' asexuality to be retained), then anxiety is so severe that a greater defensive effort is needed. This, in turn, impairs the ego functions even more strongly.

Anna Freud stressed that the neurotic mechanisms contradict the ego functions at any stage of life. "This interference with the ego functions is of greater importance in childhood than under otherwise similar conditions in the adult neurosis" (1945, p. 147).

In childhood, the damage that occurs is, however, much greater, because "the function that is most directly attacked by infantile neurosis is kept back from further development, at least temporarily, while the other ego achievements continue to mature" (pp. 147–142). One-sided and unbalanced personalities (e.g., compulsive or hysteric ones) can, according to Anna Freud, be ascribed to neurotic developments (1945, p. 147).

Which disorder of ego function that a child acquires in the course of a neurotic development depends on the specific accompanying defence mechanisms.

For example, hysterical children, in whom repression is the central defence mechanism, can be poor learners. Difficulties in remembering something (or better: in wanting to remember something), which result from the specific defence mechanism and determine the central conflict of these children, are not limited to the specific frightening content but are generalised to other memories, too. Hence, a specific cognitive style of thinking can be characterised by childhood neurosis.

Compulsive neurotic children, on the other hand, generally learn exceptionally well, but usually to the disadvantage of their emotional life.

But, owing to the excessive ego interference with the free expression of their anal–sadistic tendencies, they are estranged from their own emotions, and are considered cold and unresponsive, even when other

than these primitive aggressive sexual manifestations are concerned.
(A. Freud, 1945, p. 148)

We thus conclude with Anna Freud that if

a child shows a faulty knowledge of the outer world, far below the
level of his intelligence; if he is seriously estranged from his own
emotions, with blank spaces in the remembrance of his own past
beyond the usual range of infantile amnesia, with a split in his personality, and with motility out of ego control; then there can be little
doubt that the neurosis is severe and that it is high time to take therapeutic action. (p. 148).

Conclusion for PaCT

In estimating the need for therapy to deal with psychic problems, we
shift our view, along with Anna Freud, from the pure description of
symptoms to the significance that the neurotic symptoms have for
the process of development. For PaCT, this means that the goal of
the therapy is not primarily to eliminate symptoms, but to return the
libido orientation and defence mechanisms to the paths of normal
development. Thus, we view symptoms only in terms of their significance for the child's development. Neurotic children, and particularly
children with emotional symptoms, often show a high degree of
psychosocial adjustment. However, this marked adjustment might
also have a defensive character. It is, therefore, important to diagnose
whether good apparent adjustment is taking place on a foundation of
premature establishment of the ego. The state of the child's libido
development and the flexibility of defence formations are important
criteria in deciding for or against treatment. It is, therefore, diagnostically important to estimate whether a child with superficially good
psychosocial adjustment has depressive or anxiety feelings, or a
tendency to internalise interpersonal conflicts. Such phenomena can
be the expression of premature establishment of the relationship of the
ego or superego to the id, which entails an inhibition of the child's
developmental ability. Psychoanalytic treatment is indicated if the
libido constellations are becoming solidified and the forms of gratification rigid and monotonous. Without therapy, the child can be at risk
of remaining neurotic.

The object relations theory of Melanie Klein

In this section, we will present some central aspects of Melanie Klein's theory that are relevant to the theoretical considerations on which PaCT is based. The consequences and distinctive features of the Kleinian interpretative and therapy technique are presented elsewhere in this book (see Chapter Three, section headed "Transference and countertransference", pp. 94–96, and Chapter Six, section headed "Interpretation, transference, and countertransference", pp. 161–163). It is important to stress that the object relations theory of Melanie Klein always conceptualises "objects" as "inner objects" based on the individuals unconscious phantasies.

In contrast to Freud, Melanie Klein emphasises the primordial entanglement of drive and object. For her, the object libido is not a secondary formation; the drive attaches itself immediately to an object, that is, the person who is the relational object to the child's bodily needs. For Klein, the central task of the constituted subject is, therefore, to surmount a state in which the infant is populated by split internal (partial) objects, formed out of projections and introjections, and to transform it into a state in which whole, real, and internalised objects can be drawn upon. The individual's normal development and his or her ability to love are based on the early ego moving beyond the "paranoid–schizoid position" and reaching the "depressive position". Only in this way can the ego trust in the goodness of its (internalised and real) objects and, thus, achieve greater independence from them.

"I nevertheless attributed to the depressive position a central role in the child's early development. For with the introjection of the object as a whole the relation to the object alters fundamentally" (Klein, 1946, p. 99).

According to Klein, the unsuccessful introjection of the object is primarily due to the excess of aggressive impulses in an infant's drive constellation. Klein convincingly argued that the ego, through the repeated unification and differentiation of good and evil, fantastic and real, external and internal objects, gradually advances to a more realistic grasp of external and internal objects, and through this to a better relationship with the two. The inability to maintain an identification with (whole) internalised and real good objects could, according to Klein, lead to a state of depression. Klein says that the depressive position contains the increasing inability of the infant to identify with his or her objects. This differentiation between the self and its objects results in the subject feeling a sense of guilt for its sadistic attacks on the (partial) object. Previously, this had not been possible, because the infant was too unco-ordinated and disorganised, and because the objects introjected by him or her were only partial objects. The recognition that the primary object, against which the primary impulses are directed, is simultaneously the object of the libido, entails feelings of guilt and an urge for reparation (Klein, 1940). The early ego becomes aware that its destructive attacks, projected on to the internal and external object, have destroyed the object. The transition from the paranoid–schizoid position, in which the object is perceived as persecutory, into the depressive position, in which the subject feels guilty for its attacks against the object, is linked with the integration of good and bad partial objects into a more holistic image of the self and the object. The achievement of the depressive position, which is characterised by feelings of guilt, grief, and reparation, is an important step forward in the child's development.

If this integration of the good and bad partial objects is unsuccessful, it may lead to a disposition towards the development of depression. In this early state of the inner life, the fear associated with the good object is also the fear surrounding oneself. Whenever the mother leaves, to the small child it appears that it has eaten her up and destroyed her with its hate and love. This first and fundamental loss of a real and loved object, which is experienced before and during weaning in the loss of the breast, becomes a basis for a depressive tendency if the child is unable to set up and preserve a good internal object in this early phase of development. The success or failure of the introjection processes in the interaction with the real external mother is, according to Klein, of key importance. In the adult, real disappointments reactivate the early anxieties about being abandoned and the feelings of guilt linked to this first loss of the love object. The internal objects are not stable enough to compensate for real disappointments.

For Klein, unconscious phantasy is centrally important to the process of building up a psychic inner world. However, she developed her own concept of unconscious phantasy as a structuring medium of the psyche. Working from Freud's final drive theory, in which he described the duality of Eros and Thanatos, Klein relocates this drive polarity in the infant, effective from birth onwards as a polarised constellation of instincts. If this drive is a form of death wish, it fills the interior life with displeasure. Freud articulates an autopoiesis, a kind of self-creation under the reign of the pleasure principle, in which an ur-narcissism, purified of displeasure, describes an initial form of self-referentiality which takes itself as the object and only later comes into conflict with the outside world because of its omnipotent need for pleasure. Klein's infant, on the other hand, constructs himself from the initial birth trauma onwards through his defence against the fear of threatened destruction. In the infant, this drive antagonism, which consists of libidinal and aggressive-thanatal impulses, unfolds as a chaos of contradictory affects, and creates a phantasmatic world populated by good and evil persecutory objects. Thus, the unconscious phantasy is created by the drive itself, and, as a drive representation, it links the driving forces and psychic mechanisms.

Gast (1996, p. 167) offers a dramatic image to represent the dramaturgic setting of the genesis of the early subject, illustrating the constitution of the subject in the phantasmatic space of the Kleinian infant: in a cinema with a 360-degree screen, a projectionist alternates fluidly between horror films and romances; a director is responsible for the transitions of the scenes and the cuts, while the audience melds emotionally with the drama, sharing hate, love, fear, struggle, and suffering. All these persons, including the actors on screen, are one person; they represent the Kleinian infant, which, at this early stage of its psychic development, phantasises its polarised constellation of instincts in relation to objects in a dramatic way analogous to the image proposed by Gast. Since the drive always represents a relationship to an object, these early instincts are experienced, as the Kleinian Susan Isaacs emphasises, as "what he is . . . going to do with the desired object" (Isaacs, 1948, p. 83) At the earliest stage of drive development they are oral impulses, which are phantasised as "I want to take the (loved) object into me", or "I want to bite, to destroy the hated (because frustrating) object": "I want to take and I am taking her (mother or breast) into me" (Isaacs, 1948, p. 87). Thus, for Klein, physical drive impulses that grasp or discover their object set off a psychic movement, allowing the infant to experience a multiplicity of relationships to the object in specific phantasies. Klein suggests that feelings such as frustration, hate, love, rage, grief, and reparation are always in relation to an object. The corresponding unconscious phantasies tailor the psychic internal space.

Conclusions for PaCT

Klein teaches us the significance of internal objects. These can be distorted independently of the characteristics of the real objects, being only persecuting or only "good", according to the patient's level of integration. Even in the neurotically structured child with more mature defence mechanisms, situations of stress, overtiredness, or hyperstimulation can lead to a less integrated level of object relationship, where objects are perceived as being only "persecuting" or only "good" (splitting). Klein describes this as the paranoid–schizoid position. In Klein's psychological development concept, the transition from the paranoid–schizoid to the depressive position signifies progress in development. The subject gives up its splitting, and experiences concern and guilt for what it has done to the object. Since PaCT pursues a development-orientated treatment concept and aim, along with Anna Freud, in order to promote the developmental process we must also assume that progress in treatment may be accompanied by the temporary appearance or strengthening of depressive feelings.

The object relations theory of Donald W. Winnicott

Winnicott adds an important aspect to Klein's proposal of the significance of internal objects for the psychological development of the subject: the real object.

In his view, the way in which this real object responds to the destructiveness of the subject determines whether the subject can find a way to access the real object and, therefore, reality, or whether instead the object remains as only a bundle of projections for the subject. This would preserve a state—although he calls it an object relation—in which the subjective and the objective form an amorphous, undifferentiated mass, similar to the fantasy of the Freudian primary narcissistic infant.

> In object-relating the subject allows certain alterations in the self to take place, of a kind that has caused us to invent the term cathexis. The object has become meaningful. Projection mechanisms and identifications have been operating, and the subject is depleted to the extent that something of the subject is found in the object, though enriched by feeling, (Winnicott, 1969, p. 711)

Winnicott describes the object relation as a substantially subjective process. The nature of the object does not itself play a role. There can also be an object relation with an object that is not even perceived as such by the subject, but is made up of the projections and identifications of the subject. In order for a subject to evolve progressively and gain access to objective reality, it must have a capacity for *object usage*. This is part of the transition to the reality principle. According to Winnicott, for this transition to be achieved successfully in the early development of the infant's relation to the object, there must be room for a movement that initially appears contradictory. Winnicott describes this movement from object relation to object use as a process that, through the destruction of the object by the subject, eases the way to the individual's use of fantasy. But the object can only be experienced as separate from the infant if it survives the infant's own destructive attacks. This removes it from the omnipotent primary narcissistic control, and, thus, the subject becomes able to use the object in terms of the characteristics that are inherent to it, not just those projected on to it. Winnicott stresses

> that the position 'the subject stands in relation to the object' follows the position 'the subject destroys the object (which only thus becomes something external)'; only then can the position 'the object survives being destroyed by the subject' follow. It can survive, but need not. In other words, he will find that after 'subject relates to object' comes 'subject destroys object' (as it becomes external); and then may come 'object survives destruction by the subject'. But there may or may not be survival. A new feature thus arrives in the theory of object-relating. The subject says to the object: 'I destroyed you', and the object is there to receive the communication. From now on the subject says: 'Hullo object!' 'I destroyed you.' 'I love you.' 'You have value for me because of your survival of my destruction of you'. (Winnicott, 1969, p. 713)

Only when the infant is able to experience external reality as something that exists outside its omnipotent control, beyond illusion and projection, can it be used and drawn on to provide the infant's "not me" substance (Winnicott, 1971a, p. 130). The real object and its ability to survive the destructive attacks of the subject are central to this stage of development, which can also be unsuccessful. For Winnicott, the object's survival is demonstrated by its ability not to exact revenge. Only the good enough object has this ability to be reliable and to persist, even though it has been destroyed. Through this, the

infant experiences a continuity of being that simultaneously introduces a differentiating moment. The object that does not take revenge
shows itself to the subject through its resistance, and so enables the
infant to integrate its own aggression into an initial personality
pattern. However, only an object that is not under the subject's
omnipotent control, and thus can be perceived objectively (that is, not
just as a subjective projection), is suitable for cathexis and destruction.
Something that allows itself to be destroyed and nevertheless remains
after the act of destruction can be recognised by the infant.

An object that allows itself to be destroyed and then answers the
child's destructive impulses with refusal, withdrawal, or counter-
aggression cannot achieve real object status, because it cannot be
loved as an object that survives destruction. The subject's early
aggressiveness, according to Winnicott, therefore has a positive,
creative quality, as it leads to the generation of difference.

Psychoanalytic child therapy (PaCT) with its central element of
working through in a psychoanalytic setting, can be understood in
Winnicott's terms. Winnicott established that psychoanalysis is a
"highly specialized form of playing in the service of communication
with oneself and others" (Winnicott, 1971a, p. 41). Play, like the transitional object, is a transitional phenomenon, and opens up a transitional
space. Play involves trying things out in a space that can be assigned
neither totally to the inner world, nor entirely to the space that obeys
the reality principle and that is shared with the objects of external reality. Psychotherapy, according to Winnicott, "has to do with two people
playing together" (Winnicott, 1971a, p. 38). This playing does not take
place

> inside by any use of the word (and it is unfortunately true that the
> word inside has very many and various uses in psychoanalytic discus-
> sion). Nor is it outside, that is to say, it is not a part of the repudiated
> world, the not-me, that which the individual has decided to recognize
> (with whatever difficulty and even pain) as truly external, which is
> outside magical control. (Winnicott, 1971a, p. 41)

Conclusion for PaCT

These insights of Winnicott's are of particular significance for PaCT. In
treating children with emotional problems, it is vital that the therapist

survives the child's unconscious destructiveness and deals with the feelings of anger that he himself experiences in his countertransference, without transforming them into counter-aggressive acts. In Chapter Three, section headed "Transference and countertransference", pp. 94–96, and Chapter Six, section headed "Interpretation, transference, and countertransference", pp. 161–163, we will go into more detail about the significance of this intensive reflection of the therapist's negative countertransference for PaCT. In his treatment of Piggle, Winnicott showed how even a small number of analytical sessions (which were, admittedly, spread over a longer period) with parents and child could promote important stages of the child's development (Winnicott, 1980).

Play is an important transitional space in child development. This transitional space should not be assigned totally to the inside world, or totally to the world of external objects either. It is, therefore, important that this space unfolds and opens up in therapy. The child's play is, thus, not just a tool ("psychoanalytical play technique"), but also the goal of the treatment. This is especially important for children whose mothers suffered from postnatal depression, or whose parents had psychological problems, and whose development of the ability to play is consequently limited. One reason for this limitation could be that the child received or receives inadequate support from his object to be able to devote himself freely to playing. In such children, it is often difficult to open up the play space between therapist and child. Here, treatment should aim at creating and/or promoting the child's ability to play as an important stage of his development.

The container–contained model of Wilfred R. Bion

As Krejci stated in her foreword to the German edition of Bion's *Learning from Experience*, Bion used an "empty term" (Bion, 1992[1962], p. 20), the "alpha-function", to grasp the early communication between mother and child. At the start of his life, the infant has experiences involving his environment. The resulting sensations are first perceived by the infant as "things-in-themselves" (Bion, 1962, p. 6). These first "emotional experiences" with the environment cannot yet be symbolised, and, thus, they cannot be differentiated and potentially made unconscious. They are experienced by the subject as immediate and concrete. Only if the alpha-function develops do these raw beta-elements undergo differentiation. The alpha-function describes the transformation of internal, concretely perceived processes ("beta-elements") into tolerable experiences that can be thought about, so-called "alpha-elements". The development of the alpha-function is, however, inseparably linked to the infant's experience that there is a (motherly) object that contains his initially raw and unmetabolised sensations and not yet symbolised emotional experience. Bion describes this early mother–child unit as a kind of "symbolisation apparatus" which enables the infant to introject the symbolic function of the mother, and, thus, also to establish the function of the container within himself, and to transform beta-elements into thinkable memories, that is, alpha-elements. The container–contained model (Figure 1) should be understood as follows.

The term alpha-function indicates that the infant's initially raw, unthinkable experience (beta-elements) can only be endowed with

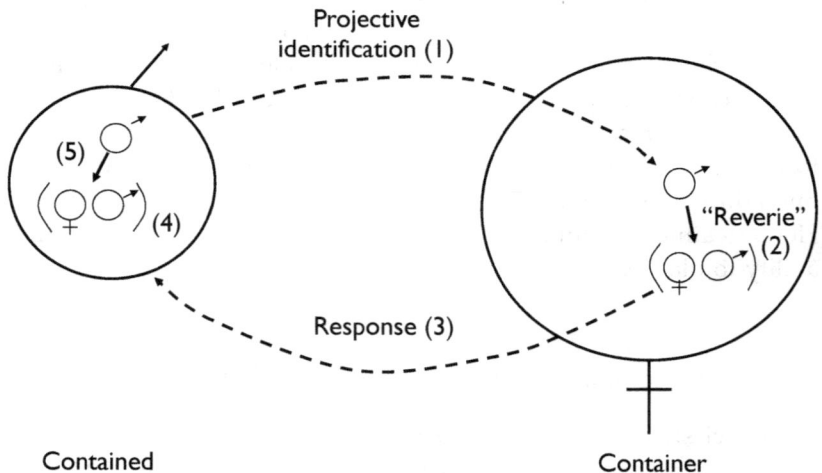

Figure 1.   The development of the mental apparatus (following Bion, 1962, 1963). Note: ♂= contained; ♀ =container; (1) the child sends out his protomental states via projective identification; (2) through "reverie" mother is able to understand and "metabolise" these protomental states and (3) gives it back to the child in a contained or "alphabetised" response; (4) the child introjects these contained psychic elements together with the "alpha-function" of the mother; (5) as long as this process is under construction, the child continues to send out unmetabolised raw psychic experience via projective identification.

meaning if the mother empathises sufficiently with these initially concrete states. Bion prefers to represent the mental apparatus through the symbols ♂ ♀, where ♀ is a symbol for the container and ♂ a symbol for the contained (Bion, 1963, pp. 40–41). The child first sends out his protomental states to the mother via projective identification (1).

> What this might be is concealed by use of the concept of alpha-function but a value may be found for this by psycho-analytic investigations. For example, when the mother loves the infant what does she do it with? Leaving aside the physical channels of communication my impression is that her love is expressed by reverie. (Bion, 1962, p. 36)

Through "reverie" (2) the mother is in a position to understand and metabolise that which the child has projected into her. In the next step, the mother gives back to the child this already "alphabetised" material in her response (3). As a result, the child introjects (4) not only the "digested" material, but also the function of the container, so that after enough repetition of this process the child himself will be in a position to think emotional experience and sensations and, thus, also to symbolise them. As long as this process is under construction, the child will continue to release "indigestible" experience (5) though projective mechanisms. Only later, when he has constructed an adequate alpha-function within himself, will he start to achieve a coherent personality that is able to symbolise by himself and is no longer dependent on the externalisation of unmetabolised emotional experience through projective identification.

The container–contained model shows how Bion situates the development of the human ability to symbolise in the early mother–child relationship (Bion, 1963, pp. 40–41). If, with the help of the mother, the alpha-function is successful, the child will be able to produce alpha-elements.

The beta-elements dominate in presymbolic thinking. If the alpha-function is disordered, sensations and emotions remain in an archaic state. In this state, they threaten to overwhelm the child. It is of vital importance for both emotional and cognitive development that the infant feels himself held by the mother acting as a "container".

At the beginning of his life, the child experiences only beta-elements. These are emotional and sensory raw material that need to be processed further. As a beta-element, a sensory experience cannot be symbolised as a phenomenon, but is experienced as a "thing-in-itself" (Bion, 1962, p. 6). Experiences in this state, before the "alpha-betisation" by the mother, are concrete and genuinely threatening to the child.

The child needs the mother to capture the beta-elements that he eliminates with her psychological receptor organ as she "thinks" (Bion, 1962, p. 84). Alpha-elements, on the other hand, may be conscious sensations that can be thought, and can be imagined as acoustic patterns, olfactory patterns, or visual images. Alpha-elements are unconscious thoughts while awake, conscious thinking, the formation of memories, and dream thoughts. If the child does not have an object that is sufficiently available to him as a container, he will be unable to construct a good enough alpha-function. People whose early emotional experiences were not sufficiently "contained" by the early object can, according to Bion, develop severe disorders of thinking. Beta-elements, that is, concretely experienced events and memories, cannot be made unconscious: the subject may repeatedly find itself being flooded with stimuli because it is as yet unable to filter and differentiate the impinging experiences. As adults, these people will still depend on the mechanism of ejection through projective identification to protect their interior world from sensory overload (Bion, 1962, p. 8).

α- function means transformation into emotional conditions that can be processed and named.

α-elements

- are available for thinking;
- are free of a surfeit of emotions;
- can be made conscious and unconscious;
- can be repressed;
- are available both awake and in dreams;
- can be formed by the child only through the mother's α-function.

β-elements are

- sensations and emotions in a not yet thinkable raw state (= emotional experience);
- unmetabolised;
- very close to the body;
- associated with a feeling of catastrophe.

Wilfred Bion's concepts of "container and contained" (Bion, 1962, p. 90) and the mother's "reverie" (Bion, 1962, p. 36) are of central significance to understanding the existential emotional content of the parent–child relationship. Bion described the infant's psychic apparatus as not yet developed enough to be able to represent intense feelings of pleasure and displeasure. If he is not to be overwhelmed by these affective valences, the infant needs the mother as a "container". The mother is, in Bion's view, the container that takes up the raw psychic material and at the same time endows it within herself with meaning, so that she returns the raw material to the child in metabolised form and endowed with meaning. The child is now able to take up these previously unmetabolised, raw affects, while being himself contained by the mother during this undifferentiated state. At the same time, he receives from the mother something that enables him, in the future, to begin to structure and differentiate his own raw affective states. Only when there is this other, who perceives the infant's distress and takes it up into herself without being overwhelmed by her own fear, can the "contained" return to the child as the thoughtful response of the mother, and be taken up. Through the mother's container function, the infant gradually becomes better able to reflect his own sensations and emotional experiences and increasingly to think independently. The processes described in the container–contained model are essential to the child's emotional and cognitive development.

If the mother (or primary relational figure) is unable to fulfil the function of containment or reverie for the baby, perhaps because she has postnatal depression or her own history of trauma, the child's development of a self constructed from differentiated representations will be inadequate. These children often apply the defence mechanism of a premature independence, or attempt to compensate for their early fears of instability and fragmentation through exaggerated sensory stimulation or physical activity.

Bick (1968) described babies' overwhelming fear of falling apart or fragmentation if they do not feel properly contained. In uncontained states, these children create their own "second-skin containment" (p. 485) as a defence against the falling apart that threatens if the mother's container is unable to provide support. Such children often emphasise autonomy and their motor functions very early on, in order to generate a compensatory support for themselves.

Conclusion for PaCT

Bion's model furthers our understanding of how important it is that the therapist is also available to the child as a container, in which the child's not yet concretely symbolised affective states can be metabolised and, thus, become understandable. Through the continuous provision of the therapist as container, the child feels himself to be held and can increasingly relinquish the "second-skin containment" (Bick, 1968), such as compulsive hypomanic defensive behaviour. As the therapist and child interact, a shared access can be found to previously incomprehensible contents of the child's unconscious, as long as the child feels contained by the therapist. For those children who have not had the experience of being sufficiently contained because their mother or father was unable to be available as a container due to their own psychological conflicts, the experience of containment in therapy is an important condition for continuing positive development.

CHAPTER THREE

More recent psychoanalytical and psychological development concepts

The concept of mentalization and its significance for psychotherapeutic practice

P sychoanalysis has several aetiological models of depression. Some focus on conflicts in which an unconscious wish towards the object has been disappointed and the self works this conflict out, not interpersonally with the object, but intrapsychically (Freud, 1917e), while other models are based on a fixation on the oral phase (Abraham, 1924; Freud, 1917e) and on an intrapsychic conflict in which one layer of the personality comes into conflict with another, when the ego ideal condemns the neurotic gratification of drives.

Our clinical experience shows us that there are children and adults whose depressive developments are based on clearly defined neurotic conflicts that have inhibited the patient's development, allowing him or her to be neurotically "stuck" while other areas of the personality remain undamaged. On the other hand, there are children (and adults) with depressive disorders where the depressive symptoms must be understood as part of a more wide-ranging structural disorder of the personality. Rudolf described these patients as having a structural disorder in which the formation of stable self- and object-representations, affect differentiation, impulse control, and the regulation of self-esteem are hampered (Rudolf, 2009).

This difference between neurotic disorder (A. Freud, 1965) and structural disorder or disorders of mentalization ability (Fonagy, Gergely, Jurist, & Target, 2004) also means that distinct therapeutic approaches are necessary. To better understand the characteristic psychological functioning of so-called early disorders, such as deficits in symbolisation, the mentalization-based approach of Fonagy and colleagues is helpful.

Fonagy and colleagues assume that the insight-promoting aspect of therapy, which brings to consciousness the unconscious desires, impulses, and their defences, is only appropriate for children (and adults) who have already achieved a certain degree of symbolisation ability (Fonagy, Gergely, Jurist, & Target, 2004). A child is able to symbolise when he can insert a third element, the symbol, between desire and the fulfilment of desire, or between drive and drive gratification. This third element can take the form of a gesture (e.g., "no", which Spitz (1957) considers an indicator of the child's entry into the symbolic world), or a visual or verbal statement. The child can then communicate with another via the symbol. Mentalization-promoting therapeutic techniques should be applied if compulsive needs, desires, and associated conflicts in the child express themselves primarily in action, physical or motor, and cannot be shaped into language, pictures, or symbolic gestures. The concept of mentalization opens up possibilities for transmitting self-awareness and psychological meaning.

The concept of mentalization

Definition of mentalization

Fonagy and colleagues define the term as follows: mentalization is the ability to interpret one's own behaviour or the behaviour of other people through the ascription of mental states.

> We define mentalization as a form of mostly preconscious imaginative mental activity, namely, interpreting human behaviour in terms of intentional mental states (e.g. needs, desires, feelings, beliefs, goals,

purposes, and reasons). Mentalization is imaginative because we have to imagine what other people might be thinking or feeling; an important indicator of high quality of mentalization is the awareness that we do not and cannot know absolutely what is in someone else's mind. (Fonagy, 2008, p. 4)

Mentalization is the ability intentionally to exchange terms about *mental states* (thoughts, feelings, opinions, and desires) so that an individual implicitly and explicitly understands the actions of him or herself and those of others as meaningful (Bateman & Fonagy, 2006; Fonagy, 2000).

Mentalization allows children and adults to "read" the psychological states of other people and the mental states on which human behaviour is based ("mind reading") (Baron-Cohen, 1995; Baron-Cohen, Tager-Flusberg, & Cohen, 1993; Morton & Frith, 1995). Baron-Cohen and colleagues, for example, developed the "Reading the mind in the eyes" test, an instrument for recording the mentalization of adults, which captures the characteristic mentalization deficits of persons with Asperger's Syndrome (Baron-Cohen, Wheelwright, Hill, Raste, & Plumb, 2001). Morton and Frith (1995), in their work on autism, give the following, much-quoted definition of the term: mentalization is

> our ability to predict and explain the behavior of other humans in terms of their mental states. . . . in our use and understanding of such words as *believe, know, wish, desire, intend, and pretend* . . . mentalizing, is primarily unconscious or implicit. It is a property of our cognitive apparatus that . . . "makes sense" of other people's and our own behavior fully automatically. (Morton & Frith, 1995, p. 363)

The concept of mentalization has its roots in developmental psychology's "theory of mind" (Gopnik & Meltzoff, 1993). In recent years, the term "theory of mind" has been defined as follows.

Theory of mind is the ability to attribute mental states such as belief, intentions, wishes, pretending, knowledge, etc. to oneself and others, and to understand that others can have convictions, desires, and intentions that differ from one's own (Premack & Woodruff, 1978). Premack and Woodruff further define the term "theory of mind" as follows:

An individual has a theory of mind if he imputes mental states to himself and others. A system of inferences of this kind is properly viewed as a theory because these states are not directly observable and the system can be used to make predictions about the behaviour of others. (Premack & Woodruff, 1978, p. 515)

More recent studies in developmental psychology indicate that it is the child's ability to imitate that enables further social cognitive performances such as the "theory of mind", adoption of perspective, and empathy (Meltzoff, 2002). In comparison with the more cognitive concept of theory of mind, Fonagy and colleagues' concept of mentalization is more concerned with the emotional aspects of social–cognitive development. Fonagy and his colleagues (Fonagy, Gergely, Jurist, & Target, 2004) systematised the concept of mentalization, making it usable in empirical research. Furthermore, in their understanding of the development of mentalization and "reflective functioning", Fonagy and colleagues present a concept that helps the clinician reach a better understanding of the genesis and manifestation of specific cognitive and emotional disorders in patients with structural disorders. "Reflective functioning" serves as an instrument for operationalising mentalization, and allows it to be measured using a scale. In this technique, narratives of the person being examined are collected, for example using the adult attachment interview (AAI (Main, Kaplan, & Cassidy, 1985)) or the parent development interview (PDI) (Slade, Grienenberger, Bernbach, Levy, & Locker, 2005)), and evaluated for their degree of reflective functioning (RF) (Fonagy, Target, Steele, & Steele, 1998). The group of mentalization researchers around Fonagy is situated in the tradition of developmental psychological theory and research within psychoanalysis, which is represented by Anna Freud, Klein, Mahler, Brody, Emde, and Stern. In terms of the environmental aspects that play a decisive role in the child's healthy development, the theory of mentalization produces similar findings to Stern's earlier theory of affect attunement (Stern, 1985) or the work of Beebe and colleagues (Jaffe, Beebe, Feldstein, Crown, & Jasnow, 2001). Stern defines affect attunement as follows, emphasising the importance of attunement compared to pure imitation:

Affect attunement, then, is the performance of behaviors that express the quality of feeling of a shared affect state without imitating the exact behavioral expression of the inner state. If we could demonstrate subjective affect-sharing only with pure mimicry we would be limited to flurries of rampant imitations. Our affectively responsive behavior would look ludicrous, maybe even robot-like. (Stern, 1985, p. 142)

Fonagy and his colleagues assume that attuned interactions between parents and infant are often accompanied by affect mirroring. By reflecting the child's own feelings in their facial expressions and vocal utterances, the parents contribute to his capacity to subdue and calm his own emotions:

> This system serves two developmental functions: the mirroring environment (a) contributes to the on-line homeostatic regulation of the infant's dynamic affective state changes and (b) provides a kind of 'teaching' or 'scaffolding' environment that results in the internalization of the maternal affect-regulative function through the establishment of secondary representations of the infant's primary emotion states. (Fonagy, Gergely, Jurist, & Target, 2004, p. 190)

This introjection of the object's alpha-function, that is, the ability of the object (container) to symbolise in concrete form perceived affective states, and thus to diminish the risk of potential inundation with raw undifferentiated affective material, was described by Bion in his container–contained model (Bion, 1962) (see Chapter Two, section headed "The container–contained model of Wilfred R. Bion", pp. 53–57). The affect regulation of the infant, brought about through affect marking, has decisive implications for the development of a healthy affective self (for definition of affective self or theory of mind (ToM) see above). The ability to form a theory of mind is connected with mentalization ability.

Let us imagine a child who has to solve the following task, the so-called "false-beliefs task" (Perner, Leekam, & Wimmer, 1987):

Maxi is shown a colourful Smarties box.

She is asked, "What do you think is in the box?" Maxi answers, "Smarties!"

The box is opened, but there are coloured pencils in it. Maxi is then asked, "Your friend Peter is waiting outside. When we bring him in, show him the closed Smarties box and ask him 'What is in the box?' what do you think he will answer?"

Between the ages of three and four years there appears to be a shift in the way that children think about their own and other people's mental states, and how they can report on them (Gopnik, 1993). Most three-year-olds will answer the question above with "Pencils!" Four-year-olds, on the other hand, generally say "Smarties". Three-year-old children are typically unable to imagine that the other child can hold a false belief. In order to solve this task correctly, the child must have acquired the ability to "mentalise" that Peter has a different perspective on the situation, and a different knowledge of the contents of the box; that something different is happening in Peter's head than in Maxi's. This ability to adopt other perspectives, together with the knowledge that the perspective in question influences the cognitive evaluation of a situation, is what distinguishes a theory of mind. To solve the "false belief" puzzle, Maxi must be able to mentalise Peter's internal mental state. Thus, what develops between three and four years of age is the idea that the other child functions mentally in a similar way to oneself, but is nevertheless different.

In acquiring the ability to read the thoughts of the other person and to grasp his or her mood, the child can furnish this other person's behaviour with meaning and so become able to predict it. The ability to mentalise thus has a crucial influence on the child's capacity for self-awareness and affect regulation: a child who observes a man walking around his car and then hitting the roof angrily three times will probably feel fear. But a child who is able to mentalise about another person's behaviour will be able to use this capacity to reduce his fear of this man, as his behaviour has become understandable and predictable.

Reflective functioning (RF) as the operationalisation of mentalization

> involves both a self-reflective and an interpersonal component that ideally provides the individual with a well developed capacity to distinguish inner from outer reality, pretend from 'real' modes of functioning, and intra-personal mental and emotional processes from interpersonal communications. (Fonagy, Gergely, Jurist, & Target, 2004, p. 25)

Mentalization describes the often pre-cognitive ability, during interactions with other people, to routinely use the knowledge that other people have an internal life, just as one does oneself, analogous to one's own feelings, thoughts, and desires. This ability is impaired in patients with borderline personality disorder, for example (Fonagy,

1995). The following illustration shows the connection between mentalization, social communication, and affect regulation: a person who trips over a foot stuck out by someone else is liable to understand this as an attack if she or he has a mentalization deficit and is unable to mentalise that the foot might just have been stretched out by accident, and that the other person intended no harm. This mentalization is easier for a person who is able to attribute to him or herself, and to others, flexible and diverse inner mental states, and can realise that behaviour may be motivated by very diverse inner mental states.

The development of mentalization ability

Fonagy and colleagues stress that the ability to mentalise develops in early childhood and is dependent on an affective relationship with the primary person in the child's life. They assume that mentalization ability begins with affect differentiation in the first year of life (Fonagy, Gergely, Jurist, & Target, 2004). They describe a close link between the ability to mentalise and the early affective interaction with the primary person(s).

It is essential that the child has adequate experience of its own mental states being mirrored in the mind of the person with whom he has his primary relationship. Fonagy calls this the central experience for the development of the ability to mentalise: "Having experienced his own mind in another's mind" (personal communication during the 14th IPA Training Programme, London, 2008).

This concept is also present in Bion's container–contained model. Without the "reverie" of the mother, who "thinks about" the infant's projective identification, the infant is unable to internalise the alpha-function and thus have the opportunity of reflecting mentally on concrete experience or symbolising it (Bion, 1962) (see Chapter Two, section headed "The container–contained model of Wilfred R. Bion", pp. 53–57).

The process of affect marking plays a key role in the development of the mentalization process. In affect marking, the child's primary person exaggerates the way in which he or she would normally express an emotion. This idea can be found in the work of Spitz (as *dialogue*) (Spitz, 1963), Stern (as *affect attunement*) (Stern, 1985), and Papousek and Papousek (1983) in their model of the *infant's basal adaptive behaviour regulation.* In affect marking, according to Fonagy and colleagues, the emotional expression is normal enough for the child to recognise the emotion for what it is. The expression must, however, also be exaggerated so that the child recognises that the emotion in question is actually the child's own, mirrored and marked by the parent, and not the parent's own emotion (Fonagy, Gergely, Jurist, & Target, 2004). In this bi-directional communication, it is important that the secondary reactions of the primary person are not too similar to the infant's primary reaction, but also not so far removed that the infant is no longer able to interpret the reaction as a response to his own behaviour or display of affect. In his affect attune-ment model, Stern also argues (1985) that the affects imitated by the primary person cannot be too similar to the child's original affects, because the child must be able to recognise that the primary person has created a relation to the internal state that underlies the externally recognisable display of affect by the infant:

> The reason attunement behaviours are so important as separate phenomena is that true imitation does not permit the partners to refer to the internal state. It maintains the focus of attention upon the forms of the external behaviours. (Stern, 1985, p. 142)

In this way, the infant learns to differentiate and modify his affects, and to relate his own affective states to the reactions of the primary person to these affective displays. Through "affect mirroring" or "affect marking", the infant gradually reaches a higher level of aware-ness and diversity of his internal states. Thus, the infant also gradu-ally acquires the ability to differentiate and control his own affects.

The more the child acquires the ability to mentalise his affects, the more he will be able to use affects in order to regulate himself, and thus reflect on the subjective meaning of an affective state (Fonagy, Gergely, Jurist, & Target, 2004). Fonagy and colleagues describe the highest form of mentalization as "mentalized affectivity" (2004, pp. 435–441).

Disorders in the development of mentalization: the alien self

In order for the child to develop a psychic internal space in which the basal valences of pleasure and displeasure can be transformed into differentiated "mentalised affectivity" (Fonagy, Gergely, Jurist, & Target, 2004), it is essential that the object makes its own psychic internal space available for successful reflection on the child's affective state.

The reaction of the primary person to the still raw and fragmented affect expression or state of the child must be contingent, that is, sensitively adapted in terms of time, space, and content (Fonagy, Gergely, Jurist, & Target, 2004, p. 201). Tronick and Cohn (1989) point out that infants themselves are already able to "reconstitute" a normal interaction that has come adrift, or contribute substantially to it, as long as they find a responsive partner. If these actions are successful, they will gradually reinforce the expectation that such reconstruction is possible even after a rupture, and that the infants themselves are powerful in this respect. The development of interaction representations in the infant is supported by the belief that these representations can be reconstructed even after disruptions. Such interactions are formed as representations, and structure the psyche of the child (Beebe, Jaffe, & Lachmann, 1992).

Fonagy and colleagues emphasise that affect mirroring must be "marked": that is, in some way exaggerated. In this way, the child can recognise that it is not the mother herself who is sad, but rather that it is the child's state that is being marked and mirrored.

If this marking fails, that is, if the delimitation of the mother's response from the child's own affect is inadequate, there will be a "failed affect marking" and, according to Fonagy and colleagues, the development of an "alien self" (see Figure 2). If the mother is unable to make her own interior psychic space available to the child, perhaps because trauma or psychic conflicts create a burden of unresolved affects so that her own fear prevents her establishing enough distance from the child's, this affect marking will fail. This mother will be so invaded by the child's fear that she will no longer be able to perform this marking. The child is then unable to recognise the mirrored fear as its own, and instead experiences it as the mother's fear. The child is thus unable to establish an interior psychic space within which his own reflected affects are available in an increasingly differentiated form; what he finds within himself are the mother's affects, not his own. Affect marking has far-reaching consequences for the development of the child's Self. A child who has not had an adequate experience of being mirrored in the available interior psychic space of the

mother because she was too absorbed by her own psychological problems will only be able to construct an "alien self", resulting in internal
alienation and undifferentiated affectivity. If the affect mirrored by
the object does not accord with the actual affect of the infant, says
Fonagy, "he will establish a *distorted secondary representation* of his
primary emotion state" (Fonagy, Gergely, Jurist, & Target, 2004, p.
194). Fonagy considers the development of the "alien self" to be a
consequence of this "deviant mirroring". There are similarities and
differences here between the concept of the alien self and Winnicott's
concept of the false self. Both are the consequence of inadequate affective attunement of the primary carer to the infant. In the concept of
the alien self, however, Fonagy is describing the consequences of
insufficient affect mirroring on the development of internal representations. In the alien self, these representations are distorted and not
congruent with the infant's original experience of himself. The development of the alien self is based on distorted self-representations.
Fonagy considers the development of the alien self to be a direct
consequence of the child's internalisation of his non-contingently and
non-congruently represented affect state on the part of the primary
person (Figure 2).

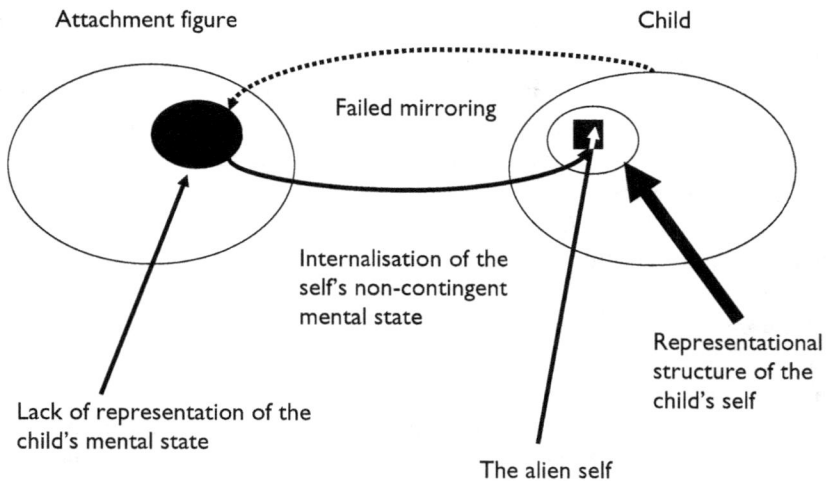

Attachment figure   Child

Failed mirroring

Internalisation of the
self's non-contingent
mental state

Representational
structure of the
child's self

Lack of representation of the
child's mental state

The alien self

Figure 2.   Development of the "alien self", following Fonagy, Gergely, Jurist,
and Target (2004, p. 419).

In contrast to Fonagy's concept of the *alien self*, Winnicott's *false self* is more of a defensive strategy by the infant, in the sense of an early defence to deal with the object's inadequate affective resonance. Winnicott describes an organisational form that aims to protect itself by hiding the true self (Winnicott, 1960). If maternal care (appropriate affective attunement, creation of constancy in social surroundings) is able to fulfil the infant's needs appropriately, protecting him from being overwhelmed by stimuli and reducing such attacks to a minimum, the infant can experience continuity of being.

> When the mother's adaptation is not good enough at the start the infant might be expected to die physically, because cathexis of external objects is not initiated. The infant remains isolated. But in practice the infant lives, but lives falsely. The protest against being forced into a false existence can be detected from the earliest stages. The clinical picture is one of general irritability, and of feeding and other function disturbances which may, however, disappear clinically, only to reappear in serious form at a later stage.

> In this second case, where the mother cannot adapt well enough, the infant gets seduced into a compliance, and a compliant False Self reacts to environmental demands and the infant seems to accept them. Through this False Self the infant builds up a false set of relationships, and by means of introjections even attains a show of being real, so that the child may grow to be just like mother, nurse, aunt, brother, or whoever at the time dominates the scene. The False Self has one positive and very important function: to hide the True Self, which it does by compliance with environmental demands. (Winnicott, 1960, p. 145)

The false self displays good social adaptation, often with an overemphasis of the intellect, but also has a strong tendency to collapse under pressure. There is a split between overemphasis of the intellect and psychosomatic existence. Under internal or external stresses, the false self may undergo a regressive separation of the bonds between body and mind, leading to the development of a psychosomatic disorder.

According to Fonagy and colleagues, a differentiated authentic self is created through marked affect mirroring by an attachment figure who is internally free enough to make his or her interior psychic space available as a kind of container of the child's undifferentiated affect states.

Winnicott argued that if the infant is unable to find himself in his mother, and instead sees only the mother, he will then be unable to find himself within himself, and will experience his own self as alien.

> What does the baby see when he or she looks at the mother's face? I am suggesting that, ordinarily, what the baby sees is himself or herself. In other words the mother is looking at the baby and what she looks like is related to what she sees there. All this is too easily taken for granted. I am asking that this which is naturally done well by mothers who are caring for their babies shall not be taken for granted. I can make my point by going straight over to the case of the baby whose mother reflects her own mood or, worse still, the rigidity of her own defences. In such a case what does the baby see?
>
> . . . Many babies, however, do have to have a long experience of not getting back what they are giving. They look and they do not see themselves. There are consequences. First, their own creative capacity begins to atrophy, and in some way or other they look around for other ways of getting something of themselves back from the environment. (Winnicott, 1967, p. 111).

Since the "self exists only in the context of the other", Fonagy and colleagues conclude that the development of the self has the same meaning as the "collection of experiences of self-in-relationship" (Fonagy, Gergely, Jurist, & Target, 2004, p. 48). They use this to describe a fundamental interactional dependence, which Emde designated as from "ego to we-go" (Emde, 2009).

Children who have been unable to experience this adequately develop a distorted "false self-image": "it is distorted because the self-experience, the self-awareness of the child has been influenced too much by its early perceptions, and the thoughts and feelings of other persons" (Fonagy, Gergely, Jurist, & Target, 2004, p. 204). Thus, the child's experiences are often unconnected to the actual experience of the child or the other person.

> This may be why many neglected or maltreated children show apparent failures of object permanence leading to primitive separation anxiety or feelings of merger with the object. In reality, they continue existentially to depend on the physical presence of the other. (Fonagy, Gergely, Jurist, & Target, 2004, p. 197)

In daily clinical life, we often encounter children who at first play in an unco-ordinated and unfocused way, and whose mothers comment on their play without actually mentalising about what is happening in the child, or about the mental state on which the child's behaviour is based. These mothers (parents) often attempt to convince the investigator, in a tone of disapproval, that what the child is doing "cannot be understood". An important goal of PaCT, therefore, is to improve both the child's direct experience of the link between internal mental states and their expression through behaviour, and the parents' ability to read the internal mental states on which the child's behaviour is based. These children often act out their emotional experiences, such as fear, hypomanically, or in temper tantrums at kindergarten or school, because their attachment figure has not made available to them the interior psychic space that would have provided a link to affective experience. Thus, emotionally neglected children are often perceived at school or kindergarten simply as "the child who hits others", or "the child with ADHD". Fonagy suspects that these children are inundated with "threatening mental states", and, instead of seeking closeness to the object and internalising the object's own capacity to contain them, they have no choice but to externalise these threatening mental states. The core of the self thus remains populated with unsymbolised mental states, and this leads to an internal alienation, which might be externalised in the form of temper tantrums. Fonagy describes this mechanism thus:

> These threatening mental states can create an alien presence within his self-representation that is so unbearable that his attachment behaviour becomes focused on re-externalizing these parts of the self onto attachment figures, rather than on internalizing a capacity for containment of affects and other intentional states. (Fonagy, 2006, p. 81)

Developmental steps of mentalization ability

The ability to mentalise develops in the first years of life in the relationship to important others. Between the ages of one and three years, the development of the ability to play, "Playing with reality", acquires the same meaning as affect mirroring in the first year of life. From the age of 1½ years, the child develops two definitive modes of thinking and feeling: the "pretend mode" and the mode of "psychic equivalence". Numerous studies have investigated the significance of "pretend play" for the cognitive and emotional development of the child. The results of these studies show that children who, at the age of three, are more willing to enter into co-operative interactions (Dunn, Brown, Slomkowski, Telsa, & Youngblade, 1991), and especially like to play in the pretend mode in tasks that require reading thoughts and emotional understanding, do particularly well later on (Astington & Jenkins, 1995; Youngblade & Dunn, 1995). There are indications that what we can classify as secure attachment in early childhood may be a predictor of a more engaged and richer pretend play at preschool age, while conversely, children who tend to avoid bonding show a rather lower level of involvement in pretend play. Overall, their pretend play appears flat and empty compared to securely attached children (Main, Kaplan, & Cassidy, 1985). Fonagy and colleagues point out that the shared pretend play, or the playful mindset of pretend, appears to promote the understanding of mental states (Fonagy, Gergely, Jurist, & Target, 2004, p. 56).

In the pretend mode, the child acts out reality, while being aware that the game is not, in fact, real. In the equivalence mode, on the other hand, thoughts are experienced as though they were reality. In patients with borderline disorder, this confusion of psychological and external reality is very apparent. Up to the age of four years, children oscillate between the two modes; in other words, the integration of these two modes, which opens up the possibility of mentalization, takes place only at that age (Fonagy, Gergely, Jurist, & Target, 2004). Where the child takes its own thoughts as being the image of reality up to this point, from now on he is able to recognise that his thoughts only represent reality, and he is able to play with the thoughts (playing with reality) (Table 1).

As already noted, this integration at the age of three to four years is considered by Fonagy and his research group as the point at which mentalization becomes possible. For Fonagy, it is clear that the parents have a decisive effect on promoting or retarding the development of mentalization. Thus, the ability to mentalise depends to a large extent on the environment. Findings about the development of mentalization's dependency on interaction with the object are therefore of central relevance to psychopathology.

It should be mentioned that Fonagy and his fellow researchers (2004) recognise that the concept of the "reflective function" is very similar to Klein's concept of the depressive position. The depressive position, according to Klein, contains the infant's growing ability to

Table 1.   Developmental stage of mentalization ability, following Fonagy, Gergely, Jurist, and Target (2004, pp. 216–274).

Child's perception and world of ideas	Age	Meaning
Purposeful mode (teleological mode)	From approx. 9 months to 1.5 years	The child is able to interpret his own and others' actions as having a purpose, but is not yet able to identify causes and motive behind these actions. All that counts is what can be observed.
Psychological equivalent	Between 1.5 and 4 years	Thoughts and external reality are not distinguished (word = thought = reality). Internal states such as thoughts, wishes, fears are experienced as real.
Pretend mode	Between 1.5 and 4 years	Thoughts, motives and fears are separated from reality (as in play).
Reflexive mode	Approx. 4 to 5 years	The reflexive mode integrates the previously coexisting modes. It enables thinking about one's own interior life and about the presumed interior life of other people. Different perspectives are recognised and that oneself and other people may be mistaken.

identify with his objects and, thus, also to acknowledge the pain and suffering that the self has caused to the object. The consequence of this differentiation of self and object is that the subject feels guilty for his sadistic attacks on the (partial) object.

Furthermore, there is an even greater resemblance to Bion's concept of "alphabetisation", in which the "alpha-function" describes the transformation of inner, concretely perceived processes ("beta-elements") into bearable experiences that can be considered—so-called "alpha-elements". For Bion, the development of the child's symbolisation ability is rooted in the early mother–child relationship (Bion, 1962) and the mother's ability to make herself available to the child as a container (see also Chapter Two, section headed "The container-contained model of Wilfred R. Bion", pp. 53–57).

Conclusion for PaCT

We assume that children of preschool and school age who are suffering from affective disorders or emotional symptoms show different levels of mentalization. As Blatt, Luyten, and Corveleyn (2005) (see "Psychoanalytical models of the genesis of depression", below, pp. 80–83) have already demonstrated in their concept of *introjective and anaclitic depression*, depressive syndromes may be aetiologically derived from a clear conflict, or from the loss of an object, or from continuing emotional neglect. In the parents' lack of emotional attunement to their children, which is often in the case with depressive children, we see why these children might have severely limited ability to mentalise. These parents can be so preoccupied with their own psychological conflicts that they are unavailable to the child. The children are then unable to form adequate mental representations of conflicts. They show limited ability to demonstrate these conflicts in play using the pretend mode. Their narratives lack coherence, and raw aggression dominates their often unfocused play.

Our intervention strategy primarily depends on which child we are treating. If the mentalization process is underdeveloped, or if the child is stuck in the psychic equivalence mode, we initially focus on interventions that verbalise affects and, thus, mark them. Here, it is essential that the child first acquires the ability to "play with reality" in the joint therapeutic process, instead of remaining stuck in the psychic equivalence mode, or only playing in the pretend mode. The experience of finding his own mental state in the mental state of the other person should help the child, in the later process of therapy, to form his own interior psychic space.

Important goals of PaCT are: to improve the parents' insight into the inner mental states of the child and to promote the child's perception of a connection between his mental states and his behaviour. Mentalization-based interventions are used according to the structural levels of parents and child.

The significance of the triad

The concepts described in previous sections are based on theories of the influence of the relational world on early development, and on findings about how relationships experienced in early childhood affect the structuring of self and object relationships. In the 1970s, Bowlby's attachment theory (Bowlby, 1969), which can broadly be classified as a psychoanalytical object relations theory, was developed on the basis of this knowledge.

Attachment is a dyadic relationship concept and is defined as instinctual behaviour that develops phylogenetically. Infants and toddlers, like many animals, will seek closeness to significant attachment figures in moments of danger. Attachment theory has been much discussed, especially since Ainsworth, Blehar, Waters, and Wall (1978) and their followers developed reliable and valid methods of "measuring" attachment behaviour in toddlers and their mothers (e.g., "strange situation procedure", and the measurement of internal attachment representations in the adult attachment interview).

The mentalization theory described in the previous chapter, popularised in recent years by Fonagy and colleagues (Fonagy & Target, 1997, 2000; Fonagy, Steele, Steele, Moran, & Higitt, 1991), assumes that a secure mother–child bond is a necessary, if not by itself sufficient, condition for the development of mentalization ability. All of these scientific results and theories are essentially based on a "two-person psychology", which assumes that the phenomena described can be observed in dyadic, and usually mother–baby, relationships. However, our own research group (von Klitzing & Bürgin, 2005; von Klitzing, Simoni, Amsler, & Bürgin, 1999; von Klitzing, Simoni, & Bürgin, 1999) has, together with several other authors (Dammasch & Metzger, 1999; Trowell & Etchegoyen, 2002), recently questioned the one-sided ascription of considerations of psychological structure to the observable dyadic mother–child relationship, and countered it with a theory of early triadic relationships.

These considerations start with the findings of developmental psychology that, from the very beginning of their lives, infants are able to develop relationships with more than one important attachment figure, and that both mothers and fathers generally show an ability for "intuitive parenting" (Papousek, 1989; Papousek & Papousek, 1983). Both fathers and mothers are, therefore, in a position to provide "a good enough environment" for the infant and the toddler. Studies by Field (1998) have shown that although babies and toddlers do identify with a depressive mother's affect, they form a quite different relationship with non-depressive fathers, one that does not focus on depressive affects. It was concluded from this that if mothers have postnatal depression, the presence of a non-depressive father can provide a substantial protective function, as long as they are active carers of the child.

There is some earlier, pioneering work that also considers the significance of early triadic relationships for the child. Klein (1928, p. 186) stated that she assumed the presence of oedipal tendencies and conflicts at the end of the first year of life to be "in consequence of the frustration which the child experiences at weaning". Thus, in Klein's view, being deprived of the mother's breast is the fundamental reason why girls in the early stage of the Oedipus conflict turn away from their mothers and towards their fathers, before penis envy later magnifies this effect (Klein, 1928, p. 193). Lacan (1953) viewed the third person, the father, as significant for human life from the outset. According to his theory, this significance is not limited to particular developmental stages. Furthermore, in his opinion, the important factor is not the real father, but rather a symbolic function that represents the third element disrupting the collusion between mother and child. The introduction of the "non du père/nom du père", which one can understand as both the father's "no" and his "name", protects the child from becoming solely the object of his mother's desire. Lacan pointed out,

> It is in the *name of the father* that we must recognise the basis of the symbolic function which, from the dawn of history, has identified his person with the figure of the law. (Lacan, 1953, p. 230)

The father's no/the father's name introduces the child into the world of symbols and language and saves him from psychosis (Borens, 1993). Winnicott (1964) devoted only a few pages of his comprehensive work to the father's influence on child development and triangular relationships. In his view, whether or not the fathers form a relationship with their toddlers depends on the mothers. But, says Winnicott, it is much easier to have two parents: "one parent can be felt to remain loving while the other is being hated, and this in itself has a stabilising influence" (Winnicott, 1964, p. 115). In Winnicott's view, one important function of the father, as a third person, consists in surviving the child's hatred, which is directed towards the father when he disappoints the child.

In her research laboratory, Margaret Mahler made the observation that child development is determined by processes of separation and individuation, and that these separation processes return throughout one's whole life. As a result of her direct observation of toddlers and their primary attachment figures, she recognised (Mahler, Pine, & Bergmann, 1975) the serious consequences of unsuccessful disentanglement and individuation. This also depends on the object's reaction to the child's strivings for autonomy. Thus, a child with primarily symbiotic organisation appears to treat his mother as a part of himself: that is, not as separate from himself, but, rather, merged with her (Mahler & Gosliner, 1955).

Mahler and Gosliner (1955) conceptualised the father's significance as a third person, primarily during the separation and differentiation phase of the second year, as a powerful and sometimes essential support against the terror of the "re-engulfment of the ego into the whirlpool of the primary undifferentiated symbiotic stage" (Mahler & Gosliner, 1955, p. 210). Abelin (1971, 1975), one of Mahler's colleagues, reported that he organised "Fathers' Days" in Mahler's research laboratory, which provided some surprising insights. He observed that a specific relationship with the father begins as early as the symbiotic phase, and that fathers play a very important role in the practising subphase, in that they stand for the "distant, 'nonmother' space, for the elated exploration of reality" (Abelin, 1971, p. 246). "During the course of the separation–individuation process, the father becomes aligned with reality, not yet as a source of constraint and frustration, but rather as a buttress for playful and adaptive mastery" (p. 249). It was Abelin who, based on these findings, produced the concept of (early) triangulation, which he defined as "the mechanism that allows the mental organization to pass from the level of relationships (acted, sensorimotor) to images (represented, symbolic)" (p. 233).

Many authors have taken up the idea and the concepts of early triangulation, and discussed them in connection with parental fantasies. Bauriedl (1980) argued that the oedipal situation exists even before the child is conceived—in the fantasies of the parents. She concluded, therefore, that, logically, development should be conceptualised in triadic terms from the outset, in that one considers the relationship between the parents and between the parents and the child at the same time. For Buchholz as well (Buchholz, 1990), development proceeds from the outset through triadic relationships. Each object can be seen from two different perspectives, a phenomenon he describes as "rotation of the triad". Even before birth, the child represents the object of parental projections (desires and fears), which must be worked through during pregnancy and after the birth. Brickman (1993) described the concept of the triad as a more wide-ranging model than that of the dyad for the understanding of development and analytical relationships. In his view, it is aspects of the triadic experience that make self-awareness in a psychic space possible at all. He defines triangulation as "the process which locates perceptions of objects (including other persons) in the world in three-dimensional space" (Brickman, 1993, p. 908). This is why, in his opinion, triangulation is vital for the survival of the subject.

The controversy over whether child development is better understood in dyadic or triadic terms may arise through confusion about the object of research. Do we view the infant or toddler as an observable behavioural unit, as an individual with its own inner world and developing representations, or as an object of parental fantasies? Soulé (1982) referred to several children, that is, the real child and the child in the parents' mind ("enfant dans la tête"). We also need to be clear whether we understand relationships mainly as interpersonal or interactional events, or as the object of intrapsychic, fantasised processes. To clarify this, Stern (1994) proposed describing the interpersonal process of forming a triad as "triadification" and the intrapsychic process of experiencing a triad internally as "triangulation".

Starting from these theoretical concepts, recent decades have seen a growing amount of research on the significance of early triadic relationships for the child's further development. We would highlight here the work of Fivaz-Depeursinge and her group (Fivaz-Depeursinge & Corboz-Warnery, 1999; Fivaz-Depeursinge, Lavanchy-Scaiola, & Favez, 2010; Frascarolo, Favez, Carneiro, & Fivaz-Depeursinge, 2004), who developed the paradigm of triadic play, an experimental methodology for standardising the observation of parents with very small babies in meaningful triadic interactions. McHale and Rasmussen (1998) focused on empirical studies of the significance of co-parenting for child development. The group of von Klitzing and colleagues (von Klitzing & Bürgin, 2005; von Klitzing, Simoni, & Bürgin, 1999) developed the concept of triadic capacity, which is the ability of parents to integrate the child into the parental relationship, both in their own fantasies and in real interactions, in order to establish triadic relationship structures that manage not to exclude one of the relationship partners. The authors have been able to show, in several prospective empirical studies, that triadic capacity acquired during pregnancy and the first year of life has a high level of predictive value for the child's later psychological development.

Conclusion for PaCT

For the PaCT approach, we will, therefore, refer not only to important concepts of object relations theory described above, but also more recent theories on triadification and triangulation processes. Both the relationship of the therapist to the child and the parent–child relationship can be conceptualised from a triadic point of view. It becomes complicated when the therapist enters into relationship both with the child and with his parents, and is, thus, confronted with the primal parental scene and has to integrate all relationship aspects into a whole. A common distortion of child analytical thinking is to undertake child therapies in the absence of the parents or of one parent, or, if something is not working well in the therapeutic relationship, to blame the parents and, thus, move to exclude them. It is sometimes difficult for therapists, particularly if they have no children of their own, to share "their therapeutic child" with his parents, to identify themselves in mutuality and to integrate these different identifications, and to make this integration ability available to the parental system and to the child. In this connection, the authors emphasise that child therapists must develop triadic capacity, and that this skill must be practised during training. We will address these concepts in the PaCT manual chapters on parental work, in order to consider concretely the idea of "limitation" in the relationships of transference and countertransference that develop within the PaCT treatment. For PaCT, it is important to support the father's potential for triangulating the child and, whenever possible, to include fathers in the treatment.

Psychoanalytical models of the genesis of depression

Anxiety and depression in childhood often co-occur up to adolescence (Sterba, Egger, & Angold, 2007). As we have already mentioned (see Chapter One, section headed "Current state of research", pp. 3–4), we use *emotional disorders* as an umbrella term for depressive and anxiety disorders. Thus, we consider the concept of internalisation and depressive processing to be core concepts for the understanding of emotional disorders.

The early models of the genesis of depression developed by Abraham, Sigmund Freud, and Radó emphasise the significance of loss, disappointment, and anger.

Abraham published the first psychoanalytical work on depression in 1911. As characteristics of this disease, he highlighted frustrated amorous desires and the resulting primal mood disturbance—*Ur-Verstimmung*—of early childhood, as well as defended-against sadistic impulses and feelings of guilt. He also indicated predisposing factors: a constitutional reinforcement of oral eroticism, a fixation of the libido on the oral stage of development, and damage to the child's narcissism through coincident disappointments in love. These patients were not only disappointed by the mother, but were also unable to elicit a response when they turned to the father. "In the child arose thus the impression of being completely abandoned; this was linked to the earliest depressive moods" (Abraham, 1924, p. 48).

In his conception of depression Freud (Freud, 1917e) also concentrates on the significance of orality, loss of the object, and the lowering of self-esteem, and embeds these considerations in his newly developed metapsychology. The melancholic person, in contrast to the grieving person, suffers a diminishing of his self-esteem, "diminution in his self-regard, an impoverishment of his ego on a grand scale" (Freud, 1917e, p. 245). However, his severe self-blame is not actually applicable to the subject, but to the object of love, which the subject has lost without knowing it. An object disappointment destabilises the object relationship, whereupon the freed libido is drawn back into the ego, in order to create an identification of the ego with the lost object and, thus, prevent the object being lost completely. The external object thus becomes an internal object, "the shadow of the object fell upon the ego" (Freud, 1917e, p. 249). Freud sees the condition for this process as a strong fixation on the love object, and, if there is little resistance from the object, its cathexis on a narcissistic basis. Although the love relationship need not be given up through the narcissistic identification, its ambivalent character unfolds in the interior of the subject. Here, the hatreds—which formerly applied to the object, even though unconsciously—now are turned against the ego. The self-torment of a melancholic person is about the satisfaction of hatreds directed towards the lost object.

Conservation of the damaged object relationship succeeds here only at the cost of damage to narcissistic integrity. Hate and anger against the disappointing object are negotiated unconsciously in the ego, with object-directed rage invisible to the outside, but showing itself indirectly in the self-accusations of the depressive.

In his work on narcissism (1914c), Freud also points out the close link between depression and the regulation of self-esteem. Thus, the self undergoes a major reduction in its self-awareness, if something in the ego does not live up to the demands of the ego ideal. The subject's self-awareness is fuelled, according to Freud, from three sources: the remnants of childhood narcissism, the fulfilment of the ego ideal, and the satisfaction of the object libido (see Freud, 1914c).

Radó (1928) described the extreme vulnerability of the mechanism of self-esteem regulation in depressive patients. He characterised depressive patients as being notably dependent on external narcissistic input.

Edith Jakobson's ego-psychological theory of depression (Jakobson, 1971) stressed the significance of the superego's character for self-esteem regulation. If the superego is archaic–rigid, self-esteem will be vulnerable, and the self will remain prone to a state of depression in which there will be intersystemic conflicts between ego and superego. The ego ideal also has decisive significance in terms of self-awareness: the more demanding it is, the more impossible it is for real behaviour to conform to its demands. Thus, there is a gulf between real-self and ideal-self.

Mentzos (2006) proposed a similar concept for the aetiology of depression, taking into account three areas of conflict: "loss of real or internal object", the "turning of aggression towards the self", and the "disorder of narcissistic regulation". These three areas become stabilised through various "vicious circles". The withdrawal of the libido from the object, which is brought about by object disappointment, effectively means that the depressive person no longer has a source of regulation for his narcissistic supply. Although it had once made sense as a protection from further disappointments, this object withdrawal now becomes damaging to the self-awareness of the subject. The desire for only good replacement objects, and then clinging to them, leads to renewed disappointments as the objects resist and fail to live up to idealised expectations. Tension within object relationships leads to further narcissistic disappointment. Finally, there is another vicious circle in which the person attempts to suppress the comprehensive aggression resulting from the object disappointment, which in turn leads to the build up of aggression within the self, and, thus, to further narcissistic weakening.

Rudolf, Cierpka, and Clement (2007) stress that the earlier in childhood the depressive disorder begins, the greater is the risk that depression will develop into a structural disorder. They describe the psychosomatic management of the depressive basic conflict. Patients with a depressive basic conflict develop a structural disorder, in which the formation of stable self- and object-representations, affect differentiation, impulse control, and the regulation of self-esteem are impeded (Rudolf, Cierpka, & Clement, 2007, pp. 117–167). In the depressive basic conflict, the desire for an object that will rescue an individual and provide security and esteem is contrasted with the hatred and despair towards the object that results from object disappointment. Rudolf detects the consequences of the early loss of an object or early neglect in the form of an orally directed longing, a hatred towards the object, and feelings of grief and resentment. The depressive somatisation has three stages. On the intra-psychic level, he suggests that one consequence of the early impossibility of making complaints or demands is the development of a permanent emotional tension and absence of release. This leads to extreme self-denial and a tendency to make excessive self-demands, resulting in both psychic and physical exhaustion.

Blatt's numerous empirical studies made important contributions to different lines of treatment for depressive patients (Blatt & Shahar, 2004; Blatt, Luyten, & Corveleyn, 2005).

Blatt differentiates two basic types of depression: *anaclitic* and *introjective*. Patients with *anaclitic depression* do not suffer from intrapsychic problems as much as from interpersonal ones, linked to issues of dependency, helplessness, and feelings of loss and abandonment. Anaclitically depressive people are often affectionate and may appear clingy. Spitz (Spitz & Wolf, 1946) described the apathetic, numbed state, accompanied by sleeplessness, loss of appetite, and avoidance of contact that he observed in infants who had been separated from their mothers over a period of three months, as "anaclitic depression". Anaclitically depressive people show, according to Blatt, an openly dependent depression. They experience massive fear of object loss and separation. Such fears can be defended against in a primitive way (e.g., through denial, or a direct search for replacement objects).

Introjective depression is experienced by patients whose depression primarily involves issues of self-esteem, self-criticism, and feelings of failure and guilt. Through the basic psychic mechanism of introjection, an interpersonal conflict does not have to be dealt with openly between people, but can be withdrawn into the intrapsychic space. Blatt concludes that in introjective depressives, this mechanism of introjecting an interpersonal conflict into one's own individual intrapsychic sphere, developed as a result of early childhood influences, has become an essential personality trait. This character type is closely associated with a rigid, punishing superego and a strong ego ideal. Measured against these internal instances, the introjective depressive feels inferior, bad, and inadequate. Introjective depressives show a self-critical depression. They are constantly preoccupied with self-doubts and have a chronic fear of being criticised and losing the approval of significant others. Initial research results show that introjective depressives, that is, self-critical depressives, respond better to longer-term psychotherapy and benefit most from psychoanalytical treatment. According to Blatt, this group of patients needs a great deal of time in psychotherapy. By contrast, Blatt's findings show that anaclitical depressives respond much sooner to treatments in which an intensive interaction with the therapist, interpersonal topics, and active and structuring interventions are foremost (Blatt & Shahar, 2004).

Case study: introjective depression in an eight-year-old boy (following Blatt)

Benjamin greeted the therapist at their first meeting warmly and almost effusively. During the examination, however, he showed increasing resistance as the therapist tried to engage with his inner world. This regulation of the relationship stood in stark contrast to the pleasure and surprise of the initial encounter. Benjamin was covering up his insecurity, and this made the atmosphere tense. It appeared to be important to him to dominate and control the situation. He dictated what was done.

He joined in the Squiggle game (Winnicott, 1971b) only with reluctance. At the third picture, communication ground to a halt. Benjamin said he "didn't feel like it" any more. He suggested playing "city-name-country" ("*Stadt-Name-Land*", a game for children well known in Germany), and got his own way, after breaking off the Squiggle game. Before they started playing, he discovered some homemade Christmas stars on the table, and described them as "Ninja warriors' throwing stars". He said these stars were not glued properly, and immediately pointed out this flaw to the therapist.

Benjamin insisted on playing "city-name-country". During the game, he was afraid that the therapist was peeking at his efforts. In their interaction, he made her into someone who was supposed to determine everything, and became annoyed when he lost. He refused any help, and, by suggesting playing this game with its strict rules, he set up a situation of competition that was a defence against closeness. He hid his solutions, telling the therapist not to look. The effect was that he was trying to provoke failure and a sense of inadequacy by entering into competition with the therapist, an adult, in a game of knowledge.

In dialogue with his therapist, he put up a clear resistance the more she tried to engage with his inner world. She resigned herself to this and dealt with him cautiously, initially acquiescing. During the game it was everyone for himself. Benjamin gave the impression of being very distanced.

At the end he wanted to play with cars and asked, "Is it bad if I drive the car into a wall?" He was startled to discover a plastic earthing wire that was poking out of the wall as part of hospital renovation work, declared, "Oh, I've broken it!", and would not let himself be calmed. He kept repeating, as if to himself, "If I do this and then that, then something will happen", or, "I would like to do this, but I'm sure I'm not allowed to", without directly asking the therapist. A constraint was presumed. Benjamin appeared powerless and unable to imagine changing anything in the external situation.

Yet, towards the end, when the therapist pointed out to him that time was up, he could not be held back. Thus, at the end, he ran out of time for talking about himself, because he had not used it at the beginning of the session with his therapist. When it was pointed out to him that now he was out of time, he replied, "But I don't care."

At the end, he gave a markedly long, open stare, and an effusively friendly goodbye, contrasting with the content of the session and confusing the therapist. The father's statement—"Well, did you spend all this time cuddling?"—with which he greeted Benjamin was also a surprise to the therapist.

Psychodynamic findings

Benjamin was a good-looking, delicate boy of good intelligence. In conversation, he appeared tired, listless, almost burnt-out. He did not speak about his inner life. During interaction with the therapist he tried to use the formally structured game to avoid engagement with his inner world. In terms of affect, he appeared dysphoric to depressive. His train of thought was fixed on rules and prohibitions, and on his inadequacy. He was not able to play (Winnicott, 1971a) (see Chapter Two, section headed "The object relations theory of Donald W. Winnicott", pp. 50–52). In psychomotor terms, he appeared restless, and fidgeted about on his chair.

It became clear that Benjamin had set up a negative melancholic introject within himself, to ward off conflict with his father intrapsychically. A few years before, the father had been unreliably available, and his own psychological illness made him react sometimes depressively, becoming apathetic and unapproachable, and sometimes aggressively and physically punishing to the then four-year-old boy. It was not possible for the child to deal with this conflict interpersonally. The conflict and the associated aggression were, therefore, introjected. This turned the anger against himself and set it up permanently directed against the self in the form of an uncompromising superego. In consequence, his ability to develop psychologically was inhibited.

On the basis of treatment of numerous cases of patients with depressive symptoms, David Taylor of the Tavistock Clinic in London developed a typology of depressive disorders and basic therapeutic principles (Taylor, 2005). Taylor stresses the need to move away from a uniform model of the disease and towards a model that takes better account of the multiple dimensions of the disorder. In his view, these include psychodynamic and developmental aspects. He argued for an empirical underpinning to the important insights into the depressive disorder gained in clinical pilot cases.

As with adult patients in this group of disorders, therapeutic closeness and the therapeutic understanding of children with emotional disorders can only succeed if particular attention is given to the young patients' efforts, which are often contradictory and directed against the object.

In the "Tavistock treatment manual for psychoanalytic psychotherapy with particular reference to chronic depression" (2010), Taylor identified a few elements (catchwords) that are still relevant to the understanding of the depressive pathology:

> the loss of an object, mourning, ambivalence, and depression; unsolvable conflicts, psychic pain, and self-destructiveness; depressive pain, the subjective experience of depression; reactivation of a good internal object; identification; deidentification and abandonment; annoyance/animosity/anger/destructiveness; triumph; devaluation and envy; feeling of guilt and self-hatred; longing and understanding of desires; the ideal and idealisation; "making good" and reparation; sadomasochism/release of bonds; developmental psychological and emotional ancestors of depression; the tendency to re-enact patterns of loss and disappointment; specific models of interpersonal relationships and personal attitudes; passivity and projection of parts of the self, narcissism, and grandiosity. (Taylor, 2010, p. 855, translated for this edition)

Taylor's "typology of depression" is intended to create a space that will enable a synthesis of psychoanalytical research, developmental psychopathology, natural sciences, and increasingly accurate epidemiological studies. He develops a classification of depressive personality types from neurotic, to moderately severe, and then to severely structurally disordered. Interpersonal or intrapsychic conflicts dominate, depending on the structural level.

Taylor reaches a profound understanding of the general difficulties of depressive patients. Depressives have problems with boundaries and dependency in closer relationships. For the therapeutic technique, this means that the therapist should also give consideration to the "subtle enactments", i.e. the characteristic dialogue of the patient. How are these depressive relationship patterns acted out in the transference relationship (Taylor, 2010)? The depressive state is generally preceded by the loss of an object, stresses Taylor, as did Freud as early as 1917 (Freud, 1917e). The unconscious hatred towards the object is transferred to other relationships. In the depressive, this has the consequence that these resentments and anger lead to severe feelings of guilt. Thus, in depressives, the destructive quality of the superego leads to severe self-reproach and self-accusation. In depressive patients with a low structural level, sadomasochistic object relationships may also dominate. In the case study of Benjamin, presented above (pp. 83–85), the child's subtle enactment consisted in bringing a submissive, self-accusatory position into the interaction, which gratifies the punishing superego, and in transference makes the therapist into the punishing counterpart. An important aspect in understanding the unstable self-assurances of depressives is that, for them, the core of the self is called into question by the self. The relationship to the good internal object is unstable and, therefore, so is the representation of the core-self as well (Taylor, 2005).

Conclusion for PaCT

In treatment of children with emotional disorders, we encounter psychic mechanisms that are the result of the internalisation of interpersonal conflicts into the child's inner life. In this way, the child protects his external object relationships or his internal relationship to the idealised object, thus enabling him to conform psychosocially. An essential part of analytical work focuses on aggression, which, in children with emotional disorders or emotional symptoms, is often directed against themselves. The goal is to detect aggressive impulses quickly in the therapist–child relationship and in the material from the sessions. It is often difficult for the child (as in the case study above) to enter into the relationship and so to make his inner world visible. The child often has difficulties entering into relationship and then separating again at the end of the session (or the end of therapy). Intensive work with the parents is necessary to resolve claustrophobia in the parent–child relationship, which often forms in tandem with the development of split-off aggressive aspects of the relationship.

The consequences of maternal depression on the early emotional development of the infant

As modern research teaches us, infants are not monadic entities walled off behind a barrier against stimuli. Small children from the outset have a remarkable wealth of perception, learning, and representation abilities, and are ready to encounter the structure of the social world surrounding them. The mother (or other primary attachment figure) and infant form an affective communication system, finely attuned to one another.

Studies using the still-face method, or with techniques of so-called feedback delay, indicate that infants perceive the contingency structure of face-to-face interaction and, from at least their fourth month, actively attempt to restore a previously available communication pattern if it is disrupted (Murray & Trevarthen, 1986; Tronick, Als, Adamson, Wise, & Brazelton, 1978). The infant's expectation that the derailed interaction can be restored supports his development of interaction representations that can be restored even after dysregulations. Such interactions are represented within, and structure, the psyche of the child (Beebe, Jaffe, & Lachmann, 1992).

This early bi-directional influencing and mutual regulation of the affective communication between mothers and infants has been demonstrated using microanalytic studies based on time-series analysis (Gottman, 1981).

The early mother–child dyad as affective communication system contains the innate basic emotions such as joy, anger, worry, fear, disgust, and surprise, which are expressed across cultures via the same facial muscles, and thus can be universally recognised. Mothers are normally very successful at reading the emotional expressions of their babies. Thus, sensitive mothers are able to exercise a modulating influence on the emotional states of the infant (Malatesta, Culver, Tesman, & Shepard, 1989; Tronick, Cohn, & Shea, 1986). Of central significance here is the alignment of time, space, and content in the facial affect mirroring, that is, the contingency structure of the maternal behaviour, which reacts to regulate the child's emotional expressions.

By observing children and their parents in her research laboratory, Mahler discovered that childhood development proceeds in cycles around recurring themes of disentanglement and individuation

(Mahler, Pine, & Bergmann, 1975). The development of one's own perceived separation from the object goes hand in hand with the formation of stable self-boundaries. The process of disentanglement and individuation is not always successful. Children with "symbiotic organisation" may be unable, or only partially able, to integrate the image of the mother as separated and external (Mahler & Gosliner, 1955). Mahler's concept takes into consideration that in discovering its early self-object differentiation from the real object, the subject feels its body contours, mirrors them, and cathects them with libido; and that this differentiation is of fundamental importance. In this connection, Mahler, Pine, and Bergmann (1975) point out the function of directly observable games between infant and mother, starting from the seventh month. The child begins to put morsels of food alternately in his own mouth and then in his mother's, or, for example, chews on the mother's necklace. These activities help the infant to begin to delimit his body schema from that of his mother. Playing peekaboo also serves the development of self-object boundaries. The child who finds his mother, or is found by her, experiences a process of separation and rediscovery, which helps the infant become aware of his own physical boundaries and the limits of the object. The playful recognition of separateness from the object in playing peekaboo has a very sensual component for the child (Mahler, Pine, & Bergmann, 1975).

The impressive studies by Tronick and colleagues (1978) on still-face show very clearly the degree of psychological distress an infant is exposed to if his mother suddenly refuses the familiar bi-directional communication structure. The infant soon begins to grimace, becomes upset, and turns away, in order to "reawaken the mother to life". If this does not succeed, the infant will consequently turn in on himself and appears increasingly despairing. Most young therapists in training shown this short video sequence are both distressed and impressed by the deep, sad affect that pictures of the "still-face" evoke. One could say that the mother's "freezing" causes a time-limited depression in the infant, with typical phases of increased activity (to reanimate the mother), protest, dysphoria, and, finally, resignation.

If mothers or other primary attachment figures suffer from post-natal depression, the child may be chronically confronted with a frozen counterpart. To some extent, depressive mothers are a "still-face" that occurs repeatedly, like a carving in stone, or a frozen, abruptly broken-off reflection. For the child's development, maternal depression signifies repeated decathecting and provokes counter-measures such as narcissistic retreat. The child experiences the mother's reactions as no longer following his expressions of affect contingently. This causes enormous stress, as the child often has no option but to see himself and his own instincts as the cause of these "psychological separations" from his mother. Numerous studies of the characteristic interaction patterns of depressive mothers have shown that postnatal depression presents a high developmental risk to the child. Studies of the facial mimicry and vocal interactions between depressive mothers and their infants indicate that these mothers react less contingently to the child's expressions of affect, and show more negative expressions of affect towards the child (Bettes, 1988; Cohn, Matias, Tronick, Conell, & Lyons-Ruth, 1986).

Postnatal depression is the commonest psychiatric disorder among mothers: 10–15% of women overall are affected, and this proportion is higher in risk populations (Harvey & Pun, 2007). Postnatal depression has negative effects on early bonding processes, the mother–child interaction and cognitive and motor development. When playing with their child, depressive mothers show less positive play behaviour, look away more frequently, show more annoyance and less involve-ment than non-depressive mothers (Tronick & Reck, 2009). Emo-tionally withdrawn or overstimulating behaviour, which is often found in these mothers, can lead to the child avoiding eye contact and retreating.

Dangers of postnatal depression:

- risk of early bonding disorders and emotional disorders;
- infant difficulty in acquiring self-regulating abilities;
- risk of regulation disorders in early childhood (e.g., excessive shouting or disturbed sleep–wake rhythm) and of later behav-ioural difficulties;
- risk of the child's narcissistic withdrawal.

In his study *The Dead Mother*, the French psychoanalyst André Green considered the consequences for the child's psychological development of the early experience of a mother absent through depression and grief (Green, 2004). For this grief for an absent or "dead" mother, Green coins the term "white grief", or the clinical symptom of "emptiness", and says this is the result of an early defence mechanism:

> a massive, radical and time-limited withdrawal of cathexis, which leaves traces in the form of 'psychic holes' in the unconscious, which are filled in with re-cathexes. These are the expression of a destructiveness which is released through the previous weakening of the erotic-libidinal cathexis. (Green, 2004, p. 237, translated by the authors)

Thus, in his opinion, this absence of the mother resonance leads to the infant shifting his cathexis of the mother to a cathexis of the self when the physical mother is present. This cathexis is a kind of "narcissistic seal": in order to escape the insecurity of the object relationship, the subject cathects itself. However, this self-cathexis ultimately has an abysmal and self-destructive quality. Our clinical experience with children whose mothers were postnatally depressed, or who suffered from lasting depressive episodes, shows that these children are often apathetic and withdrawn, with a self-esteem that is hypomanically inflated, and yet so brittle and unstable that it reacts to insults from outside with outbreaks of rage. It often appears as if these children can only experience their anger explosively.

This early withdrawal into the ego with its resulting overcathexis allows the exchange between subject and object to become rigid too early; it can lead to an early solidification of the libido and unstable boundaries between subject and object. The object's significance for the subject has to be negated early on. Thus, the child does not develop a differentiated self-object perception. Freud indicated the danger of this early withdrawal of the libido into the self in his "On narcissism" (1914c). He started by assuming that the disorder on which the psychosis is based results from this withdrawal of the libido, which is more satisfying than the "adventure of the object libido" that is accompanied by disappointment, menace, and insecurity, as well as by satisfactions (Freud, 1914c).

Green formulates the connection thus:

> The narcissists are vulnerable creatures, yes, in terms of their narcissism they are deficient beings. The disappointments that they carry within themselves as open wounds are generally not limited to one parent, but involve both of them. What object can they still love, if not themselves? (Green, 2004, p. 18, translated by the authors)

This development of self-love as a protection from further disappointments in the object is, in our opinion, a reaction to early psychic separations from, and cathexis withdrawals by, the object. Since these cathexis withdrawals by the parents are often difficult to reconstruct when taking a history, and since even normal narcissistic insults remain inevitable for the subject in its development, we agree with Green's conclusion that in the work with the child and its parents our countertransference gives important clues to whether the child has developed narcissistic defensive formations. One typical transference constellation that Green describes is that of the analysand whose ideas supply the analyst with nourishment, in order to keep him alive as the transference object of the "dead mother". The narratives of these patients are less associative than they are attempts to win the analyst's admiration. The analysand nurtures the analyst,

> not in order to be able to live outside the analysis, but to prolong it into an endless process. For the subject wants to be the mother's pole star, the ideal child, who takes the place of an idealised dead person, the rival . . ." (Green, 2004, p. 255, translated by the authors)

Green describes the defensive formation of narcissistic withdrawal described above as follows:

> Certainly, the narcissistic wound made directly or indirectly to our infantile omnipotence by our parents is the fate of all of us. But it is also clear that some never recover from this wound, even after analysis. They remain vulnerable, although analysis is supposed to help them use their defence mechanisms better and thus to avoid injury, but they plainly lack the hide that others seem to have instead of skin. No one suffers as much at finding himself catalogued under a general rubric as the narcissist, he whose greatest concern is not to be just any one, but unique, quite without antecedents or successors. (Green, 2004, p. 18, translated by the authors)

In their despairing narcissism, children exposed early on to such psychic separations or "cathexis withdrawals" as a result of their mother's or father's depressive illness also often appear to be lacking this "hide" that could shield them from attacks and insults. Their self-cathexis or "narcissistic seal" offers them too little protection, and therefore they often react with blind destructive rage to anything they perceive as a threat to their self-esteem.

Green points out that "the object—whether phantasmatic or real—concerning narcissism—comes into conflict with the ego" (Green, 2004, p. 21, translated by the authors). Sexualisation of the ego results in the desire for the object being transformed into a desire for the ego.

Conclusion for PaCT

Modern research teaches us that, from the outset, the infant is situated in a space marked by parental fantasies and real interactions, a space that it can shape actively. Even babies have the capacity to repair "derailed interactions" and dysregulated communication. Thus, in our therapeutic concept, we understand the development of the self in its subjectivity—and this essentially includes inner fantasies, wishes, and subjective mental representations—as first created through inter-subjective experiences. Gergely and Watson's social biofeedback theory of parental affect mirroring (Gergely & Watson, 1996) shows that the infant is able to represent his expressions of feeling within himself only by mirroring someone else who is present. The self is, therefore, based in the representation of the experience of another. Not all children are sufficiently represented in their primary attachment figure, particularly if this person is preoccupied with his or her own psychological problems. Additionally, not all children experience a wealth of interactions that can be internalised and lead to a differentiated affective self-representation.

Children who have reacted to their mother's early withdrawal of cathexis with a withdrawal of the libido to the ego may have switched the object of desire: the ego has become its own object of desire. The therapist who works with children whose mothers' mirroring of their emotions in the early years of their development was inadequate should always keep this movement at the back of his mind. In the child, we often experience such transference constellations of the "dead mother" as a lack of liveliness, which appears in our counter-transference as boredom, since the child does not interact with us but remains detached. This emptiness in the countertransference poses a great challenge to the therapist, who must resist the desire to fill the child with life through counter-action in order to spare it the inevitable working through of the painful experience of the dead mother.

Transference and countertransference

Transference and countertransference in adult analysis

Before turning to the specifics of transference in psychoanalytic child therapy (PaCT), we want to consider the significance of the transference relationship in adult analysis.

In 1950, Heimann tackled the classical psychoanalytic assumption that the analyst's countertransference is a kind of "disruptive influence" that hinders the course of treatment and that therefore needs to be overcome by the analyst. Indeed, in 1911, Freud wrote about the newly discovered phenomenon,

> We have become aware of the 'counter-transference', which arises in him as a result of the patient's influence on his unconscious feelings, and we are almost inclined to insist that he shall recognize this counter-transference in himself and overcome it. (Freud, 1910d, p. 144)

Freud recognised that work with transference is the essential tool of every psychoanalysis, without which the therapeutic work would be ineffectual. He describes as transference the reanimation of the patient's tenderly erotic or aggressive unconscious attitudes towards his earlier relationship object, in the here and now of the relationship to the analyst:

> It must be understood that each individual, through the combined operation of his innate disposition and the influences brought to bear on him during his early years, has acquired a specific method of his own in his conduct of his erotic life-that is, in the preconditions to falling in love which he lays down, in the instincts he satisfies and the aims he sets himself in the course of it. (Freud, 1912b, p. 99)

The individual repeats this "relationship cliché" over the course of his life with whatever love objects that reality provides. The psychoanalytical technique harnesses the re-enactment of earlier unconscious attitudes of the patient, in that, through the development of the patient's transference, it is able to detect, and therefore interpret, the central conflicts and unresolved business. Because the analyst recognises that these attitudes are not directed towards himself as a real person, he is able to perceive them as transference phenomena.

In analysis, both positive and negative transference to the analyst are established. Both transference forms may express unconscious resistance to the progress of the analysis and in particular the changes that must be made. Thus, "the strongest factor towards success is changed in it into the most powerful medium of resistance" (Freud, 1912b, p. 101). Both too strong a positive transference, for example, a strongly erotic transference in the form of falling in love, and a very negative transference, in which the patient feels persecuted or humiliated by the analyst, can lead to the patient violating the ground rules of analysis, and no longer expressing all his thoughts freely and uncritically.

On the conscious level, the enamoured patient might want to impress the analyst and therefore makes efforts to censor thoughts that could shame him. This desire not to tell the therapist any spontaneous ideas might serve a patient in negative transference as an unconscious resistance, which expresses itself in the conscious thought that the analyst wants to use what he says against him. Thus, many transference constellations develop in analysis, in which the transference of the patient becomes resistance against the making conscious of unconscious contents. Freud saw the conquest of transference phenomena as the greatest difficulty in analysis. It should be possible to manage countertransference through intensive familiarity with one's own complexes through the training analysis. This, he said, was an absolute prerequisite for performing psychoanalytical therapy: "Anyone who fails to produce results in a self-analysis of this kind may at once give up any idea of being able to treat patients by analysis" (Freud, 1912b). The analyst should analyse his own countertransference feelings and ascribe them to his own unconquered unconscious complexes. Once these are understood, he should turn again to analytical understanding in evenly suspended attention with a mildly positive attitude. He should purify himself from these disturbing countertransference feelings.

In her groundbreaking work "On counter-transference" (1950), Heimann critically examined this demand that the analyst dispose of these disturbing feelings towards the analysand through reflection on his own contributions.

She saw in this a false demand that the analyst should apply a sort of intellectually cold technique, which in her view did not satisfy the patients' needs. The claim that a good analyst should not feel anything towards his patient except a constant, mild benevolence did not do justice to the analytical situation. Rather, this requirement condemned countertransference, the most important tool of analysis, to the role of a merely disruptive element.

She wrote, pointedly,

> My thesis is that the analyst's emotional response to his patient within the analytic situation represents one of the most important tools for his work. The analyst's counter-transference is an instrument of research into the patient's unconscious. (Heimann, 1950, p. 81)

Heimann did not see the task of the training analysis as that of making the analyst into a mechanically operating brain that formulated meanings only on the level of intellectual processes. Rather, it should aim to enable the analyst to "sustain the feelings which are stirred in him, as opposed to discharging them (as does the patient), in order to *subordinate* them to the analytic task in which he functions as the patient's mirror reflection" (Heimann, 1950, p. 82).

According to Heimann, an analyst who does not make use of his feelings is restricted to formulating only weak interpretations. She went so far as to claim that it is often the analyst's feelings that can give him a pointer to understanding, and that pure thought is often further away from understanding than is feeling.

The analyst's countertransference feelings, in her opinion, also serve to condense the unfocused material produced by the patient's associations. Depending on the emotional meaning to the analyst, he will be able to select the material and point to it. If the analyst has worked through his infantile conflicts and (paranoid and depressive) fears sufficiently in his own training analysis, so that he is able to come into contact with his own unconscious in a straightforward way, he will not mistakenly ascribe to the patient material that actually belongs to him. In a reliable state of equilibrium, the analyst can thus endure the projections that the patient makes in transference to him, and make them useful in the analytical working through.

Definition of transference

Every human relationship is ruled by feelings, thoughts, expectations, and behaviours that cannot be explained solely by the current interpersonal interactions, but become understandable when seen as the repetitions of earlier relationship forms. These ubiquitous transference phenomena, however, only become interpretable in the defined setting of analytical treatment.

In 1959, Racker described the phenomena of transference and countertransference in detail. He first pointed out that being an analyst means abstaining from retaliation, not entering into the neurotic vicious circle, not submitting to the patient's defence mechanisms, and always making the effort to understand the patient (Racker, 1970, p. 73). There is a danger here that the analyst unreflectedly takes on the role that the patient's unconscious ascribes to him, and that in this way he becomes proactive. The analyst may under no circumstances give in to such an impulse, because that would mean he was acting under an "internal compulsion" and, together with the patient, would repeat but not remember and understand. This also involves continuous reflection on countertransference, so as not simply to react to the patient, but to understand his action as the temptation to repeat earlier relationship patterns. The analytical attitude also means the analyst must live a kind of "double life": he must bring about a healthy internal splitting between an experiencing, irrational ego and a rational, observing ego. Racker distinguished "concordant identification" from "complementary identification" (1970, p. 73).

In concordant identification the analyst identifies with the ego and the id of the patient. In complementary identification, on the other hand, the analyst identifies with the internal objects of the patient. Complementary identification in particular carries the risk that the analyst, in the transference–countertransference development, will allow himself to be drawn into the neurotic vicious circle and act out his possibly negative countertransference feelings.

Racker pointed out that the metaphors of the analyst as a "mirror", or taking up the "surgeon's attitude", which suggest the attitude of a cold and purely interpreting therapist, were not, in fact, used by Freud. Rather, Freud used these terms in the early days of analysis in an attempt to counter the widespread habit of the analysts to talk about themselves to their patients. Instead of expressing themselves, analysts had to try to act as a mirror for the patient. Racker warned of overextending the Freudian mirror metaphor, to the extent that the analyst suppresses feelings of sympathy and affection for the patient.

Freud himself never applied such a "cold technique", understood as the classic attitude, in his own treatment.

In his ground-breaking work "Hate in the counter-transference" (1949), Winnicott suggested that intense feelings of hate in the analyst's countertransference should be understood as an expression of the severity of the patient's disorder. In order for the patient to be able to integrate his own intense feelings of hate within himself, the analyst must be consciously aware of his own feelings of hate in the countertransference, and able to reflect on them, accept them, and tolerate them. This is only possible after a sufficiently intensive training analysis in the course of which the analyst himself has worked through deeper layers of his hatred. Winnicott compared this ability of the analyst consciously to sense hate in relation to the analysand with the mother's relationship to her infant. In his opinion, the mother hates the child long before the infant begins to hate the mother. The mother's hatred of the child is fed from many sources, since the mother sacrifices herself for the infant in caring for it, without ever being recompensed for that. The infant is voracious and needy and does not perceive the mother's sacrifice as such, but as something to be taken for granted. Once it is replete, the mother has no further significance (Winnicott, 1949, p. 72). This is how Winnicott explains the mother's hatred of her baby.

The mother, on the other hand, has the task of enduring her hatred for the baby without converting it into action or expressing it in any way: "The most remarkable thing about a mother is her ability to be hurt so much by her baby and to hate so much without paying the child out, and her ability to wait for rewards that may or may not come at a later date" (Winnicott, 1949, p. 73).

The psychoanalytical treatment of depressive patients involves processes that are analogous to the mother's relationship to her infant. Thus, the analyst, like the mother, needs the ability to tolerate the hatred that arises within the relationship. According to Winnicott, intense feelings of hatred often arise in the analyst, particularly during the treatment of patients who are not neurotic but are more severely disordered. The efficacy of the treatment depends essentially on whether the analyst can succeed in making conscious and enduring his own feelings of hatred, provoked by the patient through his hate-filled feelings towards the analyst, without acting them out.

It is, therefore, essential for therapy that the analyst can bear his feelings of hate and antipathy towards the patient, and understand them as the expression of the patient's own unconscious hatreds. The analyst must behave like the mother towards her infant and provide a holding environment without reacting to the patient's unconscious attacks with counter-aggression or the breaking off of contact.

Transference in child analysis

Anna Freud looked closely at the significance of transference in child analysis (A. Freud, 1980). She first employed a few technical considerations: the child analyst is not able to use the child's verbal report as a base, but must undertake an analysis using the products of the child's unconscious. The child's spontaneous ideas, daydreams, dreams, and play form the central contents on which the analyst can base his interpretations. The child seldom speaks spontaneously about his ideas but prefers to play, and so the analyst generally cannot base his interpretations on the child's verbal utterances. Melanie Klein's play technique became an important instrument of child analysis after Anna Freud; however, Anna Freud, unlike Melanie Klein, does not see this as a substitute for the free association of adult analysis. She distances herself from Klein's technique, which interprets the unconscious content of all the child's actions in play through constant translation and interpretation. Anna Freud holds that not everything the child says may be the expression of unconscious phantasies, and thus the child's interest in the analyst's handbag does not have to mean that he is looking for a baby in there, but could also be due to normal childlike curiosity.

For Anna Freud, the play technique is a very good instrument of observation in getting to know the child, becoming familiar with the strength of his aggressive impulses, his empathic ability, and his attitudes in general.

However, the child's play should not be compared with an adult's free association, because the child does not always "play" to the same analytical rules to which the adult "speaks". The rule of saying everything that appears on the surface of consciousness can only usefully be applied to an adult's speech. The child's play is a rehearsal of the playful expression of its drive for knowledge and the processing of the day's experiences. Not everything in the child's play has a symbolic meaning as the expression of unconscious desires. Thus, Anna Freud, unlike Melanie Klein, does not understand everything that the child does in treatment as an expression of transference to the analyst. Indeed, Anna Freud denies that the child forms any transference neurosis at all. The child continues to produce his disturbing symptoms at home, and is not prepared to re-enact his previous love relationships in the transference to the analyst, since he continues to cathect his parents in his libido positions. Unlike adults, the child does not restage his negative and positive attitudes to his parents in transference. His real relationships to the primary objects are still there, and the neurotic symptoms present themselves more in the domestic environment and less in the analytic setting; by contrast the adult in the analytic setting produces symptoms similar to those experienced with his real parents. In adult analysis the analyst remains shadowy and should ideally make himself available as a projection screen on to which the patient's behaviour patterns can be projected and interpreted as transference. The child analyst, on the other hand, cannot be a shadow. Anna Freud uses an evocative analogy to make clear what the child analyst is for the child: the transference remains unfocused, so that the analyst might find it difficult to identify the transferred picture, because there is already a picture on his "screen" on which another picture is now projected. As a result, the picture projected (by the child on to the analyst) is out of focus. How negative transference is handled also has a different meaning in child analysis than in the analysis of adults.

While the working through of negative transference in the analysis of adults is a difficult but very fruitful process, bringing much unconscious material to light, in Anna Freud's view negative transference in child analysis is more of a disturbing element, which the analyst must act to eradicate. Otherwise, the working alliance will be endangered, since the child does not experience enough psychological strain to need to hold fast to the analytical working alliance despite negative transference.

Conclusion for PaCT

We understand transference in both its positive and negative functions: transference can, as in the conventional view, disturb the course of treatment, but it can also support it. The therapist must in a way allow herself to become enmeshed in the patient's offers of transference, so that the transference can make unconscious interpersonal and intrapsychic conflicts both visible and understandable. In contrast to Anna Freud, we make the assumption that in the treatment of children the therapist represents both a real person, who accompanies the child in his development, and a transference object, often bringing defended relationship aspects back to life. In addition there is the fact that the parents may also develop a transference relationship to the therapist of their child, and this can often be the occasion for conflict. It is particularly important that negative transference aspects of the child and the parents are recognised early, so as not to endanger the treatment's positive course. In addition, short-term therapy demands a particularly careful handling of transference, as the space for a detailed working through and dissolution of transference is lacking. This has a particular impact on the interpretation technique, where transference phenomena are considered but only taken up with considerable caution.

Affective disorders and emotional symptoms in the light of psychoanalytical concepts of structural integration: the OPD-KJ axis "structure"

Since PaCT serves the treatment of children with classic neurotic constellations as well as children with early structural disorders, it is helpful to form a picture of the patient's structural level right at the start of treatment. The structural axis of the *Operationalisierte Psychodynamische Diagnostik für Kinder und Jugendliche* (*OPD-KJ*) (Arbeitskreis OPD-KJ, 2007), a diagnostic manual for psychodynamically orientated clinicians, can be helpful in this evaluation.

The evaluation of the child's structural level is based on diagnostic material from talking with children and their parents, observations during play, biographical material, and scenic representation.

Using the operationalised psychodynamic diagnosis axis "structure" (Arbeitskreis OPD-KJ, 2007) the reader can use clinical anchors to distinguish between the different levels of structural integration that, in our view, are also the basis of the clinical picture of depressive and anxiety disorders in childhood (see Chapter Five, section headed

"Therapeutic equipment", pp. 127–128). The clinician will thus be able to adapt his intervention strategies to target the child's psychological level of functioning.

What does "psychic structural level" mean?

Kernberg (1975, 1976, 1984) proposed criteria for the classification of structural level in the personality organisation of adults. These criteria classify personality disorders on the basis of three clinically differentiable types of personality organisation. Classification of the structural integration is, therefore, carried out by evaluating the quality of the internalised object relationships and the ego structure. Aspects of instinctual-drive dynamism are also considered. In the treatment of depressive and anxious children with PaCT, we use this classification:

- neurotic personality organisation, in which the symptom can be traced back to an unconscious conflict, where there is a relatively mature ego structure and mature defence mechanisms;
- borderline personality organisation, with unstable self- and object-representations and a domination by immature defence mechanisms such as splitting, idealisation, devaluing, projection, and projective identification.
- psychotic personality organisation, with disorganised self- and object-representations, psychotic fragmentation of defence, and, for example, delusional experiences when reality testing breaks down.

Conclusion for PaCT

Depressivity or depression at each of these structural levels of functioning signifies a different subjective experience as well as a different specific psychodynamic. While the evaluation of structural level in adults is carried out using a psychoanalytical–diagnostic interview, for example the structural interview of Kernberg (1984), with children we must draw on a variety of sources to gather equivalent information. In adults, the diagnostic interview places particular focus on the ability to test against reality, the integration of identity, the quality of the object relationships, and the maturity of defence mechanisms. The patient's social context, his currently significant relationship system, life story, as well as the desire for treatment, are all included. But with a child, our evaluation of his structural level must rely on the material provided to us in the initial conversations (through play, drawings, interaction, narrative).

The concept of the focus: theoretical introduction

The scientific–theoretical and treatment-related considerations of Argelander (1983) and Lorenzer (1970) on scenic understanding made clear that psychoanalytical work is fundamentally bound to attitude and not to a particular setting. Every analytical situation, whether it is an initial consultation, a counselling session, or a focal therapy with adults or children and adolescents, contains the most important elements of an unconscious scene (early forms of transference, the past, bringing it into the present), which makes psychoanalytical understanding, and the formation of a psychoanalytical hypothesis, possible. The term *scenic understanding* takes account of this understanding of the precipitation of individual conflicts in the present scene.

The conception of psychoanalytical focus is closely related to the term scenic understanding in psychoanalytical investigation. Lorenzer (1970) first described several levels of language, producing the following levels of understanding: logical understanding of the factual content of communication and interaction (understanding what is spoken), psychological understanding of the emotional relationship content (understanding the speaker), scenic understanding of the patterns of a scene that help to organise the life-expressions (understanding the situation), and understanding the desires and defence processes hidden in the scenes.

The processing of the material contained in a scene should, nevertheless, not be compared with the deeper access to unconscious contents that takes place in a long-term therapy. Transference, too, unfolds only to a limited extent in short-term therapy.

Focal therapy is based on the central components of termination, the immediate processing of the defence, and the identification of, and focusing on, the core conflict. To illustrate the complexity of the focus (Latin: hearth, fireplace, derived from this: "focal point"), Malan (1963), Menninger and Holzmann (1958), and Klüwer (1983) used triangles.

The following triangles are described:

1. The triangle of defence (conflict level).
2. The triangle of insight (life story).
3. The triangle of action (subject–object action).

The *triangle of defence* (conflict level: defended material—anxiety—defence) illustrates that psychoanalytical focal therapy addresses the immediate subject of the actual conflict, by making the anxiety that lies at the root of the defence recognisable. This focus formulation is an interpretation of the defensive movement and its content. It is developed by the therapist during the initial consultations, with the help of the conflict dynamic that emerges in the transference relationship. At an appropriate point, it is then communicated to the patient. Until that point, it serves the therapist as an internal aid to understanding.

The second level is centred in the *triangle of insight* around the acquisition of a conflict pattern in the course of the life story, and its actualisation in the transference relationship in the present. The local adverbs *here, there, then* help the therapist to illustrate how the actual conflict is realised in the transference relationship (life story: transference relationship = here; actual conflict = there; original conflict situation = then).

Focus (case study, Elisabeth, six years old, see Chapter Twelve)

"I'm controlling my therapist [here], like I also control my parents [there]. I've been doing this since my little sister was born [then]."

The third level, the *triangle of action*, concentrates on the active dialogue (Klüwer, 1983), between therapist and patient as a specific form of "immersion with each other". Here, the therapist's attention or reflective function oscillates between allowing herself to get involved in the active dialogue, which requires the enmeshment of the therapist, a calibrated playing along with the patient, and an attitude of understanding in which the therapist reflectively steps out of the current being-enmeshed interaction with the patient, so that it is possible to understand the restaging of the patient's central conflict in the current transference constellation. However, the therapist must first allow herself to become immersed with the patient.

It is important to state that the concept of psychoanalytical focal therapy was first developed in the context of adult treatment. Numerous publications have applied the focus concept to the area of child and adolescent psychotherapy. For example, a Heidelberg group evaluating the efficacy of analytical psychotherapy developed a detailed treatment guideline for short-term therapy (Hartmann et al., 2000). Chethik's considerations (1989) on the recommended line of treatment for focused psychotherapy in childhood developmental crises concluded that children and adolescents in whom an oedipal conflict is delimitable and who have a neurotic structure are most likely to benefit from focal therapy. The results of the Frankfurt focal therapy conferences also support this as a therapeutic area for the neurotic rather than the structural disorder spectrum (Jongbloed-Schurig, 2001). Windaus gives a comprehensive overview of the current state of research on focal therapy in child and adolescent psychotherapy (Windaus, 2006, 2007).

The focus represents an actualised core conflict that can be made conscious, although it is always also one interpretation selected from a multitude of possibilities. It connects focal and afocal elements of psychoanalytical work with one another. It bundles or *focuses* the material obtained from the afocal elements of the psychoanalytical setting. Starting from the initially unstructured free associations, or the child's free play, focus formulation is used to create a structure. Every interpretation is a structuring, a bundling of psychic material for the purpose of understanding.

Conclusion for PaCT

To communicate the focus to the patient, it is helpful if it is formulated in language that is both everyday and appropriate for the patient's level of development. Only in this way can an emotional connection to its internal experience be created for the child and his parents.

The difference between a focus and a classic psychoanalytical interpretation consists in the actuality of the conflict pattern addressed.

Out of all imaginable conflicts on the different conflict levels, the focus is the formulation of that which is current and active now. The treatment therefore concentrates on the verbalisation of the core conflict topic that has just been bundled in the focus formulation.

PART II

TREATMENT MANUAL:
THE THERAPEUTIC CONCEPT
OF PaCT

Introductory overview of Part II

P sychoanalytic procedures have a long tradition in the history of child psychiatry and psychotherapy. Short-term therapies take account of the need to offer therapeutic help to a large number of children with emotional disorders. The *Manual for Short-Term Psychoanalytic Child Therapy (PaCT)* comprises 20–25 psychotherapeutic sessions in changing settings (parent–child, child alone, parents alone), in which a relational theme lying at the root of the symptoms is processed and worked through. This relational theme represents a psychodynamic hypothesis about the currently active interpersonal and/or intrapsychic conflict, and integrates it with the defence mechanisms associated with this conflict. The relational theme encompasses (1) the family relationships on which the symptoms are based; (2) the intrapsychic conflicts, and (3) the therapist–parents–child relationship. We call this the *triangle of psychodynamic constellations* (ToP, see Figure 3, Chapter Six (p. 149), in the section headed "The focus of PaCT: 'triangle of psychodynamic constellations'" (ToP), pp. 147–148).

The psychotherapeutic interventions have two goals: one is to change the child's mental representations and, thus, its cognitive–emotional styles, and the other is to improve the parents' insight into the child's internal mental states (*mentalization*) through regular psychoanalytic work. The child's central conflict is worked through in verbal exchange and/or in free play with the child. Depending on the child's structural level, supplementary techniques to promote mentalization may be applied (Verheugt-Pleiter, Zevalkink, & Schmeets, 2008).

The greater the accuracy with which the focus is formulated in the initial treatment phase, the more it will coincide with the topics that surface in the course of the therapeutic process. Just as in the psychoanalysis of adults, material surfaces in child analysis in play and in the free association linked to it, giving indications of the underlying unresolved developmental issues or conflicts. What has remained unresolved reveals itself in the analytic therapeutic process. Nevertheless, a focus may shift in the course of treatment, along with the deepening understanding of the situation of the child and its family.

The course of psychotherapeutic treatment with PaCT is given below.

- Initial sessions (five sessions):
  Session 1: in the parent–child setting (subject of the session: what has brought the parents and child to the therapist? Definition of the problems from the viewpoint of the participants; psychoanalytical understanding of the "scene" of the first encounter; observation of parent–child interaction);
  Sessions 2–3: parent–therapist setting (psychodynamically orientated case history of the child, parental biography, coherence *vs.* incoherence of parents' narrative about the child and their own biography);
  Sessions 4–5: therapist–child setting.
  Sessions with the parents and sessions with the child may also alternate.
- Therapeutic work with the child (working through the focus), for example, free play: sessions (4, 5), 7, 8, 9, 11, 12, 13, 15, 16, 17, 19
- Integration of the material into a psychodynamic hypothesis, ToP (*triangle of psychodynamic constellations*) after the fifth session: focus formulated as a relationship topic;
- Parental work in the parent–therapist setting to develop, communicate, and process the focus as a relationship topic between parents and child; strengthening the parental function: sessions (2, 3), 6, 10, 14, 18, 20

Focal conference: For therapists in training, or learning about PaCT, we recommend holding so-called "focal conferences" (Klüwer, 2005) after sessions 5, 10, 15, 20. In these, we aim to formulate the focus, generate the psychodynamic hypothesis, and, in the course of therapy, to evaluate how closely one is following the manual and how the focus has been formulated, and to modify this if necessary.

CHAPTER FOUR

When to refer for PaCT

The child

PaCT is suitable to treat children with a wide range of symptoms (behavioural disorders, "hyperactivity", neurotic relationship, or learning disabilities, etc.) if anxiety and/or depression are significantly involved in the development of symptoms. Epidemiological studies have revealed a point prevalence of depressive disorders in childhood of 1–3% (Fleming & Offord, 1990). At preschool and school age, depressive disorders are characterised by fearfulness, dysphoric moods, low self-consciousness, an inability to play, impaired learning, reduced creativity and patience, a lack of fantasy, irritability, and in psychosomatic symptoms and behavioural difficulties (von Klitzing, 2008). Prior to adolescence, there is a strong overlap between depression and anxiety disorders, making clear diagnostic distinction between anxiety and depression difficult (Sterba, Egger, & Angold, 2007). Retrospective reports of adults with depression indicate that emotional symptoms were often present in childhood, even at preschool or primary school age (Kim-Cohen et al., 2003). Our clinical experience is in line with these empirical findings. At the age of 4–10 years, depressive disorders cannot be unambiguously differentiated from anxiety disorders. There is a high level of "comorbidity" of depressive disorders with anxiety disorders. Therefore, we have chosen, along with other researchers in the field, to use the umbrella term "emotional disorders" for anxiety and depression in children. Parents whose children are showing emotional symptoms often tell us that behavioural problems occur at the same time. Especially in boys, depressive experience or anxiety is often defended against through hypomanic behaviour (see case study, Julian, six years old, in Chapter Twelve of this book).

A central assumption of our psychodynamic approach is that as they develop, children with emotional symptoms turn aggression inwards, against themselves rather than towards the object. Where there are intrapsychic conflicts, it is not the objects that are condemned, but the self, which results in an inhibition of the self. The early models of Abraham, Freud and Radó established the significance of loss, disappointment, and anger in the genesis of depression. More recent models also emphasise the significance of unconscious aggression in the aetiopathogenesis of depression. For example, Mentzos (2006) proposes a similar aetiological concept of depression, which takes account of the three conflict areas of "loss of real or internal object", the "turning of aggression against oneself", and the "disorder of narcissistic regulation".

The approach of Blatt and colleagues to understanding depression in adulthood acknowledges psychologically relevant disorders of the development of object permanence (Blatt, 1995; Blatt, Luyten, & Corveleyn, 2005). Blatt's concept of introjective *vs.* anaclitic depression provides a basis for the classification of depressive developments at different levels of the individual's structural integration as neurotic pathologies or structural deficits.

The child analytical approach of PaCT aims to identify the aggression turned against the self and bring it to consciousness in shared psychic work. Thus, the child is able to find increasing access at a symbolic level to the lack, loss, and disappointment that lies at the root of the aggression turned against himself. We conclude that the absence, the lack, and the disappointment in the object will also be expressed in the transference. The transference relationship offers the child the possibility of a better solution to the conflict. It is important that the child experiences a counterpart who does not react to his aggression by retaliating and breaking off contact. The therapist tries to introduce a level of understanding through the triadic position, which can help in the symbolic expression of aggression. In the psychotherapeutic treatment of depressive children, this can then give rise to more flexible defences, less self-reproach, and less inhibition of vitality.

It is clear that children of preschool age or early school age are often not referred for psychotherapeutic treatment despite being clearly impaired in their psycho-emotional development. This is often because parents find it difficult to evaluate whether the problematic behaviour of their child is indeed the expression of psychological symptoms or disorders. The parents often hope that these problems are a normal part of development, and the child will "grow out" of them. That children of this age do not receive psychotherapeutic treatment despite having clear problems is often due to a denial of the need for treatment.

The parents

Diagnosis of a development-inhibiting psychic disorder of the child that requires intervention is a prerequisite for PaCT. This treatment is suitable for children who have emotional problems such as anxiety and depression, even if these at first masquerade as primary behavioural problems. The presence of emotional symptoms alone is, however, not enough to decide whether a child and his family can be treated using PaCT.

In addition, particular conditions must be met from the side of the parents—as our important allies—in order for PaCT treatment to be carried out successfully.

In the diagnostic phase, it is, therefore, important not only to assess the necessity, ability, and willingness of the child to undergo treatment, but also to evaluate the parents in terms of their willingness and ability to form a reliable, trusting, working alliance with the therapist.

Particular "external" and "internal" conditions must be set at the start of therapy.

Novick and Novick (2005) formulated tasks that the parents have to tackle throughout the course of the treatment. We discuss these tasks again in the section on parental work (pp. 170–183). One important precondition for the therapy is that the parents must be willing to accept the psychic and physical separateness of their child, and to work for and tolerate change. That being said, it may be important at this juncture to remind the reader that PaCT is not merely directed at a small minority of less severe or privileged families. On the contrary, by virtue of its relatively low dose and the associated time and cost-efficient qualities, PaCT is conceptualised and has proved effective as a first line of treatment with a wide range of cases from diverse socioeconomic and educational backgrounds referred for outpatient treatment of emotional problems.

"External" parent prerequisites

An important external condition is that the child's fundamental emotional and physical needs for protection, attention, and integrity must be satisfied adequately by the parents. The child must also be attending kindergarten or school, so that meaningful work can be done in an outpatient child-analytic setting.

Since the children are generally unable to manage the journey to the therapy on their own, it is important that the parents are willing and able to bring their child regularly to a fixed weekly appointment. The parents' reliability in adhering to these framework conditions is an indispensable prerequisite for PaCT.

If, in addition to emotional problems, a child also shows a tendency towards aggressive behaviour that puts himself or other children at risk, the therapist must ascertain whether the pedagogical framework in which the child is living provides sufficient support in regulating impulses. The child's ability for impulse regulation is an important pre-condition for PaCT. If, in addition to emotional problems, a child also tends to display aggressive behaviour, it should be possible for the child to regulate impulsive outbursts at school or at home with the help of limited interventions by the parents or teachers. If the child has disorganised, destructive temper tantrums that he is unable to regulate, we should first help the parents in providing sufficient pedagogical support to their child.

"Internal" parent prerequisites

It is important that the parents' care and empathy with their child exceeds the mere desire for the child to "function properly" without symptoms as soon as possible.

Parents may react to the behaviour of their child in a disparaging and unempathic way. This reaction often expresses a tendency to externalise unconscious feelings of guilt and to blame the child alone for his or her problems. If the child, for example, plays in an unco-ordinated or unmotivated way, or reacts oppositionally, some parents will make disparaging comments and try in this way to ally them-selves with the therapist against the child. Such distorting and deroga-tory attitudes are often the expression of primitive defence mechanisms such as externalisation and projection. It is an important prerequisite for PaCT to change parental attitudes of incomprehen-sion and disparagement of the child in a preliminary phase, and to improve their understanding of the inner psychic states that underlie the child's behaviour. Treatment using PaCT might, therefore, be preceded by an upstream parental module (see pp. 22–123).

It is important for treatment using PaCT that the parents do not show strong tendencies to reject their child, which would indicate that they are overtaxed by the intensive engagement with their own inter-nal psychic processes, concerns, and needs. This is often the case if the parents' own psychological burdens mean they are not in a position to engage with the child's needs as well. The initial consultations can determine whether the parents, with the help of the therapist, are in a position to think more positively about, and make serious efforts to understand, their child, or whether they would prefer to hand over responsibility for his/her problems to the therapist.

Before PaCT begins, it is also important to recognise one-sided tendencies to externalise blame in the parents. Treatment with PaCT is difficult if the parents unilaterally blame the child himself/herself, the school, the teacher, or other children, for any problems.

In addition to these prerequisites, it is important that the parents are prepared both to accept the physical separateness of the child from themselves and to acknowledge that the child is also psychically sepa-rate from them. The parental ability to allow the separation of the child can also be evaluated in the initial consultations.

It is vital that the parents are able to develop an interest in think-ing about what might be occupying their child internally. Even if they themselves find it very difficult to reflect on the internal mental processes of the child, they should be able to show an interest in these topics when supported by the therapist. Only through the parents' active work, and through our being able to bring the parents into a working alliance that jointly tries to connect the child's problematic behaviour with his internal psychic processes, can treatment with PaCT be successful.

If these prerequisites are not fulfilled after an upstream parental module, we should first attempt a treatment that helps the family manage his current problems at an interpersonal level, such as psycho-educative counselling or educational counselling for the parents, aimed at promoting the parent–child interaction and helping the parents to provide an educational framework for the child. Furthermore, in families who need a "holding environment" (Winnicott, 1965) that gives a structure to promote the educational skills to resolve interpersonal conflicts, an inpatient or outpatient child psychiatric treatment should also be considered.

In summary, in order to assess whether PaCT is an appropriate line of treatment, it is essential that the therapist not only gains a precise picture of the child's need for treatment, but also uses the initial parent sessions to determine whether the parents are willing and able to engage with a psychoanalytical process. If the dominant defence mechanisms in the parents are primarily immature and the parents' accounts suggest that they are severely distorting reality, it can be assumed that they might not be able to accept the positive effects of the treatment. Parents who suffer from psychological problems and helplessness often show unconscious jealousy towards the child for receiving more help than they do themselves.

Within such constellations, parental feelings of guilt towards the child might be so great that they can only be managed through externalisation and, thus, through accusations aimed at the therapist.

As a consequence, the parents will be unable to give the therapist much credit for the success of the therapy. Parents in such a constellation often prematurely terminate the child's treatment, without awareness that this is how they are handling their own unconscious feelings of guilt.

This overview shows that a precise examination of whether analytical short-term therapy is appropriate is an indispensable prerequisite for the ultimate success of the therapy. The therapist should take time to gather enough information about the parents' prerequisites for treatment relevant to prognosis. If two to three parent sessions as part of the preparatory sessions are not enough, PaCT may be preceded by an upstream parental module (generally sessions with just the parents). Within these sessions, the joint consideration of the child by parents and therapist should promote the parents' mentalization about their child, so that the parents develop the ability and willingness to look "behind the scenes" of the child's observable behaviour, which is indispensable for PaCT.

The parents' triadic capacity

The following considerations are based on the results of longitudinal developmental research on "early parenthood" and "development of the parent–child relationship" by our working group in joint work with Bürgin (von Klitzing & Bürgin, 2005; von Klitzing & Stadelmann, 2011; von Klitzing, Simoni, & Bürgin, 1999; von Klitzing, Simoni, Amsler, & Bürgin, 1999). Psychodynamic interviews with expectant parents explored their ability to include the still unborn child in the parents' partnership. Triadic capacity refers to the parents' ability to develop an intense relationship with their child (whether at the level of internal representations or in reality), and at the same time include the other parent. This means that the intimate relationship between the parents can mature, even when the child is integrated as a third member of the family. A mother with high triadic capacity is able to recognise that the father also has an important relationship to the child, without being overwhelmed by her fear of being excluded herself. A father with high triadic capacity recognises the mother's significance, without excluding himself from the relationship between mother and child.

As part of our research, the following five dimensions of triadic capacity were elaborated, and empirically demonstrated to be valid and predictive for the development of the child and the family relationship:

1. *Quality of partnership*: The ability to safeguard self and object boundaries in the partnership so that the family relationship is not marked by projective distortions. The subject is able to keep internal ambivalence within limits and is not forced to project his own defended and hated parts of the self on to the other. Intrapsychic conflict constellations are not displaced into interpersonal actions. Such *open and flexible boundaries of the self and object* are vital for parenthood because they help to prevent the child entering the projective field of parental distortions.

2. *Flexibility*: The ability to form a flexible relationship to the child, especially in terms of "the child in the head" ("l'enfant dans la tête") (Soulé, 1982). This constellation indicates that even during pregnancy, as well as in the further course of events, parents develop rich internal representations of their (future) child, without setting them up too rigidly. This flexibility of ideas means that the children encounter their parents as vibrant partners in the relationship, while still being able to develop autonomously.

3. *Triangularity*: A parent's ability to include the other parent in internal representations and fantasies of the child, that is, to be able to imagine vividly entering into a relationship with the child and to embellish this relationship with fantasy, while including the third party as well.

4. *Dialogue ability*: The parents' ability to have a dialogue about the child; this is Spitz's understanding of dialogue (Spitz, 1963), not just as the cognitive exchange between the parents but as an emotional exchange as well: a circular process between the dialogue partners that is full of energy and enjoyment.

5. *Transgenerational coherence*: The parents' ability to embed their parenthood in a vividly remembered transgenerational continuity of relationship. Their relationship to their own parents, with all its pros and cons, is vividly remembered. Ambivalences do not have to be split off: parents are able to identify with positive role models and at the same time develop critical views of their own parents, without demonising them and, thus, bringing the child into a transgenerational field of tension.

It is essential to gain an idea of all five dimensions of triadic capacity in the diagnostic phase before therapy commences. A certain amount of triadic capacity on the parents' part (and the therapist's) is a prerequisite for being able to work therapeutically in a PaCT setting. If there is very little triadic capacity, an attempt should be made to improve it through an upstream "parental module", involving parental and family talks. Severely disintegrated triadic constellations manifest themselves in parental disputes about rights of care and access after divorce, in which the other parent's relationship with the child cannot be allowed, especially after bitter quarrels within the partnership. The child is then drawn into the tension between the parents, and the therapy might also be crushed in this field of tension.

Case study for the working through of triadic problems in the course of successful PaCT therapy

At first, seven-year-old Kristin engaged only hesitantly in the sessions with her therapist. Little by little, however, the two succeeded in entering a positive relationship with one another, and, through artwork together, they gained access to Kristin's interior world. Kristin flourished and increasingly seemed to enjoy the sessions, smiling more and appearing not at all thrilled when the session ended. Despite this, the therapist received several emails from the mother, in which she informed the therapist that Kristin showed great resistance whenever she had to go to therapy. She was reported to have said, "I'd rather die than go there again." The therapist was initially confused, because this reluctance did not accord at all with her own impression of the therapy sessions. The therapist asked the mother to tell Kristin openly that she had given the therapist this information. Here, the mother herself at first showed great reluctance to do this, arguing that it could be a breach of confidence to her child. She did not dare to tell Kristin the information that she had shared with the therapist. The topic was also addressed in several parental discussions that included the father. The therapist explained to the parents that she was unable to work with Kristin's resistance to therapy if she had to treat this information, which had come from the mother, as a secret. The mother understood this and then told her daughter that she had told the therapist what Kristin had said about the therapy sessions. Kristin reacted to this with shame, rage, and an increased resistance to attending the session. Despite this, the parents were always able to convince Kristin to go to therapy, and the painting sessions continued to give Kristin a lot of pleasure.

The joint work, both with the child and with the parents, enabled them to understand that Kristin saw her relationship with the therapist as a betrayal of the mother, and she fantasised that her mother would not be able to stand it if she had a good time with the therapist. Hence, she emphasised to her mother how little she wanted to go to therapy. At times, the child entered in fantasy into an alliance with her mother against the therapist, so as to limit the feelings of fear and guilt that arose as part of the triad. At the same time, the mother entered an alliance with the therapist against the child, by writing emails to the therapist with information that excluded Kristin. Only when the therapist insisted that such secrets were counterproductive and that it would be possible to be open to the child about the information that passed between mother and therapist was the triadic field opened, even though for the child painful feelings were associated with it. In the end, the parents were able to say they believed that the therapy was actually every effective, because Kristin reacted to it so emotionally. The parents could also learn to understand both sides of Kristin—her pleasure in the therapy and her fear of it—and to help her integrate them. At the end of the treatment, when the therapist asked Kristin if she was looking forward to ending it or was rather afraid of the end, Kristin said, "A bit of both!" She was able to see her ambivalence: that on the one hand she really did want to continue therapy, but, on the other, she also had an urge to turn away from the therapist and towards her beloved mother. The integration of these two relationship aspects and the associated internal ambivalence was an important step towards the success of the treatment.

Triadic conflict constellations should be addressed as soon as they appear in the course of PaCT therapy, and concrete integrative solutions should be developed, for example by including fathers who have been excluded, addressing secrets and alliances openly and dissolving them, and addressing the fear of being excluded in triadic constellations. However, this also implies that the therapist's own triadic capacity is an important prerequisite for PaCT: that is, her ability to construct a relationship with the child while accepting that the parents also have great significance as they form the decisive relationships for the child.

The parent module

In some cases, the parental prerequisites for PaCT, outlined in the sections above, are inadequate. Starting PaCT immediately is contraindicated, notably in the following situations:

- the parents are unable to let the child go to individual sessions with the therapist;
- the parents' behaviour is dominated by accusations and blame, so that there is no possibility of shared concern;
- jealousy of the child and/or the therapist gets in the way of a shared understanding;

- a relationship developing between child and therapist causes the parents to feel shut out, and thus they develop anxiety (too low triadic capacity);
- the urge to eliminate the symptoms exceeds the urge to understand their meaning.

In such situations the therapist can hold several parent sessions commencing with PaCT, to find out whether the parental prerequisites can be improved. It is important here to observe how the parents react to the initial interpretations formulated by the therapist.

For example, how do the parents react if the therapist offers explanations for the child's problematic behaviour? Do the parents show an interest in having access to this level of understanding? Do they engage in this kind of discussion?

If, in the initial sessions, the parents show no effort to understand the child better, but instead expect advice and instructions on how to influence their child's behaviour as directly as possible, then intensive work with them is first needed in order to create the prerequisites for successful PaCT.

Here, we can try to improve the parental prerequisites in parent sessions inserted upstream of the therapy, and, after a few sessions, examine whether the parents' ability and willingness to engage with the PaCT procedure has improved in the course of these conversations.

Such a parental module may often be useful if the prerequisites for psychoanalytical work are present and show potential, but are not yet quite adequate. This upstream parental module also has the advantage that the parents feel their needs and concerns are taken seriously, and they enter into an alliance with the therapist. Parents whose own problems have made them very needy are often jealous of the way in which the therapist gives their child the kind of attention and care they feel they themselves have not had.

For parents who show structural deficits, such a preparatory phase of parent sessions is particularly useful in moderating the parents' unconscious feelings of jealousy towards the child.

Contraindication

Risks on the child's side

If there is a pervasive developmental disorder, such as autism or Asperger's syndrome, a PaCT procedure is unlikely to succeed. These disorders are characterised by a pervasive lack of socio-emotional reciprocity. These children cannot employ or understand non-verbal behaviour patterns well enough to steer interpersonal interaction. In order to approach such disorders using psychoanalytic therapy, a setting with a higher frequency of sessions and longer duration should be used. Children with developmental disabilities also lack the prerequisites for PaCT in the verbal and/or cognitive areas. To be treated with PaCT, children should, therefore, show an IQ of at least 80.

In addition, PaCT should not be used if psychotic illness or marked reactive attachment disorders are present. These children also require long-term treatment.

Neither should PaCT be used for children who, in addition to emotional symptoms, also show *severe disintegrated externalising symptoms*, such as severely aberrant antisocial development, as the frequency and duration are insufficient. Fonagy and Target (1994) have been able to show that only 50% of the children with severe dissocial pathology and a high level of symptoms and comorbidity show an improvement after psychotherapy. They concluded that these children require treatments with a higher frequency and over a long period. They concluded: "severe or pervasive pathology requires intensive analytic help" (Fonagy & Target, 1994, p. 45).

There is evidence to indicate that symptoms may even worsen, in children whose pathology and comorbidity exceeds a certain level, if short-term therapy is used.

If, as well as having emotional problems, a child also tends to aggressive behaviour, so that he is a danger to himself or to other children, it should first be ascertained whether the pedagogical framework in which the child is living provides enough support in impulse regulation.

If the child has disorganised, destructive temper tantrums that he is unable to regulate, we should first help the parents in providing sufficient pedagogical support to their child, before starting to work with PaCT. Here, in preparation for PaCT, inpatient child psychiatric treatments can be carried out to strengthen the regulatory capacities of the ego.

Risks on the parent's side

Custody disputes: PaCT should not be used if the parents have not agreed on a structure of access and custody during a divorce or separation. It is essential that the external conditions in which the child is growing up are not marked by parental disputes or disagreement concerning rights of access or custody. After divorce, severely disintegrated triadic constellations often present in parental disputes about rights of access and custody. In such constellations of a degraded triad, one parent cannot allow the other to have a relationship with the child, particularly after hurtful partnership quarrels. The child is threatened with being crushed in the tension between the parents. There is also a danger that the therapy or the therapist may be instrumentalised to push through the interests of one party, instead of both parents reflecting together with the therapist about the child. Therefore, the rule is: first sort out the rights of access and custody, and only then can PaCT begin (see also the section headed "The parents", pp. 115–120). Even if the parents have separated and one of them has sole custody of the child, there should be some possibility of involving the other parent in the treatment. If the therapist is forbidden to get into contact with an excluded parent, the excluding parent is usually manipulating the triadic relationships. Such a constellation must first be dissolved, before the treatment begins.

Psychosis in one parent: If one parent suffers from a psychosis, such as paranoid–hallucinatory schizophrenia, PaCT cannot practically be used. In this constellation, there is a danger that one parent will distort reality too much. It is then possible for the therapist to be woven into the parent's delusion and become a persecuting object. Since we use intensive parental work in PaCT, the parents must have the necessary psycho-emotional and cognitive prerequisites. To treat a child where one of the parents has a severe psychiatric disorder, specific therapeutic approaches are indicated (Wiegand-Grefe, Geers, Petermann, & Plass, 2011; Wiegand-Grefe, Halverscheid, & Plaß-Christl, 2011).

Neglect of the child: The child's fundamental emotional and physical needs for protection, attention, and integrity must be adequately satisfied by the parents before we can do meaningful work with PaCT. The parents' capacity to hold reliably to the specific conditions of PaCT (a fixed weekly appointment) is an indispensable prerequisite.

Risks on the therapist's side

On the therapist's side, an important condition for working with PaCT is that she has sufficient self-experience, supervision, and self-care to provide an inner psychic space for the child and his parents. Should the therapist be unable to provide this psychic space for a longer period (several weeks), because she herself is impaired by her own private problems and conflicts, if she has a psychological disorder that has not been adequately processed in the training analysis, she should not begin a PaCT treatment. In extreme cases, the therapist may develop depressive symptoms while implementing PaCT. It would then be important to have detailed supervision to clarify the cause of the therapist's inability to make use of her inner space and her therapeutic neutrality.

The therapist's triadic capacity

A particular prerequisite for PaCT is that the therapist can enter into reciprocal, triadic relationships with the family members and not simply form a relationship with the child. If the therapist is unable to do this, and enters primarily into dyadic relationships, she should not work with PaCT (and, in general, this therapist should not carry out psychotherapy with children and adolescents either). It is, therefore, particularly important that child therapists should develop triadic capacity as part of their training analysis, control analysis, and supervision.

CHAPTER FIVE

Before therapy begins

Therapeutic equipment

S hort-term psychoanalytic therapy requires, first of all, a defined period (usually fifty minutes) as well as a protected space to which no one has access during the therapy session except the therapist and the patient. The therapist is responsible for maintaining the setting, and communicating it to the patient. Before the treatment the therapist explains to the child that they will do things together (i.e., talk to each other, play, draw, etc.) for fifty minutes, and that the therapist will try to get to know the child better. She will tell the child about liberties and rules; for example, "It's up to you what we do, whether we play, talk or keep silent. It is important that we don't hurt each other physically, we both have to be careful about that." In addition the child is made aware of any taboo zones in the room; for example, "I don't want you to play on my desk, that's just for me!" Fragile, very valuable, sensitive, or hazardous objects which may potentially cause the child to injure himself, or which he might damage, should not be kept in the room. It must be possible for the child to play boisterously and without restraint: if he wants to express his aggressive impulses in a game, for instance. Every child receives a box labelled with his name and which stores everything that the child has produced during the sessions. At the end of treatment, the child is allowed to take home whatever he has made.

Toys

- Lego-Duplo house with animals (dog, cat, cow, horse);
- Lego-Duplo figures (Mummy, Daddy, Granny, and four children);
- glove puppets: fox and elephant;
- crayons, pencils, paper;
- string, glue, scissors;
- Plasticine.

Documentation of the treatment

The therapist should establish one consistent form of documentation. It is up to the therapist to proceed according to his or her individual preferences and ways of working, making notes during the sessions or from memory afterwards. In our experience, it has been most useful to write down the important play or relationship episodes, the child's ideas or the therapist's interpretations, as soon as they happen. However, the children often find this disturbing, because it interrupts their play. It turns us into "not quite optimal" play companions. None the less, the pauses that this inserts into the flow of play give us more time to reflect and understand. For instance, if the child asks, "Why are you writing everything down?" we can say, "I write down everything you do so I can think about it better afterwards."

Treatment agreement

At the beginning of the treatment, the therapist must also face the question of how to inform the parents about the content of the therapy. It is important to communicate to the parents that therapy is about gaining a better understanding, and that the rapid removal of the symptoms is not the priority, because they are the expression of difficulties that must be understood. Parents must also realise that free play with the child is about understanding the internal mental states, motives, and conflicts that underlie the child's observable behaviour. The following formulations may be suitable: "The goal of the treatment is for the child to be able to develop better. The free play situation is to help understand what internal problems lie at the root of the child's behaviour. In our (parents–therapist) conversations, too, we will work together to achieve a better understanding of your child's problem: for example, why it behaves like this and/or shows these symptoms."

Structural diagnosis according to OPD-KJ

To assess a child's structural level, we resort to the material that the child provides us in the first sessions ("first scene", sessions 4 and 5): play, drawings, interaction, narratives.

In addition to the case history as reported by the parents, we also use observation of, and reflection on, the child's play activity, his regulation of intimacy and distance in the first contacts, his capacity for pretend, children's drawings, or the squiggle game devised by Winnicott (1971b), as material for assessing the child's structural level. Overall, it must be remembered that young children are still structurally immature compared to adults. Their ego is not always able to differentiate between wishful desire and reality, the understanding of self and object boundaries is still developing, reality testing remains immature, and motor activity is still used as a way to release physical tension. The ego is too immature to anticipate all consequences of actions, and the control of the ego over the expression of affects is still incomplete. We recommend assessing the child's structural level at the start of the treatment using the criteria in the *Operationalisierte Psychodynamische Diagnostik im Kindes- und Jugendalter* (*OPD-KJ*) (Arbeitskreis OPD-KJ, 2007), taking developmental factors into account.

Below, we give a brief introduction to the theory and application of the structural axis of the *OPD-KJ* (Arbeitskreis OPD-KJ, 2007). We quote, with the kind permission of the authors of the structural axis, from pages 115–130 of the *OPD-KJ*.

The three dimensions of the structural axis

Self and object experience

The dimension of *self and object experiences* relates to the ability, in describing one's own person, to undertake increasingly differentiated attributions, starting from external variables (appearance, clothing, sexual characteristics), and becoming increasingly differentiated (abilities, qualities). The child develops the ability to experience himself as delimited from other persons and as the author of actions. In play and in conversation the child is increasingly able to perceive his own role and that of the interlocutor (self-object differentiation) and determine with increasing flexibility the setting of boundaries between rigidity and permeability (Cierpka, 1987). The child moves increasingly between the level of pretend (in play and in conversation) and the relationship level, and increasingly able to recognise and negotiate conflicts of interest. The authors point out that the child is first able to sense the needs and moods of other people, later becoming able to express them and perceive them in a differentiated way. (Arbeitskreis OPD-KJ, 2007, p. 116, translated for this edition)

Control

The dimension of *control* (*and defence*) describes the ability to buffer negative affects (bad temper, annoyance, depressive state, listlessness). At age level 2, the child reaches a balance between the various aspects of his ambivalence and is able to experience, recognise, and communicate them consciously. Self-awareness refers to the ability to self-soothe through to developing a positive sense of self-worth. The possibility of controlling impulses and de-actualising what is experienced enables the child to set impulses (e.g., aggressivity) in the service of regulating his relationships to himself and others (impulse control).

If we observe the developmental course of defence and coping, from the child to adolescent, we need to consider cognitive development and the development of the self and the self-concept as well as chronological age. Defence mechanisms require a particular maturity and development of ego and self. The question of whether each defence mechanism has its own developmental history is difficult to answer; we should, however, assume that the three defence forms – denial, projection and identification – take a different but characteristic course in their development (Cramer, 1991). (Arbeitskreis OPD-KJ, 2007, p. 116, translated for this edition)

From the second year, with the appearance of the symbolic representation mode, the baby copes with conflicts through denial, projection and defensive manoeuvres such as "clowning about", omnipotence fantasies, and other defences directed outwards. . . .

In the primary school child, feelings such as shame, guilt and fear, that are difficult to bear, can be defended against in a way that does not require such distortion of reality. The reality check remains in place despite the child's efforts at defence. Projection and denial remain important defence mechanisms: a schoolchild who is confronted about an attack on another pupil is able to claim that it was not he but the other child who did the hitting. However, at this age, supported by external help and avoiding an unbearable "loss of face", he should be able to take this back. More mature defence mechanisms (rationalisation, repression) are now permanently available and begin to characterise the child's personality.

At the next age level (from the thirteenth year), the adolescent increasingly reflects on his situation from outside. He is able to observe himself from outside and see himself with the eyes of others (perspective co-ordination from the viewpoint of a third party) . . . The defence repertoire is extended (in the engagement with drive impulses) with the addition of asceticism, intellectualisation, and sublimation. (Arbeitskreis OPD-KJ, 2007, p. 117, translated for this edition)

Communicative abilities

The dimension of *communicative abilities* comprises the aspects of 'contact', 'decoding the affects of others', 'reciprocity', and 'internalised communication'. The ability to gauge appropriate contact develops, and communication can be increasingly used for self and affect regulation. The affects of others can be distinguished with growing confidence from one's own. The spectrum of recognisable emotions encompasses first the primary affects in the sense of fundamental emotions (Izard, 1994), such as happiness, interest, contempt, disgust, fear, and sadness. Plutchik (1970) also distinguished between primary emotions that should be considered basal, and secondary, derived emotions. Later, affect is also expressed in the self-reflexive emotions (shame, jealousy, pride, guilt, etc.) and increasingly serve self-regulation (Carlson & Hartfield, 1992). (Arbeitskreis OPD-KJ, 2007, p. 118, translated for this edition).

Tables 2 to 7 present the operationalisations of the three dimensions of the structural axis using clinical benchmark exemplars (from Arbeitskreis OPD-KJ, 2007, pp. 115–130) for age levels 1 (2–5) and 2 (6–11), which are relevant for PaCT. Before the start of therapy the therapist should assess the structure of the child using the age-appropriate benchmarks for the three dimensions described.

First, a few remarks on the process of operationalisation.

> The three structural dimensions of assessment are described using particular abilities, and evaluated using a benchmark example in each case. This example describes what can be expected of an optimally structured child/adolescent in a particular situation. The assessment of the structure should always be resource-orientated, and move beyond the symptoms, taking into consideration the context-dependence of dysfunctional or functional ways of reacting. Assessment of whether the child has the capacity to respond to treatment should refer to the last half-year, and in addition to assessing the situated behaviour within and outside the examination context, requires reference to the biographical context as well. (Arbeitskreis OPD-KJ, 2007, pp. 118–119).

Table 2. Age level 1 (1.5–5 years old) "control"
(Arbeitskreis OPD-KJ, 2007, p. 120, translated for this edition).

Negative affect	The child is able to slow down and absorb negative affects (bad temper, annoyance, resentment, listlessness) that may occur when refusals or prohibitions are set or demands are made. This ability does not need to be highly developed. It may be liable to break down. It should however be possible to produce it reliably with at least one attachment figure.
Self-awareness	The child is able to comfort himself with a trusted toy, such as a transitional object, if he misses the attachment figure. The child happily accepts praise and attention and seldom appears insecure.
Impulse control	The child is able to calm down, for example after a tantrum or similar phase of confrontation and arousal. He then accepts being made a fuss of. The child is able to hold on to a toy and play idea over longer periods. He is able to stop playing an exciting and absorbing game if asked to do so.
Control agency	If another person is affected by his actions, the child is able to allow that person's state to act on him such that it changes the type and intensity of these actions. In such circumstances, he is also able to back down, moderate the force of his action, check out with the other person, or promote himself.

(*continued*)

Table 2.   (*continued*)

Control agency (continued)	The child clearly understands the prohibitions expressed to him, but whether or not he adheres to them more or less depends on the presence of his main attachment figure. The enjoyment outweighs feelings of shame or guilt.
Conflict management	The child manages conflicts through projection, denial, and "clowning", omnipotence, and other mild defensive manoeuvres directed outwards. This changes reality, and the attachment figures may even enter into this reality in order to comfort a child in trouble. The child is only able to dissolve these mechanisms if he is removed from the conflict and supported by an attachment figure in assessing the situation and moving into the other reality.

Table 3.   Age level 1 (1.5–5 years old) "self and object experience" (Arbeitskreis OPD-KJ, 2007, p. 121, translated for this edition).

Self experience	The child feels he belongs to particular groups (family, kindergarten, friends). He is able to announce and assert his wishes emphatically. He is able to describe himself using external variables (appearance, clothing, sexual characteristics) as well as starting to describe abilities (e.g. sport). Desires also contribute to ideas about himself. The child is certain about being a boy or a girl. The child is able to describe both his positive and negative characteristics. He can express his feelings appropriately, so that the investigator is able to gain a coherent picture of the child's state.
Self-object differentiation	The child experiences himself as separate from other persons and as the author of actions. He is able to recognise that he may have feelings that are different from other people's. The same situation can be experienced and evaluated differently. The child is able to distinguish between mine and yours. This ability does not remain stable, but is most measurable with strangers, for example, an investigator, and least with the closest attachment figure.
Object experience	The child has the ability to see the investigator as an independent person. The other person is recognised and accepted not just as an object that satisfies the child's desires, but has his own play ideas and needs, and the child can take them up. The child is able to recognise that objects/people are not purely good and bad, and that it is possible to turn to someone after testing their trustworthiness. (*continued*)

Table 3.   (continued)

Object experience (continued)	The child is able to hold on to his assessment of the person, even if he is feeling uncomfortable. We can observe the child continually testing out objects. There are no stereotyped attitudes to the objects. The child behaves differently towards his closest attachment figure than towards other, less intimate persons.
Empathy and object-related affects	The child is able to express object-related affects, such as solicitude, gratitude, disappointment, and concern, in a play situation. He is able to show the intention to repair or comfort. He is able to comprehend the emotions or needs of others and to let himself be guided by them.

Table 4.   Age level 1 (1.5–5 years old) "Communicative abilities" (Arbeitskreis OPD-KJ, 2007, p. 122, translated for this edition).

Contact	The child shows interest in making contact and opens up his world to the investigator with growing trust. The child involves other persons in solving problems. The child is able to create positive resonance (for example, by mirroring himself in others). Communication can be used to regulate affects, for security, and to construct the self. Approving and appreciative offers of communication have a calming and reassuring effect. (Clinical disorders, for example in the form of maintaining rigid distance, fear of contact, shyness, inhibition, angst, numbness, lack of distance in the form of superficial friendliness, inappropriate clinginess.)
Deciphering the affects of others	There is a basic ability to understand the affects of others. (However, the child is easily infected with others' affects: he cries along and laughs along.) The spectrum of recognisable emotions includes joy, interest, contempt, disgust, fear, and sadness. These can also be named. (Clinical examples of disorders: child ignores pain in himself and others, does not understand if his mother is sad. Hits other people indiscriminately, vents his feelings, does not express his feelings, or shows flat affects and only occasionally reacts with intense vegetative states.)

(continued)

Table 4.   (continued).

Communicative function of the child's own affects (continued)	Temporary, violent affects or lack of affect expression do not endanger how the child experiences the affective resonance of the attachment figure. Affects are available for communication. The child begins to name affects as reasons for his acts.
Reciprocity	The child has a basic ability to attune to others. His responsiveness to the affects of others produces interest in a two-way dialogue. Play offers are taken up and developed reciprocally. When communicating with the child, the other person feels adequately involved.
Internalised communication	The child has stable inner objects with which he is able to communicate, without the attachment figure being present in reality. This is shown, for example, in the child's being able to play on his own. Being able to be alone also includes the ability to play "alone" in the presence of the attachment figure.

Table 5.   Age level 2 (6–12 years old) "Control"
(Arbeitskreis OPD-KJ, 2007, p. 123, translated for this edition).

Negative affect	The child is able to express different sides of his feelings and stand by them in a directed diagnostic game with appropriate triggers. He achieves a balance with smooth transitions between the faces of his ambivalence. His feelings do not flip back and forth; neither does he remain rigidly in a single mood. Negative affects of fear, anger, and sadness can be endured.
Self-awareness	After experiencing criticism or failure, the child finds his own way back to feeling good. He is able to endure the hurt if someone in his circle does not share his positive self-assessment, given by his parents, without experiencing a marked crisis.
Impulse control	The child is able to disengage from playful aggression action (children's scuffle) if the general situation requires it. The aggressive affects do not continue aimlessly or without direction. The child is able to endure the delay of rewards.

(continued)

Table 5. (continued).

Impulse control (continued)	The child is able to work through a known situation (e.g., lesson at school) from start to finish in an appropriate way. In a new situation (e.g., examination) he increasingly "builds up" his control.
Control instances	The child is able to remember a prohibition, sometimes only after infringing it, and to admit a mistake. He perceives the damaging consequences for others of his own actions, although often not as anticipation but only retrospectively. The child knows the rules that relate to him specifically, but also general standards set down by parents, teachers, or persons in his immediate environment. The child wants to follow these rules. If he fails, he feels bad. There is often a certain rigidity. If a narcissistic breakdown threatens, he is able to change the standards.
Conflict management	Shame, guilt, and fear can be defended against in a way that only mildly distorts reality. The reality check remains in place despite the child's efforts at defence. Projection and denial remain important defence mechanisms: a schoolchild who is confronted about an attack on another pupil is able to claim that it was not he but the other child who did the hitting. However, after the situation is clarified, he must be able to admit to his own involvement. More mature defence mechanisms (rationalisation, repression) are now permanently available and begin to characterise the child's personality.

Table 6.   Age level 2 (6–12 years old) "Self and object experience" (Arbeitskreis OPD-KJ, 2007, p. 124, translated for this edition).

Self experience	In self-description, internal and more differentiated attributions have greater significance and, thus, give a more precise idea of one's own self, which the child is also able to express verbally. The child perceives, and noticeably engages with, how it appears to the outside world and is viewed by others. The child is able to differentiate between feelings and their expression. He can experience and describe his ownership of different feelings. The child is able to behave "as if" (particularly clearly in play) and is able to talk about it. This makes humour and lying possible.

(continued)

Table 6. (continued).

Self-object differentiation	In play and in conversation, the child is able to perceive his own role distinct from that of the investigator. He constructs his social roles by consciously copying and referring to social role models. He recognises that people have different interests and motives, and can attune himself to these with both adults and peers. The child is increasingly able to recognise conflicts of interest and negotiate them. He is able to switch flexibly between the "as if" level (in play and in conversation) and the relationship level.
Object experience	The child is consistently able to recognise the other person in his or her function and as the carrier of a particular social role. He is willing to engage with the views of the other person. There is a gradation of closeness towards other adults and peers (strangers, acquaintances, friends).
Empathy and object-related affects	The child is able to envisage the needs and moods of others, and to express them in play or in conversation. The child perceives what feelings he provokes in others, and is able to react. He distinguishes between a transient expression of feeling and a lasting emotional attitude in the other person.

Table 7. Age level 2 (6–12 years old) "Communicative abilities" (Arbeitskreis OPD-KJ, 2007, p. 125, translated for this edition).

Contact	The child shows interest (primarily via language, but also in play) in making contact and is active in building up communication. He understands and takes into account the specific situation. Contact does not lack distance, and neither is it marked by notable aloofness, shyness, or timidity. Contact shows a certain steadiness and duration, and the contact behaviour improves over the course of an encounter (rather than deteriorating). Efforts at making contact are directed towards children of the same age. Contacts to this circle outside the family are sought and maintained. In addition to affective exchange, which serves self- and affect-regulation, communication also has a cognitive informative function. The child shows intentional interest in wanting to know something. For example, he may ask the investigator, "Will you play with me?" "What is that?"

(continued)

Table 7. (continued).

Deciphering the affects of others	The affects of others can increasingly be recognised and clearly differentiated from the child's own. Distortions of interpretation through the child's own affects can be corrected within the framework of the interaction.
Communicative function of the child's own affects	A broad spectrum of affects is available for communication. The spectrum may come to the fore in play, for example. In some cases, he may be restricted by the child's reactions to previous experiences. The child's own affects do not interrupt communication. The child is able to name feelings as a reason for his actions: "I hit him because I was cross with him." Affects can be communicated spontaneously and viewed retrospectively: "I'm sad." "Three days ago I was sad."
Reciprocity	Communication with the child (e.g., during the examination) leads to a feeling of "us". Fine-tuning of the contact is possible. By negotiating the wishes of the child and the other person, a third object is created: play produces a jointly created work.
Internalised communication	The child can be separated from his primary relational object. He is able to manage the absence of this person for even a longer period without observable change in his behaviour because he can adhere to inner attitudes and orientations that were permitted to him by his parents.

Consequences of the child's structural levels for the therapeutic technique

Good structural integration

Psychotherapeutic work on the conflict requires that the unconscious material can be expressed at a symbolic level. An ideal prerequisite for this is if the child shows a good structural level at the start of therapy. If this is the case, playing in the pretend mode may serve as an instrument to increase the flexibility of the child's cognitive–emotional styles, and to identify and interpret conflictual contents, both in the symbolic material and in the transference relationship with the child. Indications of a high structural level of the child are the integration of good and bad parts of the self and the object, the suppression of narcissism in favour of object love, access to oedipal conflicts, the demonstration of triadic capacities, and the domination of a well-functioning capacity to reality test. If the structure is well integrated, the psychoanalytic understanding of unconscious conflicts using the symbolic material can form the key focus of the joint therapeutic work from the outset. However, children with a depressive disorder and an apparently high structural level dominated by a neurotic conflictual pathology might often appear very inhibited and unimaginative in play, despite their adequate ability to symbolise. The flow of play falters, or a topic being developed breaks off abruptly. This is a characteristic transference constellation of depressive children (or of children with internalising problems). In the treatment of depressive children, we encounter psychological mechanisms that result from the internalisation of interpersonal conflicts in the child's inner world. Thereby, children protect their relationships to external and internal idealised objects, thus enabling psychosocial adjustment. This mechanism is linked with an inhibition of the ability to play and be imaginative (see case study Sophie, Chapter Eleven). Since these children are concealing aggressive impulses, they are often also particularly inhibited about exploring their inner world together with the therapist at the start of therapy. If play does not get under way despite adequate ability to symbolise, it should be gently communicated to the child that all ideas may be articulated, played through, or thought in the shared play, and that there are no "good" or "bad" games. The child should feel accepted, even if he does not want to play at the start. In our experience, this inhibition of the ability to play quickly dissipates if these children experience the therapist exemplifying how to give all contents of play a neutral interpretation. For these children, it is particularly important that they experience a therapist who does not reject them if they express aggression in play or in the interaction. The analytic work in the process of therapy can then focus on the aggression that the child often directs at himself. Play is simultaneously PaCT's instrument and its goal, in the sense of restoring the child's ability to play.

Moderate structural integration

Children with a moderately integrated structural level generally show lively and uninhibited play, even at the start of the treatment. They do not appear to need to defend so strongly against aggressive impulses that their ability to play is fundamentally inhibited. These children are able to play in the pretend mode, and their play is often characterised by pronounced fantasy. Nevertheless, the contents of their play can change abruptly and their play is unfocused, which prevents the therapist from keeping play contents in mind or thinking about them. Children with a moderately integrated structure often experience the therapist in the transference as an ambivalent object, on to which they alternately project their libidinal and their aggressive transference elements. Thus, the sessions can often be very changeable, and the therapist may feel entangled in an ambivalent transference situation. These children often dominate their therapist, give orders, and often have a very rapid flow of play that does not allow the child any room for developing and controlling its own thoughts (see case study Julian, Chapter Ten). These children generally use anal sadism to defend themselves against emerging, more mature oedipal fears and against early fears of merging. In children with a moderately integrated structure, both the interpretation of the contents of the child's play (as the expression of unconscious conflicts) and the work on fostering the structure are important. Mentalization-promoting techniques are suitable for encouraging the development of structural integration (see Chapter Six, section headed "The significance of infantile sexuality in the therapeutic process", pp. 165–166).

Poor structural integration

We can still use PaCT for a child with poor structural integration, as long as the child is not psychotic and the basic elements of connection to reality are present. It is important that in the work on the differentiation of self and object boundaries, and of reality and fantasy, the application of an active, structure-giving therapeutic technique is given priority above the interpretation of conflicts. A child who does not (yet) have the stable ability to differentiate the internal reality of thoughts from external reality should first be supported in controlling his aggressive impulses, before any interpretation of the unconscious conflicts on which the destructive fantasies are based. The interpretation of a conflict lying at the root of a destructive fantasy could otherwise destabilise the child too much. For example, it could equate the aggressive fantasies linked to the conflict with a real, destructive attack on his parents. The interpretation of an aggressive fantasy could cause great anxiety in these children. They lack the secure foundation that could serve as an area to play with thoughts. Emphasising process elements—such as the explicit naming of the shared interaction and the thoughts of the therapist and child that come up within it—and with careful attunement to the child's level of psychological functions, we can slowly start to verbalise wishes, thoughts, and affects. Aggressive fantasies should be interpreted very carefully, because, if the child has a rigidly disintegrated superego, the result can be severe feelings of guilt and a self-destructive need to be punished.

CHAPTER SIX

The treatment technique

The significance of the setting

One important prerequisite for analytical therapy in general and for PaCT in particular is the survival of the child, of the therapist, and of the shared workspace—in the concrete, physical sense, as well as the figurative sense of the analytical situation. A shared area of work, defined by time and space in the "setting", is what makes a joint understanding possible at all. While the setting is established, the child and the therapist determine the content of the therapy session. It is important to communicate to the child (and also to his parents), that there is a level of psychological functioning that lies beyond observable behaviour, but which can be understood in the shared therapeutic work if the setting rules are kept. In general, the child's unconscious desires come into conflict with the rules of the social environment and his internal representation ("superego"), and the ego therefore suppresses them, at the cost of significant expenditure of energy. If this attempt at suppression is unsuccessful, then symptoms will be formed, in which, according to Freud (1900a), we see a compromise between two contradictory unconscious endeavours. The therapist's verbal interventions help to understand conflicts and make them conscious, to resolve the anxieties associated with them, and to find an age-appropriate solution and integration. Thus, right from the start, we indirectly communicate to the child that our focus is on presumed unconscious desires lying behind the behaviour, by being interested in a level beyond his observable (problematic) behaviour. If the child adopts this way of operating, which we can also call the reflective function, it will be able to expand his own imaginative world.

The two basic elements described (the analytical setting and the search for understanding) are closely linked. The psychoanalytical work of understanding and working through as part of the transference relationship between therapist and patient can only be done if the setting provides a framework, and if the work is not threatened by external or internal disorder (e.g., if the child and the therapist are too proactive). This includes keeping to the timeframe (generally fifty minutes). Psychoanalytical work is fundamentally unlike day-to-day communication, or pedagogical acts. Nevertheless, there are situations where we, as therapists, have to offer ourselves to the child as an object that provides security, by setting limits or by asking him to stop doing something that threatens the setting and the therapist/the child. If the child attacks the setting, we attempt to understand his action and to communicate this understanding through a suitable interpretation. Only if the interpreting intervention does not adequately protect the setting should a pedagogical "rescue" intervention be made.

The same applies, however, if the therapist feels impulses towards action in herself, such as wanting to reward the child, punish him, touch him, or get rid of him. In such situations, the therapist is obliged to pursue understanding and not seek to fulfil these impulses.

In child therapy in particular it often happens that these rules are broken by actions (by the child, the therapist, and the parents). Limited actions of this kind do not seriously endanger the therapy, as long as it is possible afterwards to understand their psychological significance in the transference.

Typical situations that make pedagogical intervention or limiting necessary

If a child endangers himself: Elisabeth (six years old) wanted to climb on to a cupboard to retrieve the furry crocodile that she had thrown up there. She was about to use the chair back as a rather wobbly ladder. The therapist had to intervene at this point, by limiting the child in words and actions. Giving an interpretation may also be appropriate in a situation like this, depending on context, as here: "You would prefer to be able to do everything yourself and not ask me for help. You think that I will only take you seriously if you can already do everything for yourself."

If a child endangers the analyst physically: This may be intended consciously in the course of a temper tantrum, but can also be the result of pent-up instinctual cathexis suddenly expressing itself massively and explosively. In play with Elisabeth (see case study Elisabeth, Chapter Twelve), it often happened that she threw the plastic toy figures around impetuously, often hitting the therapist in the face. The therapist then asked her to be more careful and told her that she could play as wildly as she liked as long as she took care not to hurt anyone.

If a child destroys objects: If the child's aggression cannot be expressed on a symbolic level in play, and he begins to destroy the room or its contents, it is important to communicate to the child that "We can try to understand what it is that's making you so angry, but we also have to make sure that you don't break things."

If a child shows a desire for physical closeness: On one occasion in the shared therapeutic work with Elisabeth, the therapist became the object of her pre-oedipal desires. Elisabeth wanted to be very physically close to her, in the position of a maternal transference figure, and to crawl inside the therapist in order to shut out her brother, with whom she was in competition. Elisabeth started to try to crawl between the therapist's legs. At first, the therapist allowed herself to become involved, but not without communicating a suitable interpretation: that she understood Elisabeth's desire to be close to the therapist as the desire to be close to her mother, expressed through the transference. The therapist said, "Now you want to crawl into me, just like you want to crawl inside your Mama, so that you can be really close to her." But then, when Elisabeth began to put her hand under the therapist's pullover to find her "bosom", as she enthusiastically said out loud, the therapist constrained her by saying, "You're very interested in the topic of bosoms and whether I've got one, and what it feels like. But I don't want you to grab under my pullover." Jumping at her, Elisabeth shouted, "Bosoms, I want bosoms, fat bosoms." The therapist then told her: "This topic is making you quite excited. I think you are being so rough with me because it makes you a little bit angry that your Mama and I already have a bosom and you don't." We usually reach the child by making a suitable interpretation, and often pedagogical action is not necessary.

If a child frequently wants to go to the toilet during the therapeutic sessions: Here it is appropriate first to consider what subjects have just come up, and why the child is "running away" to the toilet. Defence interpretations are suitable: " I think you are afraid/sad/angry that . . . and that's why you want to leave the room." The sudden urge to urinate could equally well be the expression of infantile sexual impulses and arousal, which can also be carefully addressed: for example, "I think that what we were just playing made you so excited that you have to go to the loo in a hurry." Of course, we should let the child interrupt the session and go to the toilet.

If a child ignores the end of the session: Before the shared therapeutic work can be done, it is essential to communicate the setting to the child: what it is allowed to do and what not, and how long each session will last. For children who cannot yet tell the time, it is important to show them, for example, by telling them, "When the big hand is there, we have to stop." This gives the child a necessary orientation. However, it still often happens that children are disappointed and angry at the end of the session, when we say we have to stop, even if we have announced the end in good time. Here, it is most important to interpret the behaviour. We could say to the child, "You are disappointed and sad that our game is already over, and it really is a pity, but neither of us can change it." For a child with an anal fixation, that is, where the drive satisfaction has bound regressively to the issue of holding tight, possessing, taking something from, or giving something to, the other person, disappointment might lead to defiant behaviour and a power struggle not to "allow themselves to be thrown out". For these children it might help to name the conflict: "You always want to be the one who decides when the session is over. It makes you angry if you can't decide that, but I set it." If after verbal interventions the child still refuses to go, we can then also say, "If you don't want to go by yourself, then I will have to take you or carry you out."

If the child insists on taking something from the treatment room: If the child wants to do this it is important to decide whether this is provocation done with the desire to irritate, in the sense of an anal power struggle, or whether the child feels its relationship to the therapist to be so insecure that it needs a physical object to guarantee the link to, and object constancy of, the therapist. In the latter case, it might be helpful for the child to take away an object from the therapist, which thus takes on the nature of a transitional object. In the former case, we would say, or interpret, to the child, for example, "It makes you angry if I take away your possibility of being in my room. You would like to be the one to decide what belongs to you and what to me." In the second case: "You're uncertain whether we will see each other again (whether we will forget each other etc.), and you would like to take this with you to be able to remember me." If an insecure child is looking for a transitional object, then this wish should be appropriately satisfied.

The focus of PaCT: "triangle of psychodynamic constellations" (ToP)

The PaCT therapeutic approach aims to connect observable behaviour and symptoms with previously unconscious or preconscious conflicts of the child and the family, and to enable them to be better understood.

In developing the focus, we are trying to integrate the complex information that the parents, child, and the resonance of the therapist provide, in such a way that it becomes possible to understand the child's symptoms as the expressions of a relational theme based on unconscious conflicts. The *triangle of psychodynamic constellations* (ToP) follows from the focal theories described above, but expands on these to include the observable relationship between the child and his social environment.

To formulate the focus, information is first gathered from the initial consultations, and assigned to the sides of the triangle shown in Figure 3: symptoms (whenever possible formulated as *relational symptoms*), *material* from the first interviews with the child and his parents (language, play, drawings), and characteristics of the developing *therapist–child–parent relationship*. This integrates the complex interplay between the experience of the child and that of the parents, as it is revealed to the therapist in work with the family. This material is taken up on the directly observable level, and linked with considerations about unconscious fundamental conflicts. The therapist's mental resonance is an important instrument of insight on all the descriptive levels shown below (relational symptom, therapist–child–parent relationship, material from the child). Our own resonance significantly influences our experience, understanding, and therapeutic behaviour.

Starting with material from the first five sessions, psychodynamic hypotheses are formulated, into which the three levels of the triangle—*relational symptom, therapist–child–parent relationship*, and *material of the child*—are integrated.

As far as possible, aspects of the conflict and the defence (fear/defended material) as well as the degree of mentalization (behaviour/physical symptom/idea) and the structural level (deficit/resource) should be considered while formulating this hypothesis.

The procedure for formulation of the focus after the fifth session is outlined below, and later illustrated using case studies. The information that the therapist receives from the three areas, *relational-symptom, therapist–child–parent relationship*, and *material of the child* in the first five sessions, is first bundled under the headings of certain predefined questions (see below). These are then included in the psychodynamic considerations of the currently active core conflict. The result of these psychodynamic considerations is the formation of an intersection (ToP focus) between the child's interpersonal and intrapsychic conflicts. The therapist can use the diagram in Figure 3 to help integrate the different levels of the triangle into a ToP focus. In regular focal conferences (if possible after each set of five therapy sessions), the focus can be tested in a joint supervision or intervision, and modified or extended as necessary.

Relational symptom

The reconstrual of the child's symptoms in terms of a relational symptom is an attempt to understand the child's problems as the expression of intrapsychic and interpersonal conflicts. We concentrate on a precise description of the problems and symptoms by the parents and the child: what is considered a problem, under what conditions does it occur, and what is not being mentioned as problematic. What is the significance of the symptoms described for the parent–child relationship? In the first sessions with the parents the central questions are:

● How can the child's symptom be construed as a relational symptom between parents and child?

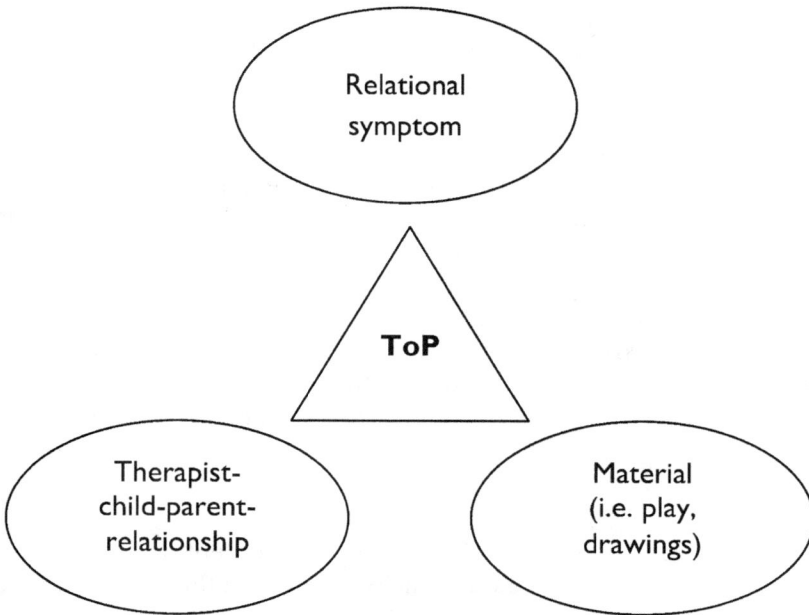

Figure 3.   Triangle of psychodynamic constellations (ToP).

- What affects and reactions do the child's symptoms evoke from the parents (e.g., if the child starts crying whenever they are separated, or wets the bed at night)?
- How do the parents talk about their child: sympathetically and empathetically, or with reproach, despair or shame?

Therapist–child–parents relationship

Starting from our own feelings, associations, and reactions to the interaction with the child and with his parents, we attempt to describe the developing therapist–child–parent relationship. We assume that the central conflict will emerge in the developing early phase of transference.

Key questions here are:

- What kind of contact does the child have with us? Do we feel warm towards her or does she provoke hostile feelings in us?

- How do the parents form a relationship with us? Are they friendly, expectant, and hopeful, or defensive and demanding, or aggressive and accusatory (suggesting projection of their own feelings of guilt)?
- What feelings do the parents trigger in us?
- Do we tend to identify more with the feelings of the child (towards his parents) or with the feelings of the parents (towards their child), or can we integrate the two?
- Do the parents perceive their child as being separate from themselves, or is their perception of the child distorted by a bundle of parental projections?
- What is the connection between the child's pathological defence and/or neurotic fixation and the central conflict of the parents?

The child's material

We understand "material" to be both the contents of the child's speech, play, and drawings, and the way in which the child forms his relationship with the therapist.

- How does the child behave in the first contact? For example, does he come close to us, or withdraw into a corner and play, without involving us?
- How does the child play? Is he loud or quiet, dynamic or monotonous?
- What are the dominant contents of the speech, the play, or the drawings that the child produces?
- Does the desire to show and tell dominate, or, rather, a sense of shame and fear of failure?
- What partial drives (oral, anal, genital) are visible in the material?
- To what extent is the behaviour dominated by primary processes? Is the child able to control his impulses, or does he function more according to primary processes?

Communication of the focus/the psychodynamic hypothesis

The focus, according to the ToP, is communicated both to the child and to the parents at a suitable point in time, using everyday language and relating it to their experiences. When it is communicated to the parents, it should, whenever possible, be "in context", that is, it should relate to previously described relationship episodes with the child. The focus should be communicated to the child in a similar way. Here, it is important to explain the focus directly to the child, for example, in relation to a play situation. This is crucial in order for the child to develop an emotional link to his inner experience. The focus should be articulated at a suitable point in the joint play, in conversation, or in the general interaction, in direct relation to what the child is expressing, and using the same colloquial expressions that the child customarily uses.

The danger of participating in play too much

While treating the child, participating in free interaction play can be risky. Here, it is important not just to play with the child, but always to oscillate between letting oneself be drawn in (to the specific way that the child interacts with the therapist to actualise his central conflict), and stepping back out of the scene in order to understand the action and resist becoming submerged in it, for example, by acting out. The therapist's constant structuring has an important function here. The therapist should not "drown" in the treatment dialogue and lose sight of his or her reflective function.

The ToP focus as intersection of interpersonal and intrapsychic conflicts

The ToP focus should reflect the intersection between the interpersonal conflicts of the parents with the child, and the child's central intrapsychic conflict. It integrates the first information, impressions, and transference feelings into a psychodynamic hypothesis, which should be formulated as succinctly as possible. The ToP focus should create the link between the child's symptom and the central transgenerational conflict between parents and child.

In the therapeutic process with the child, the ToP focus, when formulated properly, serves as a kind of matrix for the therapist, rendering it possible to understand the contents revealed through the child's expressions (e.g., play), and to link them with the pre- or unconscious conflicts of the parents.

The case studies below illustrate the process of focus formulation.

Explanation using case studies

Emmi, six years old

Relational symptom: The mother said that Emmi was "chronically dissatisfied, usually irritable and snappy", and she was constantly getting annoyed, getting into fights with everybody, particularly with her mother and brother about wanting to be first. Tiny things, for example, her mother closing the fridge although "Emmi wanted to do it first", were enough to spark a temper tantrum. She constantly provoked fights with her mother. However, at the same time, Emmi showed marked separation anxiety and clung very strongly to her mother. She showed particular anxiety when faced with strangers.

Case history: Emmi was a planned child and was showered with love and attention in her first two years, particularly by her mother and (paternal) grandmother. When her mother became pregnant again, she was afraid she would not be able to love this second child as much as she loved Emmi. However, immediately after the birth of the brother, she found that she was perfectly able to love two children. But there was one problem: Emmi (then aged 2.4) was very angry with her upon the birth of her brother, and remained so. The mother reported being very irritated that she had had only a little time alone with Emmi before the next baby came along, and that shortly after Emmi's birth the mother had the impression that her mother-in-law was going to take Emmi away from her. Emmi's bond with her grandmother was particularly strong. The family spent their first few years living in the grandparents' house, and would one day take over the family firm.

Therapist-child-parent relationship: Mother and daughter appeared devoted to each other and showed a close bond while they were playing a singing game together. When the therapist entered the waiting room to fetch them, she immediately felt shut out and experienced herself as being intrusive and disturbing. Emmi, who had been playing happily and was in high spirits, suddenly appeared to turn to stone and refused to make contact with the therapist. She did not react to being addressed, and hid behind her mother. The therapist felt she was an intruder in the harmonic mother–child dyad. Emmi then demanded the full attention of mother and therapist, by loudly slamming the lid of the doll's house with which she began to play, while the therapist attempted to get into conversation with her mother.

In contact with the father: It was equally difficult for the therapist to make contact with the father. The mother came to the arranged appointments without him, as if she would rather be alone with the therapist. He turned up for the second appointment, although this had not been agreed. He said that Emmi only rarely had temper tantrums with him. He had the feeling that her mother was very inconsistent, and failed to assert herself in the relationship to Emmi.

In contact with the mother: The therapist experienced a young, attractive woman, who appeared extremely tense and anxious although striving for harmony, and very afraid of doing something wrong. It appeared that the mother felt some guilt towards her daughter, which, in turn, meant the daughter appeared to have her mother "under control". At the same time, the therapist sensed a kind of gratification—almost *Schadenfreude*—in Emmi's mother regarding Emmi's refusal to be alone with the therapist. In effect, the family turned the setting upside down in the initial sessions. Sometimes the mother showed up alone, then again the father, although sessions with the child had in fact been arranged. The therapist felt as if her access to the child had been blocked; as if she were being prevented from being alone with her.

She also noticed that the mother was never able to insert a "No" as a limiting third party between herself and the child. Spitz understood the "No" as the child's first use of a symbol (Spitz, 1957). Overall, this state of affairs gave the impression that boundaries or limits were not tolerated between the family members. In the relationship with the parents, the therapist felt that she was often at their mercy in situations when they did not stick to the agreed appointments, or if they turned the setting upside down by unexpectedly bringing the child's grandmother to a planned parental appointment, without having previously told the therapist.

The child's material: Emmi was very intent on keeping her mother all to herself, and kept such a close eye on her mother's activity that she hardly had any space left of her own. Emmi spoke in whispers, giving the therapist the impression that she was allowing contact only with her mother and father, and shutting the therapist out. She behaved like "a little princess" whose favour had to be fought for and earned before she would grant someone attention. In the first session, which had been planned as a session with the entire family, but in fact took place without the father, as he "had to work", Emmi attacked her mother—who was trying to remain peaceful—using a large crocodile. The mother appeared embarrassed; she could not stave off this aggressive play, but smiled helplessly. When her mother left the room, Emmi wanted to be alone with the baby doll. She fed the baby, giving him far too much, and then abruptly hit the baby on the mouth. "When Mama comes back, I won't let her in," Emmi suddenly remarked. The therapist saw this as an abrupt shift from the clinging behaviour that Emmi had shown before the session began. When she played "Memory", there were only either "Mh" (good) or "bäh" (bad) pairs of cards. When she turned towards playing with the doll's house, the therapist noticed that she tried to find space in the house for all the figures at equal distances from each other. This meant that three generations were living in one room, which appeared very crammed, but also "pseudoharmonious" and ordered.

ToP

Meaning of the symptoms (relational symptom): Emmi probably linked the birth of her brother to rejection by her mother at the age of 2.4. From Emmi's vantage point, her mother focused on a new child due to Emmi's developmentally typical anal–sadistic impulses. These aggressive impulses towards her mother made Emmi afraid that the bond with her mother would be ruptured by her rage, and, in consequence, Emmi clung ever more tightly to her mother. At the same time, Emmi provoked her mother's rejection by constantly fighting with her and her little brother.

The child's material: Emmi felt "deposed" at the age of two by the birth of her little brother. Consequently, marked aggressive impulses towards her mother could not be adequately integrated and so early splitting probably could not be overcome. The scene with the baby doll in the play material may indicate this unconscious connection: first, Emmi (represented by the baby doll) was given too much, and then came the abrupt withdrawal and failure of her narcissistic claims to omnipotence through the birth of her brother. The abrupt withdrawal may be symbolically expressed by "hitting the baby doll abruptly on the mouth".

Therapist–child–parent relationship: Emmi repeatedly tested the bond with her mother and in this way time and again restaged the conflict of separation and rapprochement, destruction of the bond and reparation, in a permanent oscillation between paranoid–schizoid and depressive position (Klein, 1946). The therapist also experienced this abrupt shift in the contact with Emmi: sometimes Emmi appeared to perceive her as the good object to which she clung, and sometimes suddenly struck out at the therapist and rejected her. The therapist got the impression that it would never be calm in the transference relationship, as if she were on a permanent battleground, and felt herself to be continually "on guard".

Conveying the focus to Emmi: "You're afraid that Mama doesn't love you as much as before so you are always getting into a fight, to test out whether she still loves you as much!"

Focus formulation to the mother: "I get the impression that you find it very difficult to set boundaries, because you feel guilty towards Emmi due to the birth of her little brother. It's as though you have deprived Emmi of something. So you give her a lot, you don't set any limits or boundaries for her, and this means Emmi never has the experience of frustration. I think you want to be present when Emmi comes to me and make me feel just as you did when you weren't able to be alone with your child."

Focus formulation to the father: "Because you are materially dependent on your parents, you find it difficult to set the necessary boundaries between the generations. You notice how confused Emmi gets after family parties, and how much the children need you, her father and her mother, as the most important relational figures who are also able to set boundaries."

Max, five years old

Relational symptom: Max arrived in treatment because he was anxious around other children and showed little interest in playing with them. The other children were "so wild", he said. He was afraid of change, and also showed disordered eating behaviour. He had always been a poor eater. While breastfeeding, his mother recalled that he "didn't want" the breast. She believed sucking was too much effort for him. As a result, she gave it up. Drinking out of the bottle, he also gave the impression that sucking was giving him a lot of trouble, so the parents widened the hole in the teat. His fussy eating behaviour was already apparent at six months. When fed, he only ever wanted a kind of mush and hated it if the food contained larger lumps. Today, at the age of five years, he still only eats breadrolls with liver sausage, frankfurters, milk, and yoghurt without lumps. Mealtimes take more than one hour and sometimes up to three hours. In addition, Max often has temper tantrums at kindergarten, which his parents could not understand, as this did not occur at home.

Therapist–parent–child relationship: The parents had separated when Max was 2.6 years old. In the presence of the therapist, it felt as if the parents were making considerable efforts to give the impression of harmony. By now, both of them had a new partner. The separation had been very amicable, they said, and their relationship still was. Max had never asked why he no longer lived with Papa. This harmony was immediately noticeable in the parents' interaction with each other as well. There were no tensions. Everything appeared very rational and balanced. The mother gave the impression of being sure she had made the right decision in choosing her new partner. Meanwhile, the father indicated that he had fully accepted the situation and no longer bore any grudges. In the initial sessions, the therapist first found it difficult to believe that this could really be the case and wondered what the father had done with the anger that must have been present when the child's mother had left him for another man. Everything seemed relatively unemotional. In the father–son interaction, it became clear that the father had great difficulty in setting limits for Max. When this was brought to his attention, the father said he was always afraid that if he applied pressure, for example about eating, Max might say, "It's much nicer at Mama's, I don't want to go to Papa any more." He also felt guilty towards Max because of the separation. He had himself grown up without his biological father, and his relationship with his stepfather had been very remote.

Therapist–child relationship: Max's contact with the therapist was extremely disinterested and clearly had something reserved about it. He held everything back. His father reported that he had constipation: Max, he said, had a lot of trouble going to the bathroom. Towards the therapist, the restraint also expressed itself in his rejection of attempts to enter into verbal contact with him. This was thwarted by his repeatedly saying, "Don't know", "Don't want to", or "I hate always having to tell stories like this." The therapist felt that he wanted to hold something back with all his might; she should not obtain access to his inner life. At the beginning of the session, his play was listless, unmotivated, unfocused. He hid it from her. Later, he was thrilled about shooting at her and apparently hurting her. He was disappointed when she said that the session was over. He declared he wanted to carry on playing. One game in particular, in which he tortured a mouse and blocked its escape from a bleak prison, gave him great pleasure. The therapist felt relegated to a passive position, shot at and tortured, which Max seemed to enjoy a lot. She felt she was at his mercy.

The child's material (Sessions no. 4 and 5 with Max)

Max appeared listless. He mostly lay on the carpet limply, with little body tension. He grumbled quietly to himself, his back turned to the therapist. He would not show her what he was doing, picked up toys without enthusiasm and then put them back down again, speaking in a mixture of baby-talk and secret language, which she could not understand, so she felt shut out. If she wanted to engage with him, she had to pay great attention. Otherwise, at the start of the session he appeared extremely disinterested during contact with her.

Max turned to the doll's house and played "the loo sucks everything up". Max threw the coloured bricks, which were actually meant to symbolise flowers, into the Lego-Duplo toilet, making sucking sounds that seemed to give him a lot of pleasure. He said, "The toilet wants to eat everything up." Then he turned away and flicked the coloured flower-bricks at all possible objects in the room. Saying, "The door is shooting", he flicked a coloured brick himself at the therapist's knee, and showed pleasure in having hit her. He repeated this until she set him a boundary, informing him that it hurt her when he shot at her leg so roughly. Subsequently, he played exclusively with the toy toilet from the Lego-Duplo doll's house. Then he prepared small, secret attacks, and ambushed the therapist. This gave him great pleasure.

Max did not play with the figures in the Lego-Duplo house, but instead with the other contents: the furniture, the aquarium, and particularly the washbasin and toilet. He took a climbing plant, which was actually intended for decorating the "balcony", moved it and said "huh huh". This "creeper" thus took on a life of its own, with something rather threatening about it. Then Max suddenly threw it away, saying, "It's dead". He left the "creeper" lying in the corner. Max did not ask the therapist to play with him, but was playing in a lively way so that she watched attentively and with interest.

Then he suddenly discovered the little mouse and said, "The mouse lives under the roof, she should only have a balcony, she has a whole empty house, she lives there alone." The therapist said, "Ah, the mouse has the whole house to herself." Max was pleased and said, "Yes." The therapist replied, "You'd also like to have a whole house to yourself." Max was pleased again, gave her a conspiratorial look and nodded. Following this, he rebuilt the Lego house. Nothing was as it had been. The three-storey house suddenly turned into a two-storey house. He repeatedly crushed the little mouse between the window shutters and a cupboard he had built, so that the mouse had no room left. Then he said, "This is the mouse's cage." With considerable relish he played out various scenarios, locking the mouse up again and again, having the police come and lock the mouse up, not allowing the mouse out of prison, and pretending that the mouse had been sucked into a sack and died. All these were agonising attacks on the little mouse.

Once again, at the end of the session, although the therapist had prepared him for it long in advance, he wanted to disregard the boundaries and carry on playing as he was having so much fun. The therapist said to him, "Max, you would like to be the one deciding when the session is over, wouldn't you?"

In the next session, Max returned to the doll's house and repeatedly flew a toy helicopter into the ground floor of the house so that everything lay in ruins. The figures, furniture, cars, everything flew into the air and the whole house was destroyed. No member of the family survived, and everything was scattered in chaos. Max did not attempt to prevent this chaos and did not clear anything up. The picture of destruction left an impression in the therapist's mind even after the session was over. The helicopter made "a lot of noise and its rotors spun wildly," Max said excitedly. He found a "parking space" on the ground floor of the house, but by now the scene was in such disarray that it no longer offered any comfort. The therapist thought immediately that this might symbolise the separation of his parents when Max was 2.6 years old. His mother's new partner may have appeared to him like a "helicopter" that greedily wanted to snatch away his mother. He had made a lot of "phallic wind", and in Max's eyes, destroyed his family, that is, his sense of security. For Max, there followed the loss of trust, a change of location, and the experience of a father who appeared abandoned and grieving.

Focus formulation according to TOP

(Integration of the three triangles: relationship-symptom, material, and therapist–parent–child relationship.)

ToP

Meaning of the symptoms in the relationship ("relational symptom"): Max's eating disorder at the age of five could be seen as a compromise between the desire to be big and strong like his father and the regressive desire to be supplied orally with "baby food". Oedipal–phallic desires prompted so much fear in Max that he preferred to forgo growth and remained fixated on being small and eating baby food so as to avoid the oedipal competition with his father, who, by that time, had been jilted by his mother. Through his fussy eating habits, which demanded considerable care and attention to satisfy his every "heart's desire", he kept his father on the alert and attentive. Through regression to the anal mode of satisfaction of needs he was able to exasperate his father (as well as his mother), and use this to manage his fear of oedipal themes.

The child's play scenes (material): Max's behaviour, his babyish way of talking and his play could be understood as regression. He was stuck in the anal themes of conquering, torture, and giving orders, and of holding back. Oral themes of taking in were also dominant, but phallic themes such as the fire engine appeared very rarely.

Here, the focus could be that Max is fixated on the anal mode of drive satisfaction. Anything novel makes him afraid. Max dealt with this fear by avoiding new things and holding on fast to familiar things (pappy food, regressive language). The helicopter that destroyed the doll's house, leaving debris behind, can be understood as a symbol for his parents' separation.

Therapist–parent–child relationship: Max himself was unable to build up sufficient body tension to be focused and inquisitive (phallic). According to his parents, he avoided everything that he found to be an effort. He appeared passive, listless, and lacking energy to the therapist as well.

The therapist experienced his father as someone who was very permissive and avoided any conflict with Max or his mother. The therapist also suspected that Max perceived his father as weak and abandoned by the mother. This meant that the desire to be strong and "phallic" himself made him particularly afraid of being punished by his father. He defended against this fear through a regressive movement and developing a symptom.

Summary of focus Max (intrapsychic)

- Seeking to anally retain the status quo as a defence against fear of change and loss.
- Fear of his own oral-sadistic and anal-sadistic impulses.
- Fear of being punished by his weak and abandoned father for his oedipal desires.
- Defence against the fear through regression to oral and anal phases of satisfying needs.
- As a consequence, Max was inhibited and not adequately "phallic" for his age.
- The defence caused inhibition of development and blocking of inquisitiveness.

Focus formulation by the therapist

To the father (ToP meaning of symptom): "Max keeps you on your toes through his fussy eating behaviour and your care for him and his special desires. After the family broke up, there was no more space within it for mourning the separation. You tried to hide your feelings of rage towards your ex-wife. Max is now expressing his annoyance in a hidden way, by fighting with you about food. Max is trying to get your attention and if you devote enough time to him it will confirm that he is allowed to become big and strong like Papa. He will probably experience your insistence that he eat properly as soothing."

Focus formulation to Max: "You are afraid that if you eat like other children of your age you will become big and strong like your dad. But you're afraid that dad won't like you any more if you're as big and strong as he is. You're afraid that dad already doesn't like you any more now, because mum now lives with you and not with dad.

You are afraid if you eat something new that you will find it delicious, because then you would have to bite it and you're afraid that you will break it. Just like the helicopter when it wants to land in the house, and just like Tom (mother's new partner), when he liked mum. Then the house that belonged to mum, dad, and you got broken."

Focus formulation to the mother: "Max is afraid that he could once again lose everything familiar, just as he did as a result of the separation. Therefore he avoids all new things, particularly in his eating behaviour."

Course of treatment: Once the therapist had understood the symptoms, with their underlying unconscious desires, fears, and their defence, and interpreted them to the parents and child, Max was increasingly able to risk trying new foods. Apparently, he perceived his parents' insistence on age-appropriate eating behaviour as soothing. By making age-appropriate demands, the parents showed him that they took him seriously and that he was allowed to become big and strong.

Interpretation, transference, and countertransference

The patients Anna Freud wrote about were notable for their day-dreaming, and were also unusually articulate in the way they were able to describe their experiences. Anna Freud also showed how the children were able to create a link between new experiences and their analysis.

However, many of our patients have less verbal ability. Instead, they express their central conflicts non-verbally in play. In short-term therapy, we also encounter the difficulty that the children first have to get used to the insight-promoting technique of psychoanalysis. The fact that the treatment is limited to a period of 20–25 sessions means that the children do not have much opportunity to become familiar with the analytical method. They have barely become used to talking about their inner experience before the time-limited therapy is over.

We try to compensate for this difference with high frequency, long-term treatment by applying a focused technique.

Using this technique means we have to be much more aware of the transference and countertransference that develops from the very first sessions, reflect on these rapidly and in detail, and allow these reflections to flow into the interpretation of the conflict focus before the child can get used to the psychoanalytical mode of giving space to ideas and affording them significance.

PaCT adopts Klein's way of working, paying attention to the children's play and understanding the child's actions in the transference. Like Klein we understand play as the expression of the child's inner conflicts, but, unlike Klein, we do not immediately interpret everything the child does, but first gather the contents in order to bundle them into a superordinate theme, the psychodynamic focus, or ToP. This conflict focus is then communicated to, and discussed with, the child and his parents when a suitable point presents itself.

Like Anna Freud, too, we need regular contact with the child's parents in order to assemble a comprehensive picture of the child's behaviour and problems, because they might not arise in the therapeutic situation. We address any similarities between the relationship to the analyst and patterns described by the parents. We use the analytical play technique to interpret the child's unconscious desires and conflicts. In PaCT, it is of the utmost importance to try to understand unconscious contents and not to translate each content that the child provides. From continuous observation of, and reflection on, the child's play, we form a sort of superordinate theme, a psychodynamic focus, the "triangle of psychodynamic constellations" (see ToP, Chapter Six, section headed "The focus of PaCT: triangle of psychodynamic constellations (ToP)", pp. 147–152).

The negative transference of parents and child is particularly significant in short-term therapy. It is very important that the therapist takes note of this, especially considering whether or not it is hindering the progress of the therapy. If negative feelings occur (for example, if the parents' project guilt on to the therapist in the form of accusations), it is important that the therapist investigates their meaning and works through the parents' negative attitudes with them. It is important to respect these negative attitudes and to try to understand their meaning. If negative feelings are perceived in the countertransference, the therapist can work with the parents to try to understand

THE TREATMENT TECHNIQUE   163

and modulate them. The child's negative transference should be dealt with similarly, transforming it through an active, benign technique into a mildly positive transference. A negative transference cannot be ruled out, particularly if the child's unconscious resists bringing shameful contents to consciousness, and if the transference expresses this resistance. The contact with the parents, furthermore, has importance beyond the parental work for the child's process of working through, as we need the parents' information about the child's problematic behaviour and symptoms. Regardless of any negative or positive reactions towards the analyst, at home with his parents the child continues to show the problematic behaviour we understand as a relational symptom.

In addition to the transference relationship, the child's relationship with his parents remains the canvas on which the relational symptoms are portrayed.

Specific transference constellations in the treatment of children with emotional problems

During the PaCT treatment, specific transference constellations arise between child and therapist. These often present a major challenge for the treating therapist. As Mentzos stresses (2006), depressive patients often have a very tense relationship to the object. The object may at first be idealised in the transference. The child then carries the desire for a relationship to an object that is purely good into the relationship to his therapist. In confronting the real object, the child will almost inevitably experience the therapist as disappointing, and turn away from him or her. A tense and ambivalent relationship to the object is likely to dominate the treatment transference. In the treatment of children with emotional problems and depressive disorders, the therapist's countertransference is often severely tested through the desire to be rescued by the good object, which is typical for this group of patients, accusations directed against the disappointing object, and ultimately the devaluing and destruction of the object (Windaus, 2007).

It is important to withstand the patient's aggressive attacks, which are presumably a consequence of unconscious disappointment in the object, without transforming the aggressive countertransference feelings that this provokes into counterattacks. The therapist can become a reliable object for the patient, in a Winnicottian sense, by reflecting on her countertransference and, thus, not repeating the negatively internalised object relationship experiences of the patient. However, the strong activity in focal psychotherapeutic work might not be enough to counteract the patient's depressive affects. A therapist who experiences the inner emptiness that the child feels, that is, who experiences a concordant identification (Racker, 1970, and see Chapter Three, section headed "Transference and countertransference", p. 94) in her countertransference, might be diverted into defending against these unbearable feelings of emotional numbness through active and hypomanically distorted action. In this case, she might rationalise her own defence against depressive experience by pretending that she wants to "cheer up" the child. Such transference constellations must, in any case, be examined in detailed supervision and one's own analytical work.

Only through intensive reflection on her countertransference can the therapist make such depressive transference constellations therapeutically useful. Here, it is important that she understands these states of emotional numbness and fantasised objectlessness as a defence strategy of the child's, one that presumably helps the child to endure mental states of abandonment and disappointment by the object.

It is also important to be reliably available to the child as a container for his as yet undigested affects, so that his often very negative transference can be understood and articulated. It helps to imagine that the child is using defence mechanisms, such as emotional numbness and emptiness, in order to protect the therapeutic relationship—just like previous relationships to the primary relationship objects—from being flooded with unrestrained aggressive impulses, which are experienced as destructive.

If the therapist pays attention to the aggression that arises in the transference context in the material from the session as well, and, thus, makes an understanding accessible, the child can have a new relationship experience, which helps to change old relationship patterns.

Finally, it is important that patients should be able to receive the good object internally, despite aggression and conflicts, and not destroy it.

The repeated oscillation between paranoid–schizoid and depressive positions during treatment with PaCT can, thus, lead to a renewed introjection of the good object, which this time is successful, and enables positive and flexible relationship experiences to develop. It is only if the therapist does not turn away from the child when, in paranoid–schizoid mode, he attacks the therapist, that the child can experience the object surviving his destructive attacks. Even if the therapist often feels like reacting in her countertransference with a counterattack, she must never give in to this. Winnicott has taught us that, for the successful integration of good and bad self-object representations, it is vital that the object survives these attacks despite the child's unconscious aggression (see Chapter Two, section headed "The object relations theory of Donald W. Winnicott", pp. 50–52).

Work on the defence and the defended material is also central to the work with children. Defence should always be acknowledged, despite its dysfunctionality, as a kind of inhibitor of development. Treatment with PaCT is also about actualising previous coping mechanisms in the transference relationship in an affectively effective and scenically evident way (see Windaus, 2007, p. 339). An interpretation need not always be made verbally, but can also be transmitted in play via a particular action. This gives the therapeutic process a particular significance. Through non-verbal communication such as the tone of her voice, the therapist transmits whether she is inwardly turning away from the child or whether she remains neutrally linked to it and is able to continue applying herself to the understanding of its psychic inner world.

The significance of infantile sexuality in the therapeutic process

Chapter Two, in "The drive psychology of Sigmund Freud" (pp. 20–24), presents Freud's theory that human development runs in psychosexual phases, in which the drive constitutes the subject according to the first experiences of one's body (the erogenous zones). Thus, we attempt to understand the child's symptoms against the backdrop of conflict within psychosexual development. We assume that a child can regress to developmental phases that are no longer age-appropriate, for fear of conflicts that can lead to new psychosexual phases. The child can remain fixated on a mode of drive satisfaction, so that he cannot reach a higher level of psychosexual development. We understand psychosexual development as a drive destiny: that is, that individual human development proceeds along psychosexual phases with characteristic experiential and behavioural modalities. The drive is directed towards the object. The object relationship is determined by experiential modalities, which are derived from bodily functions. Early experiences, gained in the course of instinctual drives and forms of satisfaction in the oral, anal, and phallic phases, underpin the individual story of the libidinal (conflict) dynamic. Conflicts in the early oral phase of satisfaction of needs, for example, can lead to lasting fixations on this behavioural and experiential modality, and in the individual can later lead to a lasting oral greed, an insatiable hunger, or the "devouring" of relationship objects or "things". An oral fixation can, thus, manifest itself in a person's intemperance, in his desires to be provided for by the object, or later in development in an insatiable voracity for computer games or narcotics (addictive drugs). We assume that conflicts and failures in this early part of childhood experience have permanent effects on the development of the personality and its dominant defence mechanisms.

The therapist needs to identify which elements of infantile sexuality are visible in the child's play, and to understand these forms of expression using basic psychoanalytical knowledge. The child's sexuality is manifest, often in overt and spontaneous ways, in play and other interaction. We can use this to begin to understand the child's unconscious conflicts and, thus, move towards an understanding of his interpersonal conflicts.

Below, we discuss examples of the ways in which regressions or fixations on particular psychosexual positions are revealed through the child's play, and how the therapist can identify the currently dominant theme of psychosexual development (whether in the session, in the child's phase of development, or in a defined phase of transference).

Orality

In the case study of Elisabeth, aged six years (more detailed presentation of the case follows in Chapter Twelve), numerous oral themes were apparent in the contents of play in the first sessions: for example, a house being robbed, the human figures being devoured by animals. In Elisabeth's game, the animals gradually invaded the doll's house to build up their own kingdom. The animals raided the doll's house until in the end the human figures were left with nothing. Their house was empty. They themselves were powerless and destitute (see pp. 250–251).

The therapist should first explore these expressions of infantile sexuality for herself, and think about what this "burglary" could mean within the transference relationship, before making an interpretation. In this example, it was known from the case history that Elisabeth's mother had been depressive during Elisabeth's early development, grieving for a child who had previously been lost, and so had not been emotionally available to Elisabeth, like an "empty house". The therapist understood the "burglary" in play as the expression of an early fantasy in which oral–aggressive impulses could be expressed against the disappointing early object. She decided to articulate the oral aggression that Elisabeth's play was expressing as part of the game: "The animals are very angry with the people and want to eat them up and rob them of everything." The therapist did not consider a genetic interpretation (referring to Elisabeth's relationship to her mother) to be appropriate, because it risked destabilising the child too much. Using her knowledge of psychosexual development and its specific fantasies in this play scene, she was able to grasp something of the child's inner world and, thus, move the shared understanding process forward.

Oral themes can also manifest in the way that the child interacts within the transference relationship: for example, if he is particularly greedy, wants to have everything, or has an insatiable need for affection.

Anality

Anal themes often manifest themselves in therapy as the child being particularly retentive, for example, refusing to talk about himself, playing with his back turned to the therapist, or refusing to speak and rejecting attempts at interaction. In the case study of Max, aged five (more detailed presentation in the section headed "The significance of the setting", pp. 155–161), the therapist experienced a child whom at first she could not reach: "Max's contact with the therapist was extremely disinterested and clearly had something reserved about it. He held everything back. His father reported that he had constipation: Max, he said, had a lot of trouble going to the bathroom. With the therapist, the restraint also expressed itself in his rejection of attempts to enter into verbal contact with him. This was thwarted by his repeatedly saying, "Don't know", "Don't want to", or "I hate always having to tell stories like this." The therapist felt that he wanted with all his might to hold something back; she should not obtain access to his inner life. At the beginning of the session, his play was listless, unmotivated, unfocused. He hid it from her. Later, he was thrilled about shooting at her and apparently hurting her."

This case study shows a clear anal fixation. Such a fixation at the anal phase of libido development not only serves as a defence against anxiety, but also provides anal satisfaction. By holding everything back, Max is able to satisfy his drives in the anal mode. Since oedipal themes, for example, having to compete with his father, caused Max severe anxiety, his libido remained stuck in the anal mode of satisfaction of needs. This was how he controlled his parents, by refusing to eat, rejecting anything new, and tending to constipation.

Similar control was also apparent in the transference: by refusing to talk to the therapist, Max could retain his omnipotent ability to control everyone (parents, therapist), which, in addition to defending against anxiety, also helped to satisfy the anal–sadistic partial drive.

The contents of Max's play repeatedly revealed his pleasure in anal–sadistic drive satisfaction: "Then he said, 'This is the mouse's cage', and with considerable relish played out various scenarios, locking the mouse up again and again, having the police come and lock the mouse up, not allowing the mouse out of prison, and pretending that the mouse had been sucked into a sack and died. These were all agonising attacks on the little mouse" (p. 158, under section headed "Explanation using case studies").

Pleasure in showing and watching

This was described by Freud as the active and passive forms of a partial drive. For example, the child in the phallic phase derives a lot of pleasure from seeing what the other people's genitals look like, and what the differences are between the sexes. Looking at naked people, or showing how phallic one is, and what one can already do, are important sources of enjoyment at this phase of psychosexual development. Since this psychosexual behavioural and experiential mode can present both actively and passively, both watching and showing (exhibitionism) may be inhibited in the child. In the case study of Sophie, an inhibition of pleasure in showing and watching became particularly significant (detailed presentation in Chapter Thirteen).

Sophie (five) was brought to therapy by her parents, because she was very frightened "of exposing herself" in front of the kindergarten teacher and other children. She would refuse to make visual contact and was extremely shy. She was unable to assert herself and, when playing with other children, would always be the one to back down (see Chapter Thirteen).

In the therapy, this inhibition rapidly dissipated. Indeed, exhibitionistic tendencies became prominent. Sophie leapt wildly about the room, turning somersaults, and threw a toy horse around equally exuberantly. She wanted the therapist to see how good she was at gymnastics. In this exuberant play, Sophie's enormous pleasure in showing was quite visible, in stark contrast to the shame that had previously dominated in exposed situations.

Phallicity

In the interaction with the therapist, phallic themes manifest themselves in competitiveness, in pleasure in showing and watching, and in curiosity. In the play contents, for example, phallic themes are expressed by the swords and daggers that a child might bring to the session in order to underline his power. Julian (six years old), who showed severe castration anxiety, laid two guns beside himself during a session in which he spoke for the first time about fear, which previously he had defended against (detailed presentation in Chapter Twelve). Intensive play involving high towers, fire engines, or fast racing cars can also show that the child's (partial) drive is bound up with the phallic mode of drive satisfaction (see Chapter Two, section headed "The drive psychology of Sigmund Freud", pp. 20–24).

The point of naming such expressions and interpreting (which must be carefully done due to the time constraints) is to "deliver" the child of the pathologically bound drive energy, so that it is once more available for the child's further development (de M'Uzan, 1994). For example, a child's voyeurism can transform into a thirst for knowledge. It is important to stir the child's interest in the focus so that it becomes curious about its psychic inner world or the objects of the world outside that have been the cause of anxiety.

Work with the parents

In PaCT, work with the parents is particularly significant. It is not something peripheral to work with the child, but, in fact, a central instrument of the therapy. It aims to promote the parents' mentalization about their child, by improving their understanding of the inner states, motivations, and conflicts that underlie the child's behaviour. Parents should be helped to do this by discussing episodes that they report in terms of their interaction with the child. Here, it is important that the child's symptom is linked to the relationship problems and conflicts, as well as to the parents' own fears and defence formations. In the parent–therapist sessions, we work with the parents' biographical material and their description of family relationship episodes, as well as with what can be observed of relationship phenomenon in the parent sessions.

In the course of these sessions, parents and therapist should together develop and highlight the focus as a relationship topic in everyday language. This focus, which is formulated after the fifth session, should then be discussed in more depth with the parents in sessions 6, 10, 14, 18, 20, starting from the parental narratives of relationship episodes with the child. We use appropriate interpretations to improve the parents' insight into the child's inner world, which is the source of his behaviour. To do this, the parents need to be encouraged in their ability and willingness to adopt a perspective that takes account of the child's inner states, inner experience, and motivations.

Child analysis has long tended to neglect the topic of work with the parents, strongly aligning itself with the model of adult analysis and focusing on the individual work with the child. Virtually no systematic conceptualisation of work with the parents was undertaken in the early years of child analysis. There are some indications that Anna Freud recognised the significance of working with the parents, and was well aware of the difficulties and resistance that arose. However, there have been few attempts to conceptualise work with the parents in any detail.

One major reason for this neglect is probably that in their work with children, therapists easily succumb to the temptation to see themselves as a "better mother" for the child. This generally leads to a conflictual relationship with the real parents, as they feel devalued by the "therapist as another parental figure" and perceive it as a threat. Therapists, for their part, can find it painful that "their" child in reality still has other parents, and might react by devaluing them or feeling inhibited in the work with them. This can lead to a tendency to concentrate solely on the child and to neglect the relationship with the parents with its many transference and countertransference reactions.

A further problem lies in the possible jealousy that parents feel towards the child. If parents feel inadequate in their parental role and, at the same time, are needy as a result of their own problems, this can lead to them feeling jealous of the child because of the therapy and the attention he/she receives from the therapist.

The parents' feelings of guilt at not having given, or currently giving, their child enough often hinders productive psychotherapeutic work. Unfavourable constellations are produced when the parents externalise the guilt that they actually suffer themselves and project it to the therapist. As a result, she is then perceived as the person who is "to blame": for example, because the therapy stagnates or the child's problems do not improve, or even deteriorate. If a negative transference to the therapist that develops like this cannot be understood and influenced, it will endanger the working alliance between therapist and parents that is essential if we are to understand and process the child's symptom as a precipitate of interpersonal and intrapsychic conflicts.

Unconscious parental jealousy of the therapist

Case study 1

Jonas (eight years old) came for treatment with PaCT because he was suffering from depressive mood, and had said several times that he did not want to go on living. In the course of treatment with PaCT, the therapist was able to establish a good therapeutic relationship with Jonas, and his symptoms improved markedly. But Mrs H, his mother, although distressed at her son's problems, was unable to acknowledge any successes in his treatment. Her jealousy towards the therapist, who appeared to have better access to Jonas than she did herself, was too great. Mrs H was unable either to perceive the success of the treatment (the emotional symptoms decreasing markedly after therapy), or to give the therapist credit for it. She bore a grudge against the therapist. She could not bear the good relationship that the therapist had been able to establish with Jonas, and in which he could develop positively, to be apparent. Although previously she had attended the PaCT sessions, once Jonas' therapy had ended the mother continued to refuse to have a final parent session or to take part in the evaluation of the therapy. Thus, this negative transference constellation could not be worked through and resolved in a joint session. The therapist suspected, from the mother's previous statements, that she was acutely fearful of losing control and being unable to manage her job or bring up her children alone any more; she was filled with rage that the short-term therapy was, as agreed, concluded after twenty-five sessions.

Case study 2

Lucas (nine years old) entered treatment because he was apathetic at school, and had feelings of depression and a range of psychosomatic problems including abdominal pain and headaches. From the outset, he was very engaged in the therapy and creative in the sessions, happy to talk about his dreams, and ready to bring his internal conflicts into his play and drawings and into the parental work, too.

In the course of therapy his symptoms diminished. His parents decided on a change of school. Lucas settled down very well at his new school, forming better relationships with his peers there than with his previous ones. He was also better able to accept what was required of him in terms of performance and handle these demands more flexibly. In the final meetings with his parents, they also reported a substantial improvement in Lucas' emotional state. His mother emphasised her conviction that this improvement was due to the new school, and that the diminishing of the psychosomatic pains was probably the result of a powder prescribed by a homeopath. The therapist initially felt hurt that her therapy and its success was not being acknowledged or taken seriously by the mother, but she was also able to understand that seeing something so positive developing through her son's relationship with the therapist had made the mother feel jealous, which she countered by denying the therapist's significance for her son and her therapeutic performance. By understanding this connection, the therapist was able to accept the mother's view as a compromise. She sidestepped any conflict based on rivalry with the mother. Such a form of enacted jealousy enables the mother to permit the therapeutic work to go on, but ultimately to avoid acknowledging its success on a conscious level.

Anna Freud (1967) defined the objective of child analysis as being to restore the child's progressive developmental ability. Novick and Novick (2005) add that child analysis may also aim at enabling the parents to develop their parenthood as an important phase-typical function of their own. According to Novick and Novick (2005), work with the parents should also help them to regain a feeling of competence, to transform their feelings of guilt into useful concern, and to be able to perceive their child as separate from themselves (on this, see case study Julian, Chapter Ten) (Table 8).

The goal of treatment with psychoanalytic short-term therapy is "not only the alleviation of an individual's developmental inhibition, but also to return the parent–child relationship to its potential for a lifelong, positive resource for both, parents and child" (von Klitzing, 2005, p. 118). Parents—unlike when they seek out an analyst for their own therapy—do not encounter their child's therapist as a transference figure, but as a real person. They entrust their child to this real person, with the desire and hope of freeing him from his problems and symptoms. Despite this, transference processes do play a role in their relationship, just as countertransference reactions are sparked off in the therapist. Taking these into account and at least partially

Table 8.   Therapeutic alliance tasks (Novick & Novick, 2005).

- During evaluation, the task for parents is to begin various transformations.
- At the beginning of the child's treatment, parents have the task of allowing the child to "be with" another adult, accepting physical separation.
- In the middle phase allowing the child to work together privately with another person means integrating the child's psychological separation.
- Enjoying and validating the child's progression is the task for parents in the pretermination phase.
- During termination, parents work to mourn their loss of the therapy, to internalize mastery alliance tasks, and to consolidate their own development in the phase of parenthood.
- After treatment has ended, parents allow for continued growth in the child and grow with him. (Novick & Novick, 2005, pp. 19–20)

processing them, without finding ourselves engaged in an actual psychotherapy with the parental figures, is a particular challenge in child therapy.

Psychotherapy with children makes exacting demands on the parents' motivation and requires a high level of their compliance. For many parents of preschool and young school-age children, it will be the first time that their child has built up an intensive relationship with another adult. Allowing the child to be both physically and psychically separate, and accepting their connection to another adult, poses a great challenge to the parents. The therapist must be sensitive to the parents' fears here, and manage them appropriately, or even address them directly. It is not easy for the parents to endure the child's closeness with the therapist in the therapeutic work. It is essential to communicate to the parents how important greater psychic separation is for the child's development.

When therapy ends, it can also be a challenge for the parents to acknowledge its success and the child's progress. This may be particularly hard for parents who have difficulty in forming an inner representation of the therapist as a "good object". In the case study described above (Jonas, eight years old) the unconscious conflicts of the mother made it difficult for her to acknowledge the success of therapy and to represent the "good" internally. She was too burdened by feelings of guilt towards her child and by jealousy of the therapist, alongside her fears of losing control and of being unable to manage her job and continue to bring the children up on her own.

Work with the parents also makes use of classic psychoanalytical tools, just as the child's therapy itself does: work on defence, verbalisation, insight, reconstruction, the interpretation and use of transference and countertransference, are priorities in this work. Explanations of development psychological and psychodynamic links are also given, for example, noting that it is "normal" for a six-year-old girl to be interested in her father and to try to win him over in an age-appropriate way. Assistance in the form of pedagogical advice, support in "urgent" day-to-day issues and in the assessment of daily situations, and the modelling of behaviour are offered.

It is, nevertheless, important that the work with the parents should not focus on the complete range of the parents' individual conflicts, but be limited to the conflict topics that relate to the child's symptom. Parental work focuses on the parent–child relationship. Everything connected with the conflicts in the parent–child relationship is given attention. Thus, we process more than just the biographical information connected to parenthood and the child's symptom. Should the parents themselves be too fraught or show severe psychiatric symptoms, an individual psychotherapeutic treatment for the parent should focus on the individual conflict.

Case study: Lisa, eight years old

Relational symptom: Lisa was brought to us for treatment by her mother, because she would not allow "Mama [to] go away". She would have panic attacks and screamed and cried even if her mother was only going into the garden to hang out the washing. Lisa sometimes behaved "so stupidly" and was often unable to do anything herself, "as if she were a baby". This had been the case especially after the birth of her little brother. The mother felt pressured by Lisa's dependent, clingy behaviour.

Case history: The symptom could be understood as a relational symptom. Lisa's mother had had traumatic experiences in her own childhood, which she had not been able to process. As a result, she had frightening, intrusive memories and flashbacks, which she described to the therapist very carefully in the initial sessions, in which she relived the traumatic experiences. Fear of the flashbacks led to an inability to be alone. She clung to, and showed an open dependence on, Lisa's father or her two daughters. When she spent time with her children, she was often cold and absent, or unpredictably irascible. She used activities such as baking and cooking while the children were around to distract herself from traumatic memories.

Therapist-child-parent relationship: In the contact with the mother, the therapist experienced a friendly woman who made great efforts to maintain harmony. She had apparently learnt to use her noticeable physical attractiveness to tie men to her so as not to be alone. Increasingly, she was unable to leave the house except in the company of her husband, and she showed herself needy and dependent on him. In her psychic resonance, the therapist experienced great empathy for the mother when she related the traumatic experiences of her childhood. However, when the mother described relationship episodes with the children, the therapist sensed annoyance with the mother in the developing countertransference, because it felt as if that she was not sufficiently emotionally available for her children, and probably identified with her own early, neglecting object.

In the contact with the father, the therapist immediately noticed, with some irritation, that the mother's symptom did not bother him. The father hung on the mother's words and appeared very much in love, and proud of her as his wife. Overall, this made the father appear very submissive, although superficially he appeared to enjoy being the family's protector. The child's symptoms bothered him as much as they bothered the mother, and it seemed as if he did not dare to take up a different position from her.

The therapist experienced Lisa as a girl who was very needy and an attention-seeker. She particularly noticed that Lisa was inappropriately infantile for her age, having difficulty with tying her own shoelaces, for example. This made the therapist feel mild annoyance with the mother for not supporting the child in these important steps towards autonomy. Overall, Lisa's contact to the therapist appeared empty, "absent", and not very lively. Lisa seemed not to know how to maintain contact to the object, her mother, if she was not paying attention to her but was "cooking and baking". In her countertransference, the therapist often felt extreme tiredness and a paralysing emptiness, so that she found it very difficult to develop her own thoughts and work with them freely.

Material: In the first sessions, Lisa made a paper dragon, which she carefully painted. Lisa gave the dragon a cord, with which she bound it "so that he doesn't fly away". It became clear how important this precautionary measure against flying away was to Lisa. When the therapist looked at the dragon, she understood it as a symbol for Lisa's fear of not being contained by her mother, and "flying off into nothing", detached and abandoned to the wind. She suspected that Lisa had experienced the partial withdrawal of cathexis by the mother—who was absent during flashbacks, intrusions and depressive moods—as an existential threat.

ToP focus: The child's symptom of not being able to be without her mother was understood to result from her lack of ability to build up a good inner object that would remain even if the mother were absent in reality. Lisa was probably exposed very early on to such withdrawal of cathexis, when her mother had no inner psychic space available in which she could reflect on Lisa and her needs. Lisa's fear that "Mama is away" thus had a real and existentially threatening component, when the mother really was psychologically absorbed by flashbacks or the defence against trauma-associated affects.

To Lisa: "You don't like to show Mama that you are sometimes cross with her because you're frightened that Mama will then go away, and that's also why you cling on to Mama to tightly, to hold her fast."

To the father: "You're afraid that your wife, whom you find very beautiful and whom you love very much, might leave you. That's why you aren't bothered by her clingy and dependent behaviour, even though it considerably impairs you as a family. If your wife can't leave the house, you don't have to be afraid that she might leave you."

To the mother: "I think that Lisa's fear that 'Mama is away' shows that Lisa has sensed that you really did have to battle with your memories, and at such times could not be internally free and open to her needs, so you really were in some way "absent". Perhaps you are also afraid that Lisa will go away and that you will lose someone again. By being so afraid about going away, Lisa is protecting you from your fear of abandonment."

Course of treatment: The therapist advised the mother in this case to start individual psychotherapeutic treatment herself, to help process her traumatic experiences and so be strengthened in her parental function. Parallel to this, the treatment with PaCT used the pretend mode of play with the child to work on her fears of "falling into nothing if mother isn't here", and on her regression to infantile behaviour. This could also be understood as the child's attempt to get the mother's attention through being as small and needy as her little brother.

* * *

When working with the parents in PaCT, the focus of therapeutic interventions can only be on the interpersonal level between parents and child. Should a parent's ability to carry out the parental function be significantly impaired through their own severe psychiatric illness (such as post traumatic stress disorder in the example above, or a major depression), the PaCT therapist should not be afraid, during the initial sessions (or later, if the parents at first conceal their problems), to communicate this suspected "diagnosis" in a sensitive way and to tell them about appropriate possibilities for help.

In bundling it into a psychodynamic hypothesis, the transgenerational focus according to ToP then precipitates as a treatment focus for the child's symptoms and problems. Everything else that the parents bring with them to the child's analytic therapy, in terms of individual conflict dynamics or individual maladaptive conflictual working, is not considered directly. For example, a mother whose basic block against expressing her aggressive impulses renders her unable to assert herself against the demands of her mother-in-law might have her quality of life impaired or might tend to somatise the problem in the form of backache. The mother's individual conflict topic, "inability to set boundaries", is not, however, considered in the treatment with PaCT, except with reference to the interpersonal dimension: this mother's permissive behaviour in bringing up the child fails to limit her child's narcissistic fantasies of omnipotence, and so there is no "No" to define the boundaries between mother and child. The mother's inability to say "No" should, thus, be considered in terms of its effects on the child's development, and not as an individual problem of the mother (see case study Emmi, Chapter Six, pp. 152–155, under section headed "Explanation using case studies"). In the case of Emmi, the mother's distress was not severe enough to drive her to seek psychotherapeutic treatment for herself. Psychoanalytic work with the parents does not replace the individual analytic processing of parental conflicts. Similarly, it has little overlap with individual psychoanalytic work done by one parent who may be having therapy.

Involvement of the father

For successful therapy of the child it is important that the father is included. Many fathers are not aware of how significant they are for their child's development. All too often do fathers believe that it is mothers alone who are responsible for the emotional development and stimulation of the children. The effectiveness of the psychotherapeutic intervention depends a great deal on work with the father, in particular on his ability to be constantly and reliably available to the child as a "third object", enabling the child to separate from the object mother (Abelin, 1971). Through her direct observation of small children and their primary attachment figures, Mahler (Mahler, Pine, & Bergmann, 1975) recognised the severe consequences of unsuccessful detachment and individuation. This is also strongly dependent on the object's reaction to the child's efforts at autonomy. Thus, a child with predominantly symbiotic organisation may appear to treat his mother as part of himself. It is not possible for these children to perceive the object as being separate rather than merged with them. Children who do not have access to an early triangulating object find it particularly difficult to establish a picture of the mother within themselves as an object separate from themselves. Instead, as Mahler describes, they maintain the split between good and bad partial objects. This split is accompanied by introjective fantasies, with the desire to incorporate the good object and reject the bad one. The consequence is a funda-mental confusion of reality and fantasy:

> . . . if, against consuming introjected bad objects and the hostile world (police, dangerous psychotherapist, death of grandfather, etc.), no object image in the outside world can be depended upon—then the break with reality and withdrawal into an inner world serve the func-tion of survival. We designated this per se regressive psychotic defence, this secondary autism, a reactive restitution, because the ego thus restores, albeit regressively, the blissful oceanic feeling, the oneness with 'the object', which seems the delusional substitute for that child whose ego is unable to endure the second hatching process, the actual separation from the good object. (Mahler & Gosliner, 1955, p. 210)

If the father is disappointing or not reliably available, the child is left only with the possibility of persisting regressively in a state of partial undifferentiation from the mother, or moving to and fro in a kind of pseudo-separation between dyad and triad, without ever reaching a mature oedipality. This has serious repercussions on the child's devel-opment and on its ability to form stable self- and object boundaries; bor-derline pathology may be a result (Rupprecht-Schampera, 1995).

It is, therefore, important that, during treatment with PaCT, the therapist emphasises to the parents the significance of the father for the child's development, even if it is a single mother who brings the child for treatment. Wherever possible, the father should be involved, although this might first be presented as being "impossible". If the mother refuses such contact, we should persisting in working towards involving the father in the treatment, helping the mother with her anxieties and anger towards the father and feelings of disappointment.

Case study, Linus, nine years old

Linus, aged nine, came to us for treatment with PaCT because of depressive moods. He often complained of being unable to do anything. During the first session, he pointed to his mother and said, "She is doing the most short notice house move in the world." In his first sessions alone with the therapist, he repeatedly built "houses on wheels" with the Lego-Duplo pieces.

It quickly became clear how much Linus missed his father as "third object", as a stable house "with a foundation", with whom he could identify. The parents had never been a couple and the father lived abroad.

After several attempts and through stubborn persistence, the therapist did succeed in obtaining the father's telephone number from the mother. While processing the mother's intense feelings of disappointment and anger towards the father, as part of the PaCT parent sessions, she was able to agree that it was important for Linus to have contact with his father.

The therapist then telephoned the father and discussed the Linus situation with him. As a result, the father was very engaged and, in addition to regular contact with the child, was prepared to get together with the therapist for a talk.

Dealing with hostile accusations and denigration directed at the therapist

In dealing with serious accusations and denigration by the parents, it is important for the therapist to be aware that parents who bring their child to psychotherapeutic treatment do so primarily because they feel helpless. People often protect themselves against perceived impotence and helplessness with hostile fantasies of omnipotence. These hostile feelings towards the child who is no longer functioning properly are difficult for the parents to bear, and lead to feelings of guilt.

One way of disposing of such unbearable feelings of guilt and self-accusation is to project the aggression into the outside world. A primitive defence mechanism like this leads to some parents blaming not themselves (this remains unconscious), but other persons, such as teachers or therapists, for the fact that their child has problems. They claim the treatment is "not right", it is "the wrong therapist", or she is "not skilled enough". Unconscious feelings of guilt may often also cause the parents to feel that they do not even have the right to bring up a child, and anxiety that people might want to take it away from them.

In view of these parental feelings of guilt and failure, the omnipotent defence and the externalisation of these feelings, it is not easy to form the trusting therapeutic alliance with the parents which is indispensable for the treatment to succeed. It is also possible that parents will unconsciously try to prevent the therapist from building up a trusting and meaningful relationship with the child. In such constellations, parents may even strive unconsciously for the therapy to fail by undermining its successes: for example, by blocking the child's separating to form a close relationship with the therapist. The parents may unconsciously feel they have "won" if even the therapist cannot help the child's problems.

In such constellations, therapists can often tend to concentrate on the child alone, and to ally themselves unconsciously with the child against the "bad parents". However, for good work with the parents as part of PaCT, it is essential to apply the basic principle of understanding unconscious conflicts that underpin observable behaviour to the parents as well as to the child, particularly where a negative transference is hindering the success of therapy (Table 9).

Case study Jenny, nine years old

Jenny's mother had brought her up on her own, and in her own childhood had experienced a strict and rigid mother, who demanded that

Table 9.   Recommendations on dealing with accusations directed at the therapist.

- Don't take accusations personally, even if you feel them to be unjustified or even outrageous!
- Understand that you are a transference object!
- In case of being offended by the parents, don't react by withdrawing, but try to understand the parents' accusations as a defence against intolerable feelings or ideas.

she be ordered and disciplined and reject anything instinctual. Her own father had "never been there" and probably was not sufficiently triangulating to the mother–child relationship. In the course of PaCT therapy, the mother could not bear the fact, as she saw it, that Jenny enjoyed more empathic attention than she did (on the basis of the number of parent sessions compared to the sessions with the child, 1:4). She was jealous of her daughter. As a result, the mother defended against her needy desire to be allowed "to play" light-heartedly, and not "always having to do everything myself", as she fantasised was the case for her daughter in therapy, by directing serious accusation at the therapist: the therapy "wasn't achieving anything" and "the child carried on being a handful at home". She herself felt she was just giving out and getting nothing back. She had turned up for many diagnostic examinations but had "got no help" in return from the therapist. Only when the therapist reflected on her feelings of anger and disappointment towards the mother in her countertransference, and was able to understand the mother's accusations as a defence against her own desires for attention and help, could she empathise with the mother and interpret her feelings. In doing so, she was able to maintain her contact with the mother, and the working alliance was also strengthened by the therapist communicating to the mother that she took her distress seriously.

Therapist: "I have the impression that you feel you aren't getting enough help from me, a feeling that perhaps is familiar from your relationship with your own mother. You are annoyed, as you were with your mother, that you always have to do everything for yourself and that there is no space for fun."

It was only after this interpretation that the mother was able to confide in the therapist, who, in turn, could then draw parallels between the child's problems and those of the mother. The mother's negative transference to the therapist was thus transformed into a progressive, development-promoting intervention.

To understand the parents' negative transference to the therapist, knowledge of the parents' individual biographies, gained in sessions 2 and 3, is indispensable.

Many aspects of work with the parents have a basis in psycho-analytic object relations theory. An object relations theoretical per-spective highlights the importance of the other, the object in the models of aetiopathogensis and therapy. Going beyond the drive psychological perspective, object relations theory also accounts for the responses of the other/the object to the drive-determined activity of the subject. These others are, for instance, the parents. Parental representations and specific parental conflict solutions affect the child's psycho-emotional and psychosexual development. The direction of this influence is based on a hierarchical principle: parents have a decisive influence on the development of the child's personality and its psychological structure, while the child's influence on his parents has no structure-forming character.

It is also important here, too, that we work with the parents as real persons. To understand the child's symptoms psychoanalytically it is vital to distinguish between the parents in their function as primary objects and as real persons. The primary object is not solely the real object experienced during early in childhood, but an inner representation assembled from different facets. It is made up of the child's drive (i.e., the extent of the child's constitutive aggressivity and libido towards the early object), the personality of the mother and the father (i.e., the way in which they react to this onslaught of the child's drives), as well as the mother's/father's own desires and anxieties, which result from their experiences and memories from their own childhoods.

CHAPTER SEVEN

The therapeutic phases of PaCT

The initial period

In the initial phase of treatment (Table 10), the therapist's primary task is to establish a good therapeutic alliance. Supportive interventions are available to help here (Barber, Crits-Christoph, & Luborsky, 1996; Crits-Christoph, Crits-Christoph, Wolf-Palacio, Fichter, & Rudick, 1995) if the child is too anxious or inhibited. Fundamentally, it is the patient, in our case the parents and child, who determines the topic of the session. It is the therapist's job to explore the stressors, perceptions, and feelings that accompany the child's

Table 10. The initial period (sessions 1–5).

Psychopathological/psychodynamic findings:
- Observation: the child in the context of his relationships (with parents, teachers, peers, etc.)
- Diagnostic dialogue with the child: this should be unstructured and centre on the child's narrative; it should not be an interrogation, and no pressure should be applied to obtain information. It is also important to note what happens in the transference
- Diagnostic "trialogue" with the parents

symptoms. In an atmosphere of trust, the therapist encourages the parents and the child to talk about their relationships with other people, and then tries to identify the relationship topic that, from a transgenerational viewpoint, serves as a conflict focus, and to relate the symptoms to it. The child's problems are, thus, always understood as a precipitate of these interpersonal problems and intrapsychic conflict topics.

In the initial phase, the therapist's task is to generate a hypothesis about the role that the parents' representations play for the child's symptoms. The therapist must simultaneously pay attention to the parents (their concerns, the reconstruction of their biography, and their non-verbal manifestations of unconscious conflict material), and to what the child says and does. We are investigating the child's symptom in terms of its function for the parents as well as for the child.

The child's symptoms might also serve the parents as a defence against their own feelings of anxiety, depression, or guilt. The objective of this initial phase is to develop the focus in such as way as to clarify the transgenerational conflict that limits the parents' understanding of the child. Further objectives are to explain the child's current conflict in terms of the parents' past and present, to expand the parents' perception of their child, and to improve their empathy with him or her.

Explanation using a case study

Vivien, eight years old (first session)

Vivien would not allow the therapist to speak or play with her alone, and neither would she let her mother to speak to the therapist alone. She was not interested in any of the toys that the therapist offered her. She sat at the table with her mother and the therapist, letting neither of them out of her sight, and not daring to explore the room in case she missed something that was going on. She clung to her chair and listened suspiciously to her mother and the therapist. In the counter-transference, the therapist immediately felt an impulse to engage with her actively, to be motherly and structuring, so that Vivien would be protected from uncomfortable feelings like a "fragile little bird". When the therapist explained that she would like to talk and play with her alone next time to get to know her, Vivien reacted as though the therapist had attacked her. She turned away, hid her head in her hands, cried, and broke off contact with both her mother and the therapist. The therapist felt guilty without knowing why.

The countertransference was invaluable in the diagnostic process. Why did Vivien provoke such a strong feeling in the therapist? What did this interaction have to do with her inner world? Did the countertransference contain identification with the subject? Did Vivien herself feel guilty about something, perhaps only able to manage unbearable feelings of guilt by placing them in the other person through projective identification? When her father left the family for another woman, had she possibly asked herself: what terrible thing have I done to make my father suddenly reject my mother and me like this? Am I a bad girl?

Important: The first PaCT session is not about gathering a detailed case history or making a diagnosis by means of psychological testing! A detailed diagnostic procedure should have been carried out before referral for PaCT, including a symptom-orientated interview, psychopathological findings, systematic case history, and psychological tests.

The psychodynamic examination situation helps the therapist to form a picture of the child and the possible conflicts in his/her life, and to draw up initial psychodynamic hypotheses. The psychodynamic findings are based on the questions and topics set out in Table 11.

Designing the initial phase: sessions 4–5 with the child

The squiggle game

A tried and tested way of establishing contact with the child and his inner world is Winnicott's squiggle technique (Günter, 2007; Winnicott, 1971b), in which the therapist draws a squiggle that the child then continues. The therapist connects these spontaneous drawings with her own thoughts developed from her internal functioning, and, thus, moves towards an understanding of the child's unconscious contents as revealed in the drawing. In this way, the therapist can try to communicate with the child about his unconscious desires and fears. Meanwhile, the child becomes familiar with the psychoanalytic method from the first session with the therapist in an intermediate space (Winnicott, 1971b), and at the same time is able to experience being understood by the therapist. Winnicott described the squiggle game thus:

Table 11.   Psychopathological findings (psychodynamic).

Drive/motivation (primary–secondary process):

- Is the drive bound to a particular position of infantile sexuality (oral, anal, phallic-genital)?
- How much delay of gratification is possible for the child?
- How rigid and inflexible is the form in which the drive is satisfied?

Superego formation:

- Ego functions (imagination, memory, cognition, synthesis, and integration; the control of motor functions, impulses, perceptual functions, capacity for anticipation)
- Defence mechanisms: maturity of organisation (i.e., whether dominated by repression or splitting, projection)
- Lines of development, according to Anna Freud (1965): development of cleanliness, ability to play, quality of play (imaginative or monotonous, compulsive?)
- Levels of conflict : intrapsychic/interpersonal

> The squiggle game is simply one way of getting into contact with a child. What happens in the game and in the whole interview depends on the use made of the child's experience, including the material that presents itself. In order to use the mutual experience one must have in one's bones a theory of the emotional development of the child and of the relationship of the child to the environmental factors. (Winnicott, 1971b, p. 3)

The following case study shows how to proceed if the child is very defensive during the first sessions, and finds it difficult to communicate something about its inner world. The squiggle game can give us important information, which we collect at the level of the child's *material* in order to formulate the focus according to ToP (see Chapter Six, under "The significance of the setting", pp. 143–144).

Explanation using a case study

Ferdinand, six years old

Ferdinand, aged six, was brought for treatment with PaCT by his parents because of his extreme temper tantrums at kindergarten, during which he kicked and hit out wildly at other children. When he felt neglected or constrained by the teachers, he bit them so hard that they bled. At the time of Ferdinand's birth, his mother also had a child she had adopted ten months previously, and she reported that she had felt so overwhelmed that she often broke down in tears or was irritated and lost her temper.

Ferdinand beamed when the therapist came to fetch him from the waiting room. His mother would only allow him to leave her if he gave her a goodbye kiss. Ferdinand complied. Then he came along with the therapist.

He quickly made contact, saying he would like to play with the ball today, but did not follow the rule of taking his shoes off when stepping on to the play carpet. The therapist thought he wanted to show that he could leave the room again quickly. Playing in close proximity to the therapist on the play carpet appeared to make him uneasy. Thus, he sent a clear signal to the therapist that he wanted to play ball. The therapist thought that he was more comfortable with the movement and spatial distance from her in the ball game (they were about 2.5 m apart).

He told her that it was his birthday today, and when she congratulated him was clearly pleased and told her about his new toys. The therapist had the impression that he found it easier to talk to her if he could move around and keep his distance from her while he was doing so.

The therapist suggested the squiggle game, explained it briefly and they started to play.

Ferdinand made the therapist's first squiggle into an "African seal in the air", "a cloud sea-lion", he called out happily (Picture 1). She thought the picture looked like an embryo, the "cloud sea-lion" floating softly and defencelessly in the air, as if it had not yet found its place. Ferdinand did not want to say much about it, and asked the therapist to carry straight on.

The therapist found the defencelessness of the "cloud sea-lion" very touching, as Ferdinand was also showing her that he, too, often felt at someone's mercy and that his rages and motor excitability at kindergarten were often a manoeuvre to face this fear of "falling apart".

The therapist acquired a sense Ferdinand's early fear of falling apart or becoming fragmented at a point when he did not feel held by his overwhelmed mother.

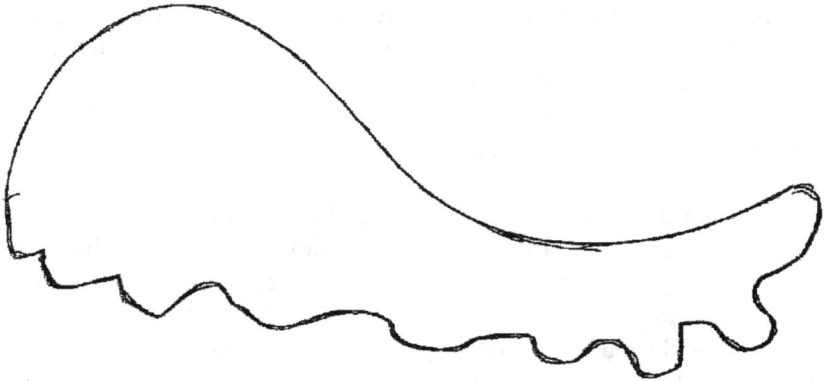

Picture 1.   The "cloud sea-lion".

Ferdinand turned the second squiggle into a submarine (Picture 2). There were two people in it, who could "look out at the land". One could observe while the other could steer the submarine.

Ferdinand appeared to want to rescue himself from going under and from the falling apart of his psychic existence by taking over the rudder.

He explained to the therapist how the one who was watching the land climbed up the steps out of the peephole, and showed her exactly

Picture 2.

where the other one was standing and taking charge of the steering. Then he thought of a television story in which two cartoon characters were in a boat and one forgot to steer. They "almost rammed a bridge", said Ferdinand excitedly. The therapist thought: if someone uses their motor functions to protect the ego (as Ferdinand did at kindergarten) there is a danger of collisions with the object. The object libido could thus come into conflict with the ego libido.

Then Ferdinand said, "Oh, I forgot, there are also torpedo holes, they can shoot out of there, they need something to eat, seals and so on."

The phallic "shooting" allowed him to compensate for the lack of support from his mother.

At the same time, Ferdinand also seemed to want to be "held" by the controlling object, in a way that would enable him explore freely, to look around the world, without "biting down firmly" on something, as he did literally with his kindergarten teacher, in order to defend against his fear of falling apart.

Was he in the process of moving beyond the symbiotic relationship with his mother? The two of them defended themselves by "shooting" at the outside world, and finally using the torpedoes to get food. But if one did not "steer" one's impulses, an accident or collision might occur.

Out of the third squiggle, Ferdinand drew a "stag cloud", which really did look like a deer's antlers (Picture 3). But then he said, "I don't want to tell you any more now." This picture appeared to frighten him, and he tried to avoid talking about it. The therapist tried to persuade him to tell her something about the deer or the "stag cloud", what ideas he had about it, and whether he liked deer? Lost in thought, she began to draw the outline of a deer with eyes and a mouth, thus breaking her own rules. She caught herself being intrusive and challenging him. The stag was strong and powerful like a father figure. Ferdinand said, "This is boring", and again wanted to deflect attention away from the drawing. Then he said, "When we talk I get hot in my tummy, it's uncomfortable," and showed the therapist his tummy while he stroked it. Then he got up and wanted to return to playing ball.

First he played on his own, quite wildly, making black streaks with his shoes on the therapist's floor. When she pointed this out, he stopped immediately and meticulously rubbed the marks off with his

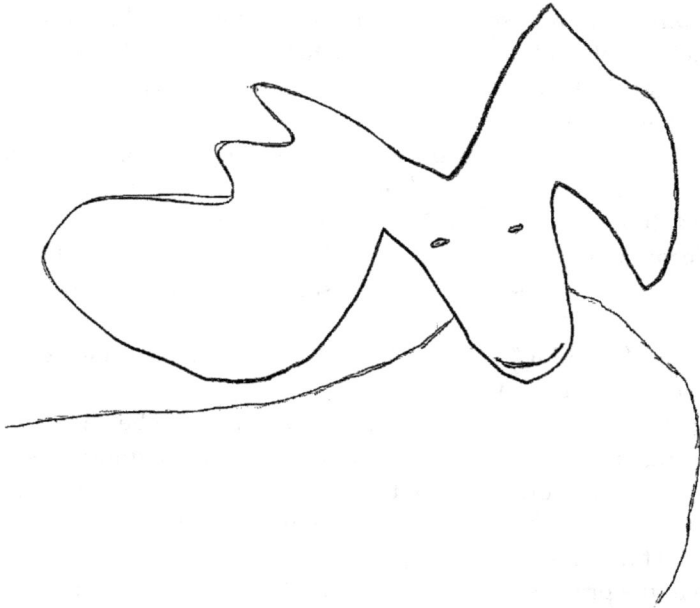

Picture 3.

finger. She interpreted, "You want to make up for the way that you were so wild." Ferdinand nodded. He then asked her to continue playing ball with him. She interpreted to him, "Ferdinand, you find it easier to talk to me if we have some distance from one another and if you can be moving around while we do it." Ferdinand acknowledged, "Yes, but the squiggle game was nice too."

Interpretation

This brief play sequence gave the therapist an insight into Ferdinand's inner world. Ferdinand was preoccupied with issues of identity and delimitation, as well as the regulation of closeness and distance. Becoming close to the therapist through talking made Ferdinand feel physically warm, which made him uneasy. This could be understood as reflecting Ferdinand's fear of losing his differentiation from the object. He experienced this as extremely frightening and precarious, particularly as he was in the process of opening up the significance of the (male) third object and of establishing his identity outside the symbiotic relationship with his mother. His father appeared to him both as rescuer and as someone who threatened to block his oedipal desires to be "alone in the submarine" with his mother. The regulation (steering) of impulses also came up here.

Focus formulation according to ToP

Focus formulated to Ferdinand: "It is important for you to know where your place is. You always want to be the first, because otherwise you are afraid that you will disappear altogether. This makes you angry enough to want to push everyone else away from you."

Considerations of the meaning of the symptom in the family relationships: Immediately after his birth it was difficult for Ferdinand to find a place in the family, since a ten-month-old baby, his adoptive sister, was already there. His mother was not only overwhelmed by this, but also had difficulties in setting her own boundaries from the needs of others. As a result, she was unable to contain Ferdinand's impulses adequately, and, for his part, he did not acquire the ability to regulate them within the relationship to his mother. He used impulsive, physically aggressive behaviour to recreate the boundary between himself and the object. The aggression actually served to ward off fear and to re-establish ego boundaries.

Focus formulated to the parents: "Ferdinand uses his temper tantrums to push people away, because he is not able to detach himself from his Mama in the way that would be appropriate for his age. Being very close to Mama, and therefore small and dependent, makes him feel frightened. This is exacerbated because you as his mother often treat Ferdinand like an adult, and in return he treats you without respect when he sees that you are feeling helpless and overwhelmed. So, it becomes difficult for Ferdinand to find out where he is and discover whether he is already big and strong, like his father, or really still small and dependent."

The middle period

This phase is summarised in Table 12.

Table 12. Overview: the middle phase (Sessions 6–19).

Psychotherapeutic work with the child
(Sessions 7, 8, 9, 11, 12, 13, 15, 16, 17, 19)

- Work on the focus (working through the central conflict):
- Naming the focus at a suitable point in free play
- Circling the focus in analytical work with the child, with the main attention on:
- How does the focus appear in the child's play?
- How can it be communicated to the child in the form of a verbal intervention?
- Testing out possible solutions with the child in free play.
- Being available to the child as a real object, transference object, and developmental object.
- Preparing the child for the fact that the therapeutic contact is time-limited, putting this into language that the child understands: "Today and next week we still have time to play together and tell each other things, but after that we will have our last session and say goodbye to each other."

Accompanying parental work:
(Sessions 6, 10, 14, 18, 22)

- Promoting the parents' insight into the child's inner mental states (mentalization) using events that occur within the relationship between them and the child.
- Explicit formulation of focus in a vivid interpretation as part of the therapeutic work with the parents.
- Strengthening the parents in their parental function.

Sessions 6–19

Each section consists of three sessions with the child in which we focus on the child's central conflict focus. In the accompanying parental work every fourth session, the therapist uses the knowledge she has gained about the child's inner experience from her work with the child and his parents to help the parents towards a better understanding of the child's developmental problems.

In the work with the child, the therapist oscillates between focal and afocal psychoanalytic techniques. She immerses herself in the game and abandons herself to her associations in the "reverie" (Bion, 1962, p. 36), in order to bundle her thoughts into a further focus and to formulate them as an interpretation. During play, the therapist focuses on the child's inner reality and his/her predominant mode of defence.

The therapist always directs her attention to the child's inner experience, which she accesses indirectly through its verbal utterances, stories, play contents, and relationship behaviour. It is vital that the therapist develops an understanding of how libidinal and aggressive impulses, unconscious desires and their defences are depicted within the child's play. The goal of the therapeutic work is to create a link between the child's conflicts and the central conflict topics in the relationship between parents and child, and to integrate them into a focus. The connection between feelings (e.g., "I am sad"), thoughts (e.g., "because Mama/my kindergarten teacher likes my sister/the other children more than me"), and symptom/behaviour (e.g., "and that's why I hit other children, to get back into first place") should be unfolded in play or in words, and thus made conscious. Verbal interventions during play with the child should be directed towards articulating feelings and desires, enabling unconscious conflicts to be made conscious.

The concluding period

Table 13 sets out the work of the final stage of therapy.

The concluding period of therapy with the parents

If the parents have experienced the work with the therapist as useful, this phase will entail mourning the end of this helpful relationship. Without the direct presence of the therapist, but through identification with her therapeutic function, the parents' task is now to consolidate what has been achieved so far.

The penultimate session is the final parent session. Looking back, the therapist spells out her view of the developmental progress that has been achieved in the shared work, as well as describing any continuing blocks to development and the important stages of the therapeutic process. She also warns the parents of potentially difficult developmental steps yet to come. It is important to communicate to the parents that they must continue to keep an eye on the child's

Table 13.   Overview: the concluding period (Sessions 19–25).

Content of the final sessions with the child:
- Preparing to say goodbye and the end of therapy
- Summarising the focus
- Stating explicitly the way in which the child deals with parting from the therapist and the associated affects (such as disappointment, sadness, and anger)
- Often the child defends against the pain of parting in the final sessions, for example, by frequently leaving the room and leaving the therapist alone. This turning of passively suffered into active abandoning can be interpreted to the child by formulating it, for example, thus: "It makes you sad and angry that we're seeing each other for the last time today, and that you can't come again. You would rather run away from me, so that I have to come looking for you and don't forget you!"
- Final session in the therapist–child setting: taking up and circling the focus, mutual looking back on what has happened, and looking forward into the future!

experiences and the behaviours that underlie the symptom, so that the child's development in a healthy direction is encouraged.

Final session in the therapist–child setting

After the final parent session, a last session is held with the child. In the concluding sessions, the therapist symbolically hands the child back to the parents, thus proving to them that they now have the necessary resources (they are "good enough") to continue alone on the journey they have begun together with their child and to consolidate the successful therapy as a family.

In the last session with the child, what has been processed and experienced must be finalised while at the same time directly addressing the topic of parting. It is important to understand the individual way in which the child handles the process of parting in the context of its intrapsychic conflicts and their expression, and to acknowledge what it does as an active and mostly progressive attempt at coping. The management of parting and the associated affects must be discussed with the child in terms of the developed focus.

Explaining the process of parting using a case study

Lena, eight years old

Lena suffered from depressive moods and insecure self-esteem when she began PaCT a year after her parents separated. It quickly became clear that Lena's mother felt exploited by Lena's father and had been unable to process her feelings of sadness and anger towards him. Already, before the separation, Lena's father had been unreliable and rarely available to her. After the separation, in fact, he broke off contact with his daughter for over half a year.

As a consequence, Lena had developed internalising–externalising symptoms consisting of a mixture of self-reproach and self-abasement, pathological lying, difficulties in concentration, and a drastic deterioration in her performance at school.

Course of treatment: In the transference relationship, Lena showed intense annoyance if her therapist was even a few minutes late, and would criticise her severely. In the course of treatment, the transference developed a sado-masochistic pattern. Lena wanted the therapist to like her, and submitted to her devotedly. The therapist understood her corresponding countertransferential feelings of being powerful, elevated, and courted as an identification with Lena's father-object. In contrast to her submissiveness, Lena began to torment and subdue the therapist, by ordering her to play her maid and to carry out unexpected and impossible tasks. The therapist felt helpless and worthless in the complementary identification in her countertransference, and despairing annoyance as well. She was able to use the developing transference to understand Lena's desire to be loved by her father, and her anger at being at the mercy of her father's disregard. She turned this anger against herself as a means of holding on to the relationship to her father. Thus, an introjective depression developed. Once, when playing in the treatment room with playdough and water, she refused to let herself be stopped from "splashing". She disregarded the therapist's attempt at setting limits, leaving her helpless in the face of the mess being made. Lena told her to be "the servant", who had to obey the tyrannical "king" (who was played by Lena herself). Lena enjoyed splashing and smearing the therapist. As a result, the therapist was able to interpret to Lena that this desire to make her angry was related to Lena's anger with her absent father, whom she loved but experienced as unreliable.

Concluding period with Lena: Five sessions before therapy was due to end, the therapist introduced the topic of ending the treatment to Lena and her mother (and, shortly after that, to the father as well). Two sessions before the end of therapy, the therapist noticed that when she went to fetch Lena from the waiting room she appeared both submissive and uncertain, but at the same time was reluctant to come with her. The therapist thought that Lena might be trying to cope with the passive experience of being abandoned by carrying out her own active abandonment, so that the therapist would be left alone and Lena would be the one who did not go to her. The therapist also interpreted Lena's submissive and well-behaved attitude as her desire and belief that therapy would continue if only she were good: "Yes, it's stupid that I won't be able to see you any more," said Lena, and suggested playing "splashing again". The therapist then said: "It makes you very angry that our time together here is nearly over, and so you want to splash and annoy me too."

These impulsive acts were, however, well regulated and kept in check in the remaining sessions. The therapist could name both grief and annoyance to Lena. She was sad as well, as she had become very fond of this little girl, whose self-esteem wavered so much and who turned her anger with her father so obviously against herself.

On parting, Lena insisted that the therapist give her something of her own to take away. The therapist was reminded of what Lena's mother and Lena herself had said, and she interpreted, "This is like with Papa. You want him to buy you something nice, as proof that he really loves you." The therapist sensed Lena's despair. The child nodded and started to cry. But she continued to insist that the therapist should give her something, and waited for her goodbye gift. Lena herself had brought the therapist a picture she had painted, and some chocolate. The therapist hesitated, but then thought that Lena was in such distress because she was so dependent on this concrete gift (Table 14). Thus, although she considered the treatment to be successful, and that the family would be able to acknowledge the success of therapy and consolidate it, the therapist was left with a feeling of guilt that she had not given Lena enough. The therapist understood this countertransference as identification with the father and also as the result of an aggressive act by him, being repeated in the relationship with the therapist.

Table 14.   Summary: content of the final sessions with the child.

● Prepare for parting and the end of therapy.
● Summarise the focus.
● Explicitly name and acknowledge the way the child manages the process of parting, as well as the associated affects of disappointment, sadness, and anger.

Different ways of saying goodbye

Even if the treatment length has already been extensively discussed with both parents and child, in our experience it is important to remind parents of the end of therapy five sessions before the therapy actively finishes. Depending on where the child is in the process of working through, the therapist and the parents together can decide when to aim for the end of therapy in this previously agreed 20–25 session period. Five sessions before the planned end, at the latest, the parents and child should again be reminded of the date of the last appointment, so that the parting can be sufficiently prepared for. In short-term therapy, the therapist, child, and parents are confronted with the problem of "slow understanding at double speed" (Emanuel, 2011). They face the paradoxical situation that, once the analytical process is under way and the child and its parents have become used to psychoanalytical work, no sooner have they become attuned to the attitude of precise observation and understanding than the process comes to an end. Ideally, the parents themselves will have developed the confidence to continue the process on their own. In our experience, this is often the case for families whose conflicts and their processing were clearly delimited and for whom the focal work led to an improvement in the symptoms (see case studies Julian, Sophie, and Elisabeth, Chapters Twelve, Thirteen, and Fourteen). In these constellations, the therapist's countertransference at the end of therapy can also be used positively. In general, the therapist does not feel guilty and is able to trust the child's further developmental process. These constellations also reassure the therapist that prescribing psychoanalytical short-term therapy had been the right choice. Her feeling at the end of therapy can thus be summarised, "For a while I joined them, accompanying the child's developmental process, and now I'm leaving them to go on their way."

However, there are also cases where, during the termination of therapy, parents become afraid that they will be unable to contain themselves or their child. Some parents defend against the fear of being abandoned by the therapist with anger and reproach. The therapist might equally well feel guilt at not having given the family enough. Here, it is important for the therapist to acknowledge her own feelings of guilt, and recognise that in this case short-term therapy was not sufficient, but was just a "taster" of the psychoanalytical method: in a way, a preparation for long-term therapy. The message to the parents and the child during the final session should then not be that the therapy has failed (and that the therapist, or the child, or the parents "are to blame"), but that the child and his parents may come again, or that the child can enter long-term therapy in which what has already been achieved can be continued.

CHAPTER EIGHT

Summary: therapeutic process of PaCT

The therapist gathers information and significant insights from the first sessions with the parents and with the child (narrative, play behaviour, relationship episodes with the child, counter-transference) making use of evenly suspended attention.

After the five initial sessions, the therapist bundles the material acquired, the developing countertransference and transference, and information from parental sessions and play with the child. (For psychotherapists in training, the focus is formulated in joint intensive supervision during the "focal conference" following the fifth session. Further focal conferences follow the tenth, fifteenth, and twentieth sessions.)

In formulating the focus, the child's intrapsychic level should be linked to the (parent–child) interpersonal level. The psychodynamic hypothesis, consolidated in a focus formulation, should depict the way in which interpersonal conflicts between parents and child intersect with the child's own intrapsychic conflicts. The therapist integrates all this information, these impressions and countertransferential feelings, into a psychodynamic hypothesis, formulated as comprehensibly and succinctly as possible, thus creating a link between the child's symptom and the central transgenerational conflict of the family.

The focus according to ToP is communicated to the parents and the child in the succeeding sessions, using language that is as concrete as possible, and illustrated with examples. After the initial session in the parent–child setting, one or two sessions are held with the parents, and then a few sessions with the child alone to make an assessment and plan the treatment. The focal procedures require concentration on a single conflict level. This means that the central conflict that stands out in the first conversations and sessions with the child and his parents is integrated into a focus. A precise knowledge of the psycho-dynamic basic conflicts and the defences mounted against them is necessary in order for the therapist to recognise unresolved conflicts, one-sided accentuations, or fixations of the personality, or rigid defence mechanisms in the child's material. To understand how conflict underlies the symptom, we have to assume that behind the manifest (play) behaviour there is a latent, unconscious level consist-ing of instinctual desire and defences against it.

Once the focus has been formulated, the therapist uses it during the psychotherapeutic work with the child as a kind of matrix against which it is possible to understand the contents of the child's play. The more precisely the focus is formulated, the more it will reflect the topics that arise in the process of working-through. The rule here is that in free association and in free play in the psychoanalytic work with the child, material emerges to indicate unresolved develop-mental themes and ongoing conflicts. What remains unresolved is revealed in the analytical process. The focus can be modified or refor-mulated whenever fresh knowledge makes possible a better under-standing of the child. The focus initially serves the therapist as an internal aid to understanding, and at a suitable point is communicated to the child and the parents in vivid and everyday language. The focus should always be communicated to the parents where it can be related to the parents' descriptions of relationship episodes with the child. In a similar way, the focus is communicated to the child in the form of a verbal interpretation. Unless the focus is discussed in the context of a play situation, the child will be unable to connect it emotionally to his inner experience.

As treatment goes on, the therapist evaluates the focus and modifies it if necessary. She should reflect continuously on the three points of the triangular *relational symptom*, *therapist–child–parent relationship*, and *the child's material*, thinking about the child and his situation, and identifying the central conflict as it comes to light.

Therapy with the child should then work through the child's central conflict, improving his defences and increasing the flexibility of his representations and conflict resolution. The focus is communicated at a suitable point in free play in the form of an interpretation relating directly to the experience and the expression of the conflict. Taking psychoanalytical therapeutic concepts as a starting point, we assume two things: that the therapy aims to change the child's mental representations and, thus, its cognitive–emotional styles; and that psychoanalytical work with the parents aims to improve their insight into their child's inner mental states, that is, the parents' mentalization about their child.

The focus is communicated to the parents in the course of sessions 6, 10, 14, 18, and 22 as a relationship topic, again using everyday, concrete language. Our interpretations are based on the parental narratives of relationship episodes with the child, so that the parents' insight into the child's inner world, where the child's behaviour has its root, is improved. To do this, we need to promote the parents' ability to adopt a perspective that takes account of the child's inner states, inner experience, and motives.

The model of the *triangle of psychodynamic constellations* (ToP) then helps us to structure a process that integrates the complex information provided by the parents, the child, and our own perceptions, developing an understanding of the child's symptoms as related to underlying unconscious conflicts.

In short-term therapeutic work, the therapist is always faced with the difficulties of speeding up the diagnostic process without impairing her ability to "dream" ("reverie", Bion, 1962, see Chapter Two, section headed "The container-contained model of Wilfred R. Bion", pp. 53–57). Through her psychoanalytical listening and observation, and her evenly suspended attention, she must first try to access preconscious conflicts that present on the surface of the material, and then—using a focal technique—bundle this material relatively quickly by formulating a focus that serves as a psychodynamic hypothesis. She must let herself become involved in the child's play, while simultaneously keeping a distance from it and from the shared interaction in order to introduce a psychodynamic level of understanding.

CHAPTER NINE

Prerequisites for the therapist

P articular prerequisites are required of the therapists who perform PaCT. As this is a short-term therapy, the therapist must be able to acquire an "accelerated" understanding within a short timeframe, without this impeding her ability to respond.

The psychotherapeutic concept of psychoanalytical short-term therapy (PaCT) reflects classical psychoanalytical treatment methods. Nevertheless, the following points remain distinctive.

1. The therapist is much more active in psychoanalytical short-term therapy than in traditional psychoanalysis, both in terms of making verbal utterances and of observing the interactions between the therapist and child, parents and child, and parents and therapist. Moreover, the theoretical assumptions that implicitly accompany the therapy mean that the therapist must be more active in questioning, researching, and formulating psychodynamic hypotheses that could serve as a basis for inter-pretation.

2. Apart from this, the therapist also works more selectively. She limits her interpretations to the conflicts between mother/father and child and their equivalent in the mother's/father's/child's

biography. She also limits her interpretations in the therapeutic work with the child to the most obvious intrapsychic conflicts.

PaCT should be performed only by therapists who have been trained in psychoanalysis (if possible, of both children and adults). Psychotherapists undergoing advanced training can also use PaCT if their own training analysis is sufficiently advanced and they are authorised to carry out treatment of children under regular supervision. A therapist's own training analysis provides the basis for making use of his or her own countertransference in a targeted and disciplined way. For therapists in training, we recommend supervision in focal conferences (Klüwer, 2000). Here, a therapist can present her case, and the psychodynamic focus she has identified can be evaluated and modified if necessary as part of the supervision. A further prerequisite, which child psychotherapy has often tended to neglect, is that the therapist must be able to enter into mutual, triadic relationships with the family members and not just establish a relationship with the child alone. Triadic capacity should therefore be fostered in the training to become a psychotherapist for children and adolescents.

To perform PaCT, it is important that the therapist has a basic psychoanalytical training, as a solid knowledge of the subject's underlying conflict, his fantasies and mental mechanisms, and of the phases of psychosexual development and the ways in which infantile sexuality are expressed, are prerequisites for psychoanalytic understanding and interpretation. It is equally important to maintain the ability to work focally, that is, "keeping hold of the thread" and concentrating on the subject's central themes. Another goal of PaCT is to help the parents' conscious and unconscious representations of their own parental function, of the child, and the parent–child relationship become more flexible. By changing the child's and the parents' representations in this way, the child can further its developmental possibilities appropriately, without identifying with the parents' malign projections and without turning undesired aspects of his self-related negative affects aggressively towards himself.

CHAPTER TEN

Limitations of a short-term psychotherapeutic approach

The treatment guideline in PaCT that we have developed fits within the tradition of psychoanalytical short-term therapy, with a treatment duration of 20–25 sessions and a low treatment frequency of once-weekly appointments. PaCT can be used to treat children with various symptoms (behavioural disorders, "hyperactivity", neurotic relationship, and other disorders), if anxiety and/or depressive moods have played an important part in the genesis of the symptoms. In the outpatient child psychiatric and psychotherapeutic clinics we meet children and their parents who report a wide range of difficulties and problems. The family is often so fraught with psychological distress that it is difficult to work on eliminating specific symptoms in the usual disorder-specific procedure. In view of the abundance of problems described by the family, clinicians often do not know which symptom they should identify as the main symptom, and which family and interpersonal problems they should define as the main problem, because the stresses and difficulties are so complex.

The concept we present in PaCT is intended to provide first aid for psychotherapists, particularly those in training, in the form of a treatment guideline. It aims to provide concrete instructions on how to understand a complex problem. Taking the focus concept of the *triangle of psychodynamic constellations* (ToP) as a basis, the therapist in training will be empowered to use the focus to develop a profound understanding of the problem with which he or she can work on the processing of the child's intrapsychic problems and the family's interpersonal conflicts.

As it is effective both for children with anxiety and depressive symptoms and for those with accompanying behavioural problems, PaCT is suitable for treating many of children and their families who present at child psychiatric and psychotherapeutic practices and outpatient clinics. These children often also suffer from structural deficits or mentalization disorders. Experienced child analysts will ask why we are presenting a guide to short-term therapy, since experience shows that structural changes may be made only over time as part of a long-term treatment.

We assume that the different phenomenologies of depressive symptoms in childhood follow different aetiological paths. A depressive phenotype may be the expression of a neurotic conflict, or of a disorder in the ability to mentalise—that is, a structural disorder. If emotional symptoms are strongly associated with familial or individual risk factors (e.g., the parents' serious psychological illness, chronic family conflict, sustained neglect of the child, etc.), a longer therapeutic intervention may be necessary. In children who are exposed to severe psychosocial stress, and who tend to express their difficulties in action rather than mentally, the effectiveness of short-term therapy may be more limited than in children whose symptoms are connected to a clearly delineated conflict (Target & Fonagy, 1994).

More wide-ranging structural changes require a longer-term therapeutic approach, as has been shown in numerous studies.

As a basis, PaCT prescribes structuring the therapeutic approach into twenty-five sessions, but it is certainly also feasible to apply this approach to therapies where sessions are more frequent or held over a longer period (more than twenty-five sessions), and we would, in fact, encourage this.

In families for whom short-term therapy is not enough, it has nevertheless been shown that they benefit substantially from 20–25 sessions of PaCT, which is shown in a reduction of the symptoms, even if this reduction does not achieve diagnostic remission according to the relevant definitions of diagnosis (*DSM-IV, ICD-10*) after treatment in children with a high starting level of deficit. The aim of PaCT for these families is to promote their interest and motivation for a further, long-term psychoanalytical treatment.

One reason why we have decided on a short-term therapeutic setting is that inexperienced therapists in the child psychiatric services often have had no experience at all of long-term psychotherapeutic treatment, and yet have to perform it as part of their clinical work. We want to give these therapists a tool that makes use of the richness of psychoanalytical theory and practice, without shortening it in its complexity. Even inexperienced therapists, if they have enough self-awareness of evenly suspended attention and under attuned empathy from their own training analysis, can develop an understanding of the child's unconscious conflicts and promote the child's mentalization.

A further reason for choosing a short-term therapeutic setting for PaCT is that short-term therapy is easier to research. Because of the limited number of sessions, PaCT is very well suited for a systematic empirical investigation of its effectiveness in controlled clinical studies.

CHAPTER ELEVEN

Risks and side effects of PaCT

Externalising behaviour by the child

As well as causing an improvement in the symptoms, treatment with PaCT often changes the child's tendency to resolve interpersonal conflicts by turning aggression against himself. This process, however, may be accompanied with an increase in oppositional, externalising behaviour. The parents should be prepared for the possibility that their child may become more bad-tempered or aggressive, having more temper tantrums, or being disobedient. Part of the parent sessions should offer help from the therapist on how to deal with this behaviour. The focus should be particularly on the question of who is troubled by this "side effect" of PaCT. The child might use the shift in behaviour to express his desire to exert more influence on his environment, which is a sign of developmental progress. The child no longer feels at the mercy of conflicts with his environment. In the treatment with PaCT, he has experienced the therapist being able to withstand his aggressive impulses, and will now try to repeat this with his familial relationship objects. We should also explain to the parents that this behaviour might go through phases, and that this may represent important developmental progress.

Attempts by the parents to block the child's efforts towards autonomy (because they fear that the child might distance himself from them) must be worked through in the parent sessions.

Danger of the child's regressive disintegration

It might happen that the contents of an interpretation cause the child such fear that he disintegrates. This is a particular risk for a child who shows structural deficits in self–object differentiation, especially if the therapist focuses on oedipal topics too early on. The child does not yet have the structural prerequisites for this, and is at risk of disintegration and regression.

This in no way means that the therapist should hold back from giving interpretations. Rather, after each interpretation, she should carefully observe what follows it. Are there indications that the child has been able to incorporate the interpretation? Or are there signs that the play is coming off the rails, or the child can no longer control his impulses? It is very important for the therapist to observe what effect her interpretations have. It might happen, for example, that the therapist overestimates the level on which she can make an interpretation, so that the child is unable to integrate it. This is why observation of what happens in the treatment room between therapist and child after an interpretation is of particular significance.

Deterioration in one parent's previously unknown psychopathology:

In rare cases, a previously unknown or ignored parental psychopathology may deteriorate, so that the parental situation destabilises, and possibly leads to breaking off the therapy. Generally, however, the PaCT parent sessions do not aggravate the parental situation even where there is an existing psychopathology in one parent, but, by contrast, tend to bring about stabilisation. In their sessions, the parents receive support in the management of their parental function and their burden is thus eased as well.

Suicidal tendency

In general, any suicidal tendency present in the child will be reduced through PaCT treatment. Suicide attempts in childhood are quite uncommon. In rare cases, however, a suicidal tendency may be reinforced within the framework of PaCT. If a negative therapeutic reaction with predominantly destructive elements should develop in the transference, the destructive impulses cannot be ignored for the sake of pseudo-harmony. Genetic transference interpretations are not appropriate in such cases, as they could destabilise the child. It is, nevertheless, extremely important to name the child's aggression. Where there are indications of an acute suicidal tendency, for example, with striking behavioural changes such as neglect of appearance, giving away personal objects, or an excessive preoccupation with death, the therapist should address this directly with the child. The suicidal tendency often diminishes if the child's negative feelings are addressed in the transference and the child experiences a therapeutic relationship in which the therapist offers appreciation and recognition, combined with acknowledgement of, and space for, the child's destructive feelings. It is important for the therapist to emphasise to the child that she is working for the survival of the relationship. The parents should always be informed if the child shows a suicidal tendency. In severe cases of acute suicidal tendency, the child should be temporarily hospitalised for his own protection.

Risk of boundary violations (narcissistic and/or sexual abuse)

In their therapist, children should find a person who is concerned with their problems and anxieties, but also with their desires. This rapidly produces an intensive relationship between child and therapist. Children are also especially spontaneous in showing their affection for the therapist and often express the desire for physical closeness. There is a danger here that the therapist, because of her own insufficiently worked-through desires for closeness and attention, or because of an unfulfilled desire to have children, will allow the child to get too close. This might lead to an inappropriate intimacy that originates in the therapist. If a child cathects the therapist as a transference object and expresses strong desire for closeness, the therapist might expose herself to an inappropriate intimacy with the child, particularly if she has failed to reflect on her own desires and needs in training analysis and/or supervision. The therapist might accept an invitation to the child's birthday party, for example, thereby creating too much closeness to the child and/or his parents. Children in the age group we treat with PaCT can easily awaken the desire for this "cute little girl/little boy" to be one's own child. The temptation to step out of the analytical role of abstinence is thus particularly great with this age group—especially because the expressions of infantile sexuality have an incremental quality. Equally gradual are the forms of possible abuse, from a narcissistic gesture up to a manifestly sexual encroachment.

This danger is not specific to PaCT, but is present in all psycho-therapeutic procedures and any relationship-orientated work with children. Such therapies should only ever be performed within a well-established, institutionalised framework. The institutionalisation of the psychotherapy enables us to monitor the ethical criteria of psycho-therapy, in which the imperative of abstinence may not be violated under any circumstances. The quality of the training can be monitored through integration into the circle of one's colleagues and supervisors. Candidates for training must, therefore, be prepared for these topics and reflect adequately on their own needs and desires through exten-sive self-examination in training analysis and supervision, so that they do not succumb to the temptation of inappropriate closeness to their patients.

Furthermore, professional bodies, training institutes, and clinical institutes that work psychotherapeutically with children should estab-lish a system of contact persons and procedures to deal with any complaints from parents, children, or colleagues.

PART III
CASE STUDIES[3]

CHAPTER TWELVE

Case study 1: Julian, six years old

Relational symptoms

J ulian (six years old) had a marked fear of going to kindergarten. Taking him there often resulted in dramatic scenes in which he clung on to the radiator in the entrance hall, cried, and even vomited. His mother also reported that Julian had no interest in playing with other children.

Therapist–child–parent relationship (countertransference)

Therapist–parent relationship

Independently of one another, father and mother said that they did not want to come to the parent sessions together. The mother said that she suspected that in her presence the father would be too inhibited to speak openly with the therapist. The therapist and the parents therefore came to an agreement that, in addition to the initial parent sessions with the mother, there would be two sessions with the father. The father said he wanted to be available for parent sessions; however, he rarely was, and the therapist had to make strenuous efforts to make appointments with him. In practice, he showed little interest in the parental work.

Julian's parents had separated when he was one year old. Mother was a single parent, was not in paid work, and had not completed professional training, despite obvious above average intelligence. Julian had regular contact with the father, although the mother described him as being disinterested and mildly apathetic. She said quite openly that she did not need anyone except Julian, her "sunshine". There was another son from her first marriage, with whom she had almost no contact. This son had been addicted to drugs since he was fourteen years old.

In the first contact with the mother, she spoke about her child in a tender voice, very lovingly and sensitively. At the same time there was something about her that highlighted her independence, and she often seemed to be crossing boundaries and expressing some kind of aggression towards the therapist. She stated that she did not need therapy herself, as she had already "processed" the traumatic experiences of her childhood and adolescence. In the parental sessions, she hardly gave the therapist a chance to speak, often finishing her sentences. This provoked feelings of anger in the therapist. She felt cut off and rendered impotent because she had no place in the mother–child dyad. The mother also emphasised that Julian did not enjoy coming to the therapist. The therapist sensed the mother's jealousy when Julian was alone with her. At the end of each of the first sessions, the mother burst into the treatment room to fetch Julian in a way that the therapist experienced as an attack. The mother seemed unable to bear her son being with the therapist, and so could not allow him to experience separation from her.

In the contact with the father, the therapist experienced a good-natured, large-framed man, who spoke lovingly and with interest about his son. He reported that he had already felt shut out of the dyadic relationship by the mother during Julian's infancy. He now regretted that he had given up custody at that time. At the same time, the therapist felt that his relationship with his son was much more distanced than that of the mother, and she began to wonder whether Julian also sensed that he had a far more existential significance for his mother than for his father, who was leading his own, quite distinct life. The therapist also noticed that her own relationship with the father was more distanced and passive than with the mother. It was

as if the therapist had only a negligible, or even questionable, significance for him.

Therapist–child relationship

In contact with Julian: Whenever his mother was present, Julian
demonstrated to the therapist that he did not like coming to see her.
However, when he was alone with her, she could sense his curiosity
and pleasure in the contact. Nevertheless, he immediately indicated to
the therapist that her clumsy Lego-Duplo toys were not good enough
for him, and brought his own along, "the little Legos for bigger children". Although age-appropriate, the therapist's clumsier figures and
bricks were apparently not of interest. He made it clear that he did not
want to play with the more childish toys.

As much as he did not want to show interest in the therapist's toys,
he did not want his mother to notice that he was interested in the therapist: before the second session on his own with the therapist he looked
at her—unnoticed by his mother—through the window of the waiting
room, looking enthusiastic and happy. In the presence of his mother,
while they were saying hello, Julian made a gesture of shooting the
therapist, at which the mother said, "You shouldn't shoot people!"
Nevertheless, the therapist had the feeling that the mother, in fact,
obviously enjoyed his destructive gesture towards the other woman.

Material of the child

In free play, Julian dominated the therapist and relegated her to a
passive and helpless position. The therapist's toys were only allowed
to do what he dictated, leaving the therapist feeling trapped and
powerless. Over and over again her toys were switched, shot,
tortured, and bombed to death. The experience was of a monotonous,
cruel game, with no room left for her to manoeuvre. Julian was the
lord who dominated her, and she his slave, with whom he could do
what he liked. It appeared that the therapist and her reactions were of
no interest to him. She felt robbed of all her functions as a subject, and
experienced his wild playing as an attack on her thought process.

When the therapist wanted to talk to Julian, he rummaged noisily
in the toy box. He tried to make her nervous by throwing everything

about the room and destroying the Lego-Duplo doll's house with great relish. Bombs and cannons were constantly exploding. He told her to be quiet, and forbade her from making written notes during the session, threatening that otherwise "he would go away".

Psychoanalytic understanding of the therapist–child relationship (transference relationship)

Julian apparently did not want to allow the relationship with the therapist to be important for him and, thus, for her to become an important third party in his life. To counter his fear of her, he made her into a partial object robbed of speech, which he could have at his command. The therapist wondered whether Julian was repeating the relationship with his father in the transference with her. He took away her potency, her competence, and her central instrument: the spoken and written word. Thus, he castrated the therapist. She suspected that he was seeking and simultaneously fearing her as the phallic father, the symbolic third person in the symbiotic-appearing mother–child dyad. She, as the third person in Julian's relationship world as well as the spoken word as third party, was forbidden by Julian.

He fended off his own castration anxiety by castrating the therapist. The defence mechanism expressed itself in a reversal of passive to active, which prevented this fear becoming conscious. Julian avoided experiences with third, triangulating objects (therapist, other children, kindergarten) so as not to be confronted with the castration anxiety. In his fantasy, he had already beaten his real father and was now afraid of his father's revenge. The potential danger of aggression from the counterpart provoked enormous fear in him. In a contraphobic defence manoeuvre, he turned himself into the one who set limits and controlled the therapist.

He was angry with the therapist because she decided on the end of the session or the end of treatment, and thus constrained his primary-process desires and childish fantasy of omnipotence.

Theoretical considerations

According to Lacan, through the father's "No" ("*le non du père*") the child receives the father's "Name" ("*le nom du père*") and is, thus, assigned a place within the symbolic order. By playing with this homophony, Lacan emphasises the simultaneous legislative and prohibitive functions of the symbolic father (Lacan, 1953, p. 230). Accepting the No, that is, the restriction, would mean that the child must limit his childish fantasies of omnipotence and claim to the mother. On the other hand, the father also names the child, giving it a position within the symbolic order and situating it within the generational and gender boundaries. Thus, the restriction is associated with a gain in subjectivity and relativisation in the relationship to the mother. At the same time, the dyad loses the dangerous possibility of dissolving the boundaries between subject and object. Fears of fragmentation, meaning the child's fears of merging his contours with the pre-oedipal mother and forfeiting his own boundaries, are reduced by the presence of the father as a symbolic third party. However, being situated within the symbolic is only guaranteed if the child gives up his incestuous desires and acknowledges the father's incest prohibition.

According to Lacan, the Oedipus complex should be understood as a metaphor for the prohibitive and, at the same time, legislative function of the phallic other. It indicates that which the child must reject in order to obtain the status of a subject. The symbolic father establishes the law and uses it to regulate the oedipal desire for the mother; in this way he becomes involved in the dyadic relationship with the mother and introduces a necessary symbolic distance between mother and child. Where the name of the father is excluded or discarded, the speech cannot be meaningful, the threat of the destruction of language brings with it the possibility of psychosis (Lacan, 1993).

Focus

Julian and his mother defended against the developmental process of letting go by establishing a relationship-symptom: fear of the kindergarten. Here, the child's unconscious wish corresponds with that of the mother: both wanted, and at the same time feared, giving up the pre-oedipal internal merging. This is why the child's symptom was not just the expression of the oedipal anxiety of being castrated by a punishing third person (e.g., the father), but also of the mother's fear of being alone, which she experienced as irreversible and existentially threatening, if the child turned towards others—as symbolised by attending kindergarten.

Julian's fear of the kindergarten was of the third party who sets limits, but, thereby, also introduces him into a symbolic order. In the wishes of the mother, Julian was to be her better partner and make good all the negative experiences in her life, like a child "Messiah". As a child, Julian could not possibly satisfy this demand. Yet, at the same time, it confirmed his childish fantasies of omnipotence and oedipal megalomaniac fantasies, failing to set them appropriate limits.

At kindergarten he saw his megalomania under threat. Being one of many scared him, as it put at risk his position as the most important person for his mother.

He defended against his fear of the restricting third party, the symbolic father, by refusing to enter the kindergarten, vomiting and saying, "I hate kindergarten!"

Julian's development-inhibiting symptom of not wanting or being able to go to kindergarten was an impressive expression of the conflict in which he found himself. Although the father and his symbolic significance bestows subject status, that is, boundedness, this relativises the child's significance as the only object that the mother loves. For Julian, acknowledging the significance of the third party also meant acknowledging a power that set limits to his childish fantasy of omnipotence. Julian should have gone through a mourning process in which he became aware that he was not the only important person for his mother. However, as the mother did not represent a "third party" internally, but, because of her own traumatic experiences of "boundary-crossing third parties", saw her relationship with the child as the only fulfilment in her life, there was in reality no one who could have taken on this function for mother and child. Julian had not had the experience of being shut out in the oedipal triangle, together with the experience of being rescued from his pre-oedipal merging with his mother. Therefore, encounters with third parties triggered massive anxiety in Julian (i.e., of being punished by the third party for his amorous desires towards his mother), which he defends against contraphobically, by demonstrating to his counterpart that he is the stronger.

Communication of the focus to the mother

"Julian has not yet had much experience of people other than you. For you, your son is the centre of your life and he can see how important he is to you. Because you live alone with Julian and do not have a partner or a job, Julian experiences himself as being something very special. He does not have to share you with anyone, and is always together with you. At kindergarten he is less important for the other children and he senses that. Through a lack of experience of third parties and, thus, of experiences where he is not always at the centre of people's attention but is just one of many, contact with others, like his peers, is a source of great anxiety for him. He is afraid of being humiliated, and no longer being the most important person. He is also uncertain of how to behave with his peers, because he has had so little contact with other children up to now. Therapy is giving Julian the experience of a third person—me as therapist—whom he does not know as well as he knows you and for whom he is not the most important person. This may exacerbate the conflict at first, and bring out feelings of anxiety in Julian."

"You may also want to protect yourself and Julian from the world out there, in which bad things happen. But being isolated with him, even if it initially seems the best thing for both of you, will have a very negative effect on his development. It is also important that you as his mother help him to have regular contact with his father."

Communication of the focus to the father

"Julian and his mother, with whom he lives, have a very close relationship with each other. You may feel shut out of that relationship. Because you find this painful, you don't actively seek contact to your son. But, as his father, you are an important person who can show him the world and with whom—as he becomes more independent from his mother—he can have experiences that are important for his development. You should resume regular contact, which you actually want. But also it may be that Julian is afraid of this. We can talk about this fear in the parent sessions."

Communication of the focus to Julian

"It frightens you if someone is stronger than you, because then you think that you aren't special any more, and realise you are very small.

So you are scared of going to kindergarten, because you're afraid that someone there might be stronger than you are. You like coming here to play, but at the same time it frightens you, because then you're no longer totally there for your mother. When I want to talk to you, you're afraid that we will talk about all the difficult feelings and then I will go away and won't be here to fulfil your wishes."

Treatment plan

First, techniques to promote mentalization were applied, so that Julian could eliminate his fear of contact with the therapist (the phallic father, the third person) and get used to the experience of separation. This was done during play by carefully mentioning affective states of the toys in the pretend mode.

The therapist allowed herself to become involved in countertransference while at the same time reflecting on it, managing to stay attuned to the child's communication level. The annoyance that the therapist felt in the countertransference about the expected loss of her own subjecthood was first internally represented and understood as concordant transference, in order to be turned into a verbal intervention at a suitable point. The child's annoyance at being restricted by the therapist was verbalised.

In such situations, the therapist thus repeatedly named the focus to Julian, adapted to the play context: "If you are always the stronger one and can always knock me out, then you don't need to be frightened." At the same time, regular therapeutic work processed the central conflict of mother and child by verbalising the fear of separation/castration anxiety, while experience of separation from the mother in therapy represented a kind of "exposure" to a third party.

The accompanying regular parental work was intended to help the mother develop a shared understanding that the child's fear of separation was her own separation problem, which had already been expressed with her first son. That son had probably solved his autonomy–dependency conflict by developing an addiction.

In work with the mother, the therapist attempted to develop the focus that, for Julian, contact with third parties, for example, his peers, was frightening, because he lacked experience of separation and autonomy and, thus, of not being at the centre of attention.

In addition, the mother (and the father) were to be strengthened in their parental function, and given advice on helping Julian to become more independent. The therapist offered understanding and contained the mother's fears of being alone. In addition, she promoted the mother's perception of Julian as developing increasing separation and independence from herself, and to tolerate it.

When the focus was communicated, the mother reacted as if the therapist was saying something that she herself had already thought. The mother said she often felt disappointed by other people. She well understood that Julian could not remain with her forever, but she found it difficult, as he felt like a part of herself. She did notice how firmly Julian clung to her. She knew that this was not good, and was also afraid that Julian could develop in the same way as his older, drug-addicted brother. Quite soon after the initial sessions, she reported to the therapist that she had a new partner, whom Julian had immediately taken to. The therapist was surprised and asked herself whether the mother was reporting this relationship in order to show that she was working with her and was now allowing relationships between Julian and third parties. Her impression was that the mother felt guilty about Julian because she realised that her own fear was inhibiting her son's development. Was she now trying to make everything better by rapidly entering a relationship with a third party? The new relationship lasted only a few weeks. The therapist understood this abrupt formation and breaking off of attachment as an enactment by the mother. In later work with the mother, she was able to acknowledge that this relationship had been an effort towards "normality" in the family, as she put it. But now she knew that the problem lay deeper, and she actually did not want anyone close to her except her son; she had not really wanted the new partnership at all. The therapist also saw the negatively coloured descriptions of the mother's new partner as a kind of self-fulfilling prophecy: yet another new third person who turned out to be a disappointment, confirming her unconscious dyadic relationship pattern of being safe and happy with her son alone. The therapist did not, however, express this thought to the mother, as she suspected that at such an early stage, and as part of short-term therapy, the mother would not be able to process it or address it meaningfully.

The communication of the focus encouraged the father actively to define contact with his son. The therapist had the impression that it

did him good to have the importance of his function as father emphasised. He said he thought that he had excluded himself from the close
relationship between mother and son out of jealousy, and neglected
his fatherly function—as if he wanted to punish mother and son.

In the initial treatment sessions, Julian reacted very dismissively
whenever the therapist stated the focus. He continued to forbid the
spoken word, thus taking away the therapist's most important treatment tool. Even though he repeatedly said, "Don't talk, or I'll go", the
therapist sensed Julian's increasing interest in her. He was gradually
more able to allow her to be important for him in the relationship.
When she stated the focus: "If you're always the stronger, you don't
need to be frightened of me," he just replied, "I'm never frightened."
Nevertheless, he wanted more contact with the therapist and
frequently expressed the wish that she should come home with him
and visit him and his mother. The therapist understood this as the
child's wish for a third object, which he was slowly getting close to,
but of whom he was still afraid.

The course of treatment is described below.

Course of treatment

Julian brought a little teddy bear to the first session of his treatment,
put it on a chair and pulled the chair very close to both himself and
the therapist. He still tried to appear very "cool". The therapist understood this teddy as a transitional object that he had brought with him
for triangulation, to manage the distress of separation from his mother
and his fear of the therapist. The therapist tried to get into conversation with him about his little companion:

Therapist: "Is he sitting there and watching?"

Julian countered dismissively, "No, he's having a little sleep!"

In the course of treatment he brought a huge number of "wea-
pons", such as sticks or toy guns, to demonstrate his power to the
therapist.

Julian's defence against a father transference, that is, against
acknowledging the symbolising function, appeared very tellingly in
the first sessions of treatment. He repeatedly robbed the therapist of
her key tool, language, and castrated her by repeatedly insisting,
"Don't talk (or write), or I'm going."

He constantly instructed the therapist to play the part of the tormented victim in their games. He threw bombs at her from which she could not escape. The therapist played along, taking on the role of the victim, with a pleased and aggressive affect, laughing and imitating the sound of a shot.

The therapist tried repeatedly at suitable points to interpret Julian's fear of her (and of "the third party"), and to pick up on the focus:

Therapist: "If you're always able to knock me out, because you're always the stronger one, you don't need to be frightened!"

Julian countered, cheekily, "I'm not frightened! I'm only frightened of spiders!" while flinging a stuffed rat disdainfully at the therapist.

In the meantime the therapist was told by the mother that Julian now went to kindergarten regularly, if not with great enjoyment.

Only at a late stage of therapy did it slowly become possible for Julian to allow the third party, spoken language, words, and contact with the therapist.

Julian started one session by talking about a Lego figure that he had brought with him to show the therapist. They both sat on the floor and looked at the figure. Julian controlled the conversation. The therapist succeeded in talking with Julian about his fear of the children at kindergarten. It became clear to her what kind of distress he had when he was one child among many and not the special and important one, as with his mother. The therapist tried again to interpret to him his hypomanic defence, by saying: "If you can't be the strongest or the only one, you get frightened. That's why you don't want to go to kindergarten."

The course of treatment will now be presented, using an actual session. More important than the explicit dialogue was the emotional movement between the therapist and Julian, which indicated that Julian was beginning to become interested in her as a third person, and in the words of understanding as a symbolic third party.

Julian had laid beside him two guns that he had brought to the session.

Julian: "Look, has the robot got a head?" [The therapist allowed herself to become involved.]

Therapist: "He has a head. No, he doesn't have a head! You're right!"

Julian: "Has he got eyes?"

Therapist: "I think so, yes"

Julian: "Has he just got eyes beside his head?"

Julian: "I'll show you! Look, he's got no nose!"

Julian: "It's a robot!"

Therapist: "They [the Lego figures] all have no nose!"

Julian: "He looks cool!"

Therapist: "Is he new?"

Julian: "Scared, isn't he?"

Therapist: "He looks scared, you think."

Julian: "Hm. He was in with the single figures!"

Therapist: "Did you choose him?"

Julian: "Yes!"

Therapist: "You chose the scared one!"

Julian: "No, my mummy chose him." [The therapist wondered whether he was defending against his fear by attributing the choice of the scared figure to his mother].

Julian: "Yes, but you can't see how he is when you buy him, he's in a bag!"

Therapist: "Look, you've got a scared one, but he doesn't look scared from the outside, only when you take his helmet off can you see that he's scared."

Julian: "The face looks a bit fierce."

Therapist: "A bit fierce, but actually you said he looks scared! Maybe it's the same as you, you don't want anybody to ever see that you are scared sometimes."

[The therapist noticed the boy's defence against admitting his fear to the therapist and his efforts not to make conscious his fear of the therapist in the transference relationship.]

Julian: "Look, he's got screws everywhere. Another hand."

Therapist: "He's made of metal. If a bullet hits him, he won't even notice."

Julian: "Hm".

Therapist:	"He's wearing armour."
Julian:	"Yes! and look. I'll take the hand off and then he can shoot!"
Therapist:	"Ah. The hand isn't actually a hand, it's a gun."

. . .

Therapist:	"Do you know what, when we play like this, you're always the one who decides what to play."
Julian:	(demanding from therapist) "One flat square and one small Lego piece!"
Therapist:	"At kindergarten you're sometimes afraid of the other children. You don't like going there."
Julian:	"No, I don't like kindergarten! It's just crap! Look at the clock!" [The therapist understood this reminder of the approaching end of the session as his need to limit her and not to be limited by her.]
Therapist:	"It's not that late!"
Therapist:	"Why is kindergarten crap? Can't you play like you do here?"
Julian:	"I hate all the children at kindergarten! Because I'm not on my own there."
Therapist:	"You're not alone there, ah, that's why."
Julian:	"I want to be on my own."
Therapist:	"You want to be on your own."
Therapist:	"You like playing best when you've got a grown-up to yourself."
Julian:	"Not a child!"
Julian:	"Well you can look here, how you can build stuff!" (focusing on the Lego).
Therapist:	"When you're on your own, then you are the one who can decide everything and that's why you also destroyed what the other girl made out of Plasticine, do you remember?" (Some sessions previously, Julian had angrily destroyed a Plasticine figure that another child had formed, when he saw it on the therapist's sideboard.)
Julian:	"Yes (contritely). I hate girls. But you aren't one."

Therapist: "But I am a girl."

Julian: "But you're already grown up."

Therapist: "I'm already grown up, that's true!"

Therapist: "And with Papa?

Julian: "Look, now it's a real cannon!"

Therapist: "Oh!"

. . .

Therapist: "I just have to think about what you've told me. That you're a child who doesn't like to go to kindergarten, because there you're not the most important one, and that isn't any fun."

Julian: "Hm. They don't want to play with me at all (sad)!"

Therapist: "They don't want to play with you at all?

Julian: "Yes! Hm. I can play so well with you!"

Therapist: "You can't play so well with the other children. Oh."

Julian: "Uhuh [nods]. Look and see if you can find a small black Lego piece!"

A few sessions before the end of therapy, the therapist told Julian that there were only a few more sessions left. In the twenty-first session he entered the treatment room and immediately said to her angrily, "I'm so angry. I'd like to smash up everything in here."

The therapist sensed his agitation; he was sweating and trembling. She sensed how his sadness about the end of their time together was hidden behind his rage. The therapist understood his anger as the defence against his castration anxiety, because she was the one who had set the limit to their joint sessions. He did not accept the restrictions she placed on him. So, he started to destroy things on the sideboard, which he assumed were important to the therapist. He tried to frighten her by threatening to smash a glass, a present from a colleague, which was on a high shelf, and some patient files that were also lying on the sideboard. The therapist interpreted to him that he was getting angry with her and about the fact that their sessions would soon end, so that he wanted to smash all her things.

Language created a connection between the therapist and Julian. After his attempts at destruction, Julian approached the therapist, as if to reassure himself that she was still there. He tried to get close through fighting, suggesting that she should fight with the big stuffed crocodile and the "greedy frog". Julian tried in this way to intimidate the therapist with his threatening gestures. He stood upright, while she was sitting cross-legged on the rug. The therapist said to him, "You're so angry with me today, you probably want to hurt me a lot." Julian replied, "Yes, because I had to come here, I couldn't eat up my strawberries [at home]. Now they'll go bad." He experienced the therapist as the one who placed restrictions on his gaining narcissistic pleasure.

End of therapy

In the final (twenty-fifth) session of joint therapeutic work, Julian was well able to control his annoyance towards the therapist and his desire to be close to her. In the transference, he oscillated between a position in which he dominated the therapist and one in which he submitted to her and wanted to sit on her lap "like a good boy". He pursued a power struggle around boundaries and restriction by suggesting— like an adult—what they should play in the final session, and would not be stopped from sitting at the computer with her and looking at Lego animations on the Lego-Star Wars homepage with her. The therapist acceded to this unusual request, but limited it to ten minutes. She offered him a little child's chair, while she sat on her big chair and worked the computer—her instrument. But Julian wanted to sit on her lap, to be very close to her and operate the phallic instrument, the computer, like her. He kept wanting to move the cursor, and click functions that he already knew. Julian engaged in a power struggle with the therapist, but finally recognised her limiting function. The therapist thought he could sense how comfortable he might be on his Papa's lap, being protected by the powerful Papa when having adventures with spaceships and robots on alien planets. Being a child and not a substitute partner for his mother would also allow him to be as he was, with all his fears, weaknesses, and limitations.

After twenty-five sessions, the short-term therapy was over. By then, Julian had progressed to the extent of being able to spend the night with the other children at the kindergarten party. After the end of therapy, as well as at follow-up six months later, Julian no longer showed symptoms of a separation anxiety. His mother told the therapist she was pleased and proud that Julian was able to integrate well into his class, and enjoyed contact with the other children. When saying hello, Julian cheekily asked the therapist, "Can't you see that I've grown?"

At first, Julian showed no interest in his father; even when invited to spend the weekend with him, Julian initially refused. His mother explained this in terms of his continued fear of separation. Only when the therapist presented Julian with the interpretation that he was afraid his father would not be as interested in him as his mother, and was also afraid of feeling homesick and therefore of "being weak", did change begin to happen. "Mama always says that Papa doesn't want to do anything," said Julian. The therapist countered, "And now you're frightened that Papa won't want to play with you. You're actually very interested in playing with Papa and seeing where Papa lives now, but you're also afraid that Papa won't always fulfil your wishes in the way that Mama does. But you've stayed here with me, even though I don't always fulfil your wishes like Mama does either." As at the beginning, the therapist had to be a symbolic father for Julian, at least transitionally, and thus enable him to experience separation and triangulation for the first time. This included exposing him to minor frustrations, and thus imposing a "No" and a limit to his fantasies of omnipotence and his desires (e.g., the end of the session, which frustrated him every time because it constrained the flow of his play). Increasingly, this helped him to experience a form of relationship in which two people are not one and do not always have the same wishes, unlike his relationship with his mother, who rarely frustrated his desires. These experiences with the symbolic third person— which became possible through the therapist as triangulating third person—helped him to dismantle his fear of third persons, and consequently made it easier for him to use his own father as a triangulating object.

Over the course of treatment, Julian was then able to spend whole weekends with his father. However, his relationship with his father continued to resemble a further dyadic relationship. His mother reported that Julian did not phone her, and in fact did not even express the wish to reach her by telephone while he was at his father's. Apparently she was then "out of sight, out of mind": she complained that when he spent time with his father, she was no longer present for her son. He then had difficulty in managing the renewed encounter with her: for example, by looking away. She said she believed her son was now excluding her. "It appears that one of us always has to be shut out." Both Julian and his mother continued to find it difficult to manage separation from the object. Julian is apparently unable to represent internally the object that is absent at any one time (whether father or mother), because he still experiences himself as merged with the object.

Sometimes there were mornings when he said he had stomach ache, which the mother saw as Julian's attempt to stay at home with her. Of course, she did not give in to this, she explained, in order to reassure the therapist. The therapist was confident that the time-limited short-term therapy had turned out to be helpful for the development for both mother and child.

CHAPTER THIRTEEN

Case study 2: Sophie, five years old

Relational symptom

S ophie's parents contacted the child psychiatric clinic because their daughter started bursting into tears, "because she was so sad, but didn't know why", as she said. She became very afraid of doing something wrong, particularly of not being able to do things perfectly at kindergarten. Tense, terrified of failure, she would start crying here, too. She was very frightened of exposure in the presence of the teacher and other children; she avoided eye contact, and was extremely shy. She was unable to assert herself, and always backed down in any confrontation with the other children. A change of teacher at kindergarten caused her enormous separation anxiety, as did simply being taken to kindergarten by her mother in the morning. The scenes there made the mother feel uncomfortable and embarrassed.

Therapist–child–parent relationship

The parents

Sophie's mother was a busy, achievement-orientated woman, who appeared to be very pressured by the attempt to balance her professional and family life. In the first session, she complained of the day-to-day constraints she experienced. For example, her (female) boss curtly rejected her request for shorter working hours in order to have more time for her daughter. The mother gave the impression of being pedantic and rigidly structured. The therapist got a picture of a woman under extreme tension, unable to find a tolerable balance of the demands in her life. Little time remained in the evenings for Sophie. The family quickly had their evening meal, and, after watching a short children's television programme, Sophie then went to bed. Sophie's dad fetched her from the day-care centre every day and then took her out to play. Her dad struck the therapist as laid-back and prudent. He was less strict and rigid. The therapist warmed more to him.

During the first parent session, the father hardly got a word in; the conversation was dominated by the mother, who appeared to be trying to win the therapist over to her side. The mother seemed afraid of being shut out if she did not make extreme efforts at communication. Behind this almost childish competition for attention, the therapist sensed the mother's clear anxiety that her husband would be preferred, and she herself be rejected.

Sophie was a "cry-baby" and had been "very sensitive" from birth. Despite this, she had been put in day-care for eight hours a day at the age of only three months. She found it difficult to settle there, but, nevertheless, father and mother continued in their full-time jobs. In taking the history, the therapist had the impression that the mother identified very strongly with her daughter, whom she described as sensitive, weak, and anxious. In contrast to this anxious disposition, between 2½ and three years of age she had undergone an "extreme" period of defiance. Sophie had been given to lashing out and screaming, until her parents shut her in her room, saying, "You can come out when you're good again."

Therapist–child relationship

Sophie was a delicate, pretty girl with long, curly hair, whose play showed a significant need for harmony. Sophie made great efforts not to do anything wrong, talked in a childish voice, and appeared to be very shy. It was clearly very important to Sophie that the therapist should like her.

Material of the child

In the first session, oedipal themes in particular became visible in Sophie's play: a prince and princess kissed each other lovingly. There were several "princesses", but they expressly did not compete for the prince. All the figures were always in agreement and would refuse to assert their own interests rather than fight. Play also brought out fantasies of omnipotence, as well as pleasure in showing and telling: the dolls danced and could fly, showed off these abilities to the audience with great pride. Sophie painted a picture and described it: "I'm sitting behind Papa in the car, Mama is driving, we're going on holiday, and one suitcase is poking out." The therapist felt happiness when looking at the picture and thought Sophie was probably experiencing her mother as taking the lead. The therapist understood the drawing as the expression of Sophie's desire for more time to be playful, free of the tight everyday schedule, and that "one suitcase [could be allowed to] poke out" so that not everything had to be always orderly and perfect. At the same time, the therapist interpreted the suitcase that was "poking out" jauntily as a symbol for Sophie's warded off desire to show herself (exhibitionism).

In the second session with Sophie alone, she was asked what she would wish for if a fairy granted her three wishes: "For the weekend to be five days long and kindergarten only two days", and not the other way round, as in reality. In her countertransference, the therapist felt deeply sympathetic that Sophie experienced so little pleasure in her daily life, that she longed so much for more time with her mother, and just to be a child with more time to play. Sophie played solicitously with the dolls, combing their hair and stroking them. This harmony was, however, indirectly disrupted at the end of the session, when Sophie suddenly drew a picture and showed it to the therapist with the comment, "I have drawn a creepy ghost." This ghost had a pink shell, beyond which the sun was shining. However, within the shell there was a lot of ugliness: red pimples, an enormous mouth, and big black teeth. Red and black were the only colours used. The therapist understood this as indicating that Sophie's libidinal and aggressive impulses were shielded from the outside by a pink shell. The therapist understood the harmonious "pink façade" as a symbol of Sophie's aggressive inhibition. The pink façade blocked the black and red (libidinal and aggressive) impulses from penetrating through to the outside.

The therapist suspected that in Sophie, the relationship between id and superego had become rigid early on, without a stable, mature ego being able to mediate between the two demands. At the same time, the therapist understood Sophie's picture as an indication, directed at her, of what was lying dormant in Sophie's psychic inner world, and also as a test of whether the therapist was able to deal with this sinister ghost of suppressed drives.

Sophie came to the next session in higher spirits and, as soon as they were alone together, attacked the therapist with a stuffed "rat" and a "shark". She leapt exuberantly about the room, turned somersaults, and made a toy horse cavort equally wildly alongside her. Her enjoyment in displaying herself became apparent in this boisterous play, a far cry from the shame that otherwise dominated her in exposed situations. The therapist asked herself whether Sophie had realised that the therapeutic relationship sometimes allowed a "suitcase [to] poke out".

Sophie and "the crowded bus"

Sophie came to the next session beaming with pleasure. She was brought by her grandmother, as in the previous session, and pressed a big bouquet of lilies of the valley into the therapist's hand. While the grandmother chatted to the therapist, Sophie sat quietly at the table, but jiggled her feet impatiently at the same time. The therapist brought the conversation with the grandmother to a friendly close and then turned to Sophie with the words, "You can hardly wait to start, but you don't dare to tell Oma to hurry up and leave." Sophie nodded and appeared surprised to hear the therapist say this out loud. She immediately went over to the play figures and bricks and started building. She took control, relegating the therapist to a passive role, not paying attention to her and letting her drop out of the game. Gradually Sophie's construction took on the form of a bus, which she patiently and meticulously rebuilt when it fell apart. "The bus should take all the people and animals," she said. The therapist thought of Noah's Ark. The bus grew taller and appeared stuck, unwieldy and unstable. It kept collapsing under the load of the many animals and people. There was no question, however, that even though the occupants could barely move, and even if it was extremely uncomfortable, everyone had a place. To play, Sophie also found herself an extremely uncomfortable space, squashed into a corner. Sophie meticulously rebuilt the bus, which kept falling apart. This gave her play a repetitive character, lacking any development. Defiantly, she kept trying anew to stop her construction from collapsing. The bus never started driving. Right on top of the bus sat a little girl, in a very unstable but exposed position. This position was as commanding as that of the bus driver, but it was also the most insecure and dangerous position. The therapist suspected that this was Sophie herself.

Focus according to ToP

From the *relational symptom*, the developing *therapist–child–parents relationship* and the child's *material*, the therapist derived the following understanding of the transgenerational conflict topic: the active participant was to blame. In Sophie's pictures and in the therapist's perception, the mother was the active one, who paid too little attention to Sophie and, therefore, also felt guilty herself. She externalised this feeling of guilt by complaining, for example about her boss, or about how hostile to children "society" was in general. Yet, passivity was a dangerous position, as it brought the risk of exclusion.

The defence against activity and aggression resulted in a position of passive suffering. Thus, depression became one way of avoiding the guilt of being aggressive and active (phallic). What was making Sophie anxious in her everyday life—showing herself, exposing herself—appeared in play sessions to give her great pleasure: she played without involving the therapist, whom Sophie turned into a passive audience. She wanted the therapist to observe how well Sophie was playing, and thus relegated her to a passive position. The therapist felt shut out and controlled. She suspected that Sophie had a marked defence against the pleasure of exhibitionism, which presumably resulted from oedipal competition with her mother. Sophie was afraid that, if she showed anyone how great she was, Mama might reject her. Renouncing exposure through inhibited and extremely shy behaviour, however, means the loss of phallic development ability. Drive was suppressed, and appeared in the symptom. The depression was, thus, a defence against aggressive-active positions. It appeared that Sophie had been aggressive at one time (e.g., in the markedly defiant phase), but this capacity had been lost. She turned this aggression against her own self. In Sophie's perception, the other children, especially those who took anything away from her or demanded her active participation, were the aggressors. She herself was the helpless victim who could "not show her teeth", as her defence would not allow her to do so. A person who was aggressive and demanding, who wanted to show all she could and wanted to do, put herself in the wrong. The desire to be punished for active positions expressed itself in depression.

Focus formulation to the mother

"When you are active and go to work, you feel that you are at fault because you take something away from someone else—your daughter, for example. So instead, you blame your boss for not allowing you to have a more family-friendly work schedule. You are careful not to make mistakes and are generally very controlled. But you also wish you did not always have to take responsibility for everything, and simply had time to play with your child. On the other hand, you do not feel comfortable when you are just playing and not working all the time, because you are afraid you might lose control of things."

Focus formulation to the father:

"You are afraid that your wife will reject you if you highlight your relationship to her daughter. To avoid conflicts, you prefer to let your wife 'muzzle' you."

Focus formulation to Sophie

"If you hide away and are quiet and sad, you don't have to be afraid of getting into a fight with Mum about, for example, wanting to be alone with Dad sometimes. You feel ashamed and you hide, although you would really rather draw attention to yourself. You think that if you behave shy, anxious, and sad, you will protect your parents from your anger. But at the same time, behaving so shyly is boring and hinders you from playing happily with your kindergarten companions."

Course of treatment

In the following session, Sophie came up the stairs and for the first time she asked the therapist actively and challengingly, "When is it my turn?" When she entered the room, she was more spontaneous than before, looked around, picked up the hand puppets and simply played with them. The therapist instructed her as to which toys she could play with and explained why, thus also placing restrictions on her behaviour at the same time. She was surprised at how unusually quickly Sophie responded. The therapist realised that in the developing transference she had become the object that swiftly controlled the child's behaviour, which was lively and sometimes cheekily transgressed boundaries. As the therapist noticed the transference constellation of *complementary identification* (Racker, 1953, see Chapter Three, section headed "Transference and countertransference", p. 94) into which she had fallen with Sophie, the girl slumped physically, appearing once more to be depressive, gaunt, lifeless, and withdrawn, and returning to playing repetitively on her own. It was as if this sequence, in which pleasurable and spontaneous things always had to be curtailed, had repeated what she had experienced with her parents.

During this session she again played very repetitively and compulsively. Everything had to be in order. She chose to sit on the uncomfortable cold floor, and not on the play rug. She did not involve the therapist. No shared play was created; rather, the preparations that Sophie made were so painstaking that no time or space was left for play itself. This play inhibition was a central symptom of her depression. Sophie's play "got stuck" and could not unfold spontaneously, as preparation and organisation took up too much time.

For example, Sophie instructed the therapist to "arrange all the things, all the toys, that are in pairs". The therapist started to feel bored and thought, "Oh, this is boring, having to arrange everything." She asked herself if she was now identified with Sophie's position, in *concordant identification* (Racker, 1953, see Chapter Three, p. 94) in the transference, where Sophie experienced a burnt-out, "lifeless" primary object with whom she wanted to play but who did not play with her and to some extent ignored her needs. Was the therapist now identified with the subject pole in the transference, experiencing—as Sophie did—a maternal object in the transference that (after a strenuous working day) was unresponsive to Sophie's lively desires? Was the therapist experiencing in her countertransference—again like Sophie—a mother who was uncomfortable about enjoyable and spontaneous things, like the "pink ghost" that hid all turbulent feelings inside itself?

Sophie then told the therapist to arrange the objects in rows, while Sophie herself prepared something for their joint play—which she would not reveal to her. The therapist felt that Sophie's instructions to arrange everything were a punishment for having set boundaries so quickly at the beginning of the session. Was Sophie's crying before kindergarten and the sudden tears during the day also a way in which Sophie punished her mother, expressing aggressive impulses towards her while at the same time turning them against herself? As the play continued, the therapist felt extreme tiredness and boredom in her countertransference, and also felt shut out. Sophie determined what there was to do, and thus took on the dominant position. At some point in the process, she established rules of the game, which she adhered to so strictly that there was no space left for enjoyment.

The therapist announced that the session would soon be over, whereupon Sophie continued with her preparations and built an enormous sofa out of Lego. The therapist protested, "Sophie, we aren't playing together at all, each of us is playing on our own." Sophie responded, "Oh, you're not used to playing on your own, I always have to play on my own. I'm used to it."

Then she came to the therapist with the Lego sofa she had completed, and put two play figures on it. Suddenly, she decided that it wasn't enough and that she needed to build another little Lego sofa. The therapist said, "Oh, but it'll take a long time if we want to build it." Sophie said, "Yes, but that's just how it is. Let's do that together." She insisted that every gap had to be painstakingly filled. In her countertransference, the therapist again felt forced to carry out a tedious task.

Once all the preparations had been made, Sophie suddenly started to play. She said, "This is the kitten," and took a cat figure. She wanted the therapist to take the dolls and try to stroke the cat with them. But Sophie kept intervening in the play, biting the dolls. Sophie seemed pleased when the therapist said "Ow!" and added, "I didn't think the cat could bite like this." The therapist gave her this interpretation: "The little kitten is so angry, just like Sophie sometimes, although you can't tell from looking at her, because she looks so nice and she's often very sad." Sophie nodded and was pleased and became more exuberant.

She wanted the game to be repeated up to the end of the session. She appeared disappointed that the session was over.

The transference elements and the play contents made it clear to the therapist how many aggressive impulses were bound up in Sophie's compulsive behaviour. This aggression could be expressed in pretend play. Again and again, Sophie produced play situations with the therapist in which the dolls or clay figures had to fight each other. She enjoyed this a lot. In her daily life, Sophie's aggression was extremely inhibited. For example, the mother reported in the parent sessions (from which the father repeatedly excluded himself, even when the therapist insisted that all three should talk together) that Sophie, who had in the meantime started school, set herself very strict rules. She often cried during lessons when she thought she had not understood something as quickly as the others. The teacher said Sophie would never put her hand up voluntarily, yet when asked, she always knew the answer.

Thinking about the session just described, the therapist considered that Sophie initially wanted to play uninhibitedly with "the forbidden". After the therapist had limited her, the play became tedious and unenjoyable, with Sophie identifying herself with the prohibitive position and denying the therapist everything enjoyable. Thus, she put the therapist in the role of the passive person who wants to be more spontaneous, as Sophie herself had been at the beginning of the session. Sophie, on the other hand, now used the rule that all jobs had to be completed before play could begin as a defence manoeuvre. In the transference, Sophie thus became the maternal object, prohibiting all enjoyable impulses.

In the next session Sophie again was controlling the therapist and played the prohibitive part. The therapist described this movement in their relationship in an appropriate scene within their interaction: "You always make it so that I can't have any fun playing, because I always have to do something. It means I can't play with you at all!" The therapist was surprised at how readily Sophie accepted this intervention. She said, "I know that, too. I'm always so sad in the evening when I want to play with Mama, but she never has time and is always just tired!" The therapist said, "That makes you sad, and angry too, but you only dare to show that you're sad. If you show that you're angry, you're afraid that Mama won't like you any more and won't play with you any more."

In the subsequent sessions, the therapist was repeatedly able to name Sophie's feelings of disappointment and anger at her mother. In this way, she was also able to explain the difficult situations in the mornings when she had to leave her mother in front of the kindergarten. On the one hand, this expressed her desire to stay with her mother and spend time with her. But on the other hand, Sophie expressed her anger by embarrassing her mother by crying and screaming, and refusing to be "handed over".

The parent sessions also worked on this conflict topic. These sessions took place together with the father only after the therapist had given an interpretation to the mother: that she was afraid a three-way triadic constellation of therapist and her husband would shut her out. The mother said she had always had this kind of fear. As a child, for example, she had been afraid that her parents would prefer her little sister and that this would shut her out. This interpretation and the conversation about the feelings of exclusion brought about a change. The warnings and pleas to bring the father with her, to which the mother had previously only responded with excuses, were now successful.

In the joint parent sessions, the therapist explained to the parents that Sophie's bursting into tears was the expression of both her sadness and her angry disappointment that her parents, and particularly her mother, had so little time for her. Sophie was upset that she always had to conform and perform perfectly, but generally turned this against herself, thereby inhibiting important development-related needs.

The therapist pointed out that it was normal for a six-year-old girl to show feelings of rivalry and anger towards her parents, especially to her mother. She explained that usually six-year-old girls have strong feelings of love for their fathers and want to be alone with them sometimes.

The therapist explained to the parents that Sophie was particularly frightened that she would lose her mother if she showed that she wanted to be alone with her father; she suppressed a lot of things she actually enjoyed, such as being open or at kindergarten about the many great things she could already do—in fact, show off a bit. The therapist was pleased that the parents responded positively to this interpretation of Sophie's conflict. The mother said she could recognise this in herself. As a child she wanted to win her parents' approval by trying to do everything perfectly, unlike her much less disciplined little sister. She saw now that this strategy had not made her happy, and in comparison with her sister or her work colleagues she still felt at a disadvantage.

In the sessions with Sophie alone, the therapist named the conflict in play moments when, for example, the play protagonists were ashamed or behaved passively because of their fear of punishment and loss. And when negative transference elements arose, the therapist named them immediately, so that Sophie could experience how aggressive impulses towards her did not lead to a rupture in the relationship.

During the course of treatment, the therapist always presented the conflict to Sophie by relating it to the concrete play situation, and in context-related and child-friendly formulations. For example, the therapist first described Sophie's play and then interpreted: "The princess doesn't want to show that she is in love with the prince, because she's scared the other princess won't like her any more. So she would rather hide behind the curtain, being quiet as a mouse." Sophie nodded at this, appeared very cowed, and said quietly, "Yes", as if she identified with the play figure of the princess in hiding. The therapist then interpreted: "That's like with you, when you're scared that Mama doesn't like you any more because you love Papa so much and would like to be alone with him." Embarrassed, but also a little relieved, Sophie nodded. Then she suddenly sprang up and turned a somersault. The therapist suspected that she was showing with this displacement activity how well she could move and how much she enjoyed it, and she said so. Sophie nodded proudly.

After twenty-five sessions of PaCT, Sophie showed neither separation anxiety nor lasting sadness with sudden bouts of crying or overwhelming fear of failure. Sophie was able to express her enjoyment of standing out among her peers, by becoming the "group leader" of her "gang". Some time after the end of the treatment with PaCT, the mother wrote to the therapist to say that Sophie had continued to develop very well. In the meantime, she had started school. According to her mothers report, the treatment effects were stable. At school Sophie was now class representative.

CHAPTER FOURTEEN

Case study 3: Elisabeth, six years old

Relational symptom

E lisabeth would not speak outside her family context. Elisabeth's grandmother suspected that this was mutism, or even autism, and therefore advised the parents to bring Elisabeth to our outpatient clinic.

In the first meeting, the parents reported that at 1½years old, Elisabeth had developed the habit of banging her head repeatedly on the hard surface of a wooden chair. She even removed the chair cushion to do this. The mother suspected that she did this so that the chair was "nicely hard" when banging. Overall, Elisabeth was very shy and was able to play on her own for hours, without needing contact with others. Her little sister (four years younger) was the complete opposite: open, outgoing, and warm. At kindergarten, Elisabeth was extremely shy about presenting anything, and was especially awkward when doing sports. If pressured by teachers or parents, she would defy them and refuse. As well as shyness at saying or doing things in public, her parents sensed that Elisabeth enjoyed a "power struggle". She insisted on still sleeping in her parents' marital bed at night. While there she often wet herself, which gave her mother a lot of extra work changing bedclothes.

Therapist–child–parent relationship

The parents

The therapist experienced the mother as very friendly and making great efforts towards keeping things harmonious. A calm, disciplined woman, who was pleased to continue paid work, she spoke in a quiet voice. She apparently placed little value on her outward appearance; she dressed simply, and seemed somewhat pallid and nondescript. In her first contact (which took place with Elisabeth, but without the father), the therapist had the feeling that the mother was hiding something that she appeared to be ashamed of. The therapist suspected a family secret or taboo. And, in fact, the mother reported in the next session—which was also the first session with the therapist but without the child—that she had developed postnatal depression after Elisabeth's birth, and had found it very difficult to accept Elisabeth. The child felt so alien to her, and she herself had felt numb and "as if dead". In her countertransference, the therapist had a strong sense of the sadness around this unhappy start to the relationship between Elisabeth and her mother, and had the impression that the mother felt a strong degree of guilt towards Elisabeth.

The mother began by talking about the death of her first child. This child, Elisa, had died unexpectedly one week after birth. The sudden death had been a great shock for the family. The mother went back to work immediately afterwards and tried to distract herself through work. She became pregnant again a year later, and bore Elisabeth. She had never grieved properly for her first daughter and "threw herself into work" to compensate. Elisabeth had been very restless, "yelled a lot", and "fed poorly", whereupon her mother quickly stopped breast-feeding her and switched to bottle-feeding. At the age of seven months, Elisabeth was sent to day care for eight hours a day. In the eyes of her mother, she had "acclimatised well" and had fitted in. Hearing this description, the therapist felt exasperated at this obvious contradiction between the early stresses on the child and her apparent "fitness for day-care". The therapist surmised that Elisabeth, as a result of her early experiences of loss, had entered a kind of narcissistic withdrawal. To all outward appearances she was quite an easy child, until, at 1½ years old, she was psychomotorically able to harm herself, which her parents then had to notice.

The therapist's annoyance grew when she realised that it had been the grandmother who had noticed that Elisabeth's development was not proceeding normally, and who had urged the parents to have Elisabeth's symptoms investigated at the child psychiatric clinic. The therapist had the impression that the grandmother took more note than the parents did of what the child needed. It was also the grandmother, and not the parents, who often brought Elisabeth to the sessions.

The mother recounted that she came from a family in which feelings were not talked about, and her own mother had always been very strict and achievement-orientated. Elisabeth's mother had always conformed to her own mother's demands here, and had never dared to show anger towards either of her parents. She was now very happy with her husband, and lived together with him and the children in a large house.

In the next meeting the therapist experienced the father as a friendly and intelligent man who was proud of his wife and children, and emphasised that he did not have an "intellectual" job like the mother, joking in a friendly manner at his wife. He spent a lot of time with the children. He appeared not to find the situation worrying, except for the nightly bedwetting. However, it sometimes irritated him that the mother gave in too easily when Elisabeth demanded to sleep in her parents' bed night after night, and did not set any boundaries to this behaviour.

Contact with Elisabeth

Elisabeth was a pretty girl, who appeared very shy and who pointedly ignored the therapist in the first contact. She noticed that Elisabeth did not look at her at all during their first meeting, although the therapist showed great interest in Elisabeth. Being ignored and rejected like this was thus in marked contrast to her own strong interest in the child, and gave a painful and sad quality to her experience of the first individual session.

Material of the child

During the first session in the therapist–child–parent setting, Elisabeth sat down on the play carpet and began spontaneously to play with the Scenotest figures in a sustained and precise way, and to build the house in which her family lived, with several stables for the animals. The therapist noticed at once that these stables had no exits. Elisabeth built walls and each animal received its own stall. There was, therefore, no exchange between the animals or with the humans. Elisabeth did not speak to the therapist either. When asked, "Is that your house?" Elisabeth nodded, and beamed at the therapist happily with big eyes, as though pleased that the therapist had recognised this. In her play, Elisabeth appeared as if sealed off from her parents, who were sitting with the therapist at the table. Occasionally, she sat briefly on her mother's or father's lap and exchanged cuddles, before abruptly retreating into her "own world".

Over the course of the first two individual sessions with Elisabeth (sessions 4 and 5), there was an interesting development.

In the first session (session 4), Elisabeth turned immediately to the Lego-Duplo figures, and played on her own with the animal figures, then instructed the therapist, mutely but decisively, to play with the humans. It was as if Elisabeth did not even want to touch the human figures, as if they were so alien to her that just touching them made her uneasy. In play there was now an endless battle of "humans against animals". The humans did not stand a chance. Everything they did was punished and everything, such as their cars and their "treasure", was taken away from them. Whenever the humans moved, they were punished mercilessly by the animals. In her countertransference, the therapist found it was difficult to develop her own thoughts and use them freely. She felt herself carried along by events that Elisabeth dominated. The therapist experienced this rapid transference as an attack on her thought processes and asked herself what it meant. During the battle scenes that Elisabeth had take place in her game, a lot of blood spurted as the animals ate up the humans. The toy figures the therapist played with were brutally attacked again and again. Sometimes Elisabeth even slightly hurt the therapist in her vigorous play. For example, her figures once scratched the back of the therapist's hand. Even feeling only mild physical pain, the therapist felt tense and that she had to protect herself. She set Elisabeth boundaries, by asking her not to harm herself or the therapist in play (see Chapter Five, under "Typical situations that make pedagogical intervention or limiting necessary", p. 150).

When the game finished, all the humans were dead. Elisabeth justified this as follows: "Because they have cars, which are dangerous for the animals. And also the people captured the wild horse, and now this is their punishment." At the end, the therapist stood with empty hands and a lot of dead toy figures scattered on the floor, positioned opposite a threatening "animal army", arranged in rank and file. In her countertransference, she felt helpless in this game and powerless against the persecuting objects. She understood that Elisabeth had used projective identification to place her own paranoid–schizoid fears in the therapist. In that the therapist, rather than Elisabeth, felt persecuted and helpless, she was able to get rid of her unbearable and frightening feelings through externalisation, and protect her inner self this way.

In the second session (session 5) with Elisabeth alone, Elisabeth resumed the game and took up an empty cardboard box. First, she took a small figure and named it Berta, like her little sister. Berta pushed Linda, the little kitten, in a wheelbarrow towards the cardboard box. Elisabeth commented on it: "This is Linda, the little cat. She's already dead, like my sister. They are now together in heaven." The therapist asked, "What's your sister called?" Elisabeth said, "Luise". The therapist replied, "I thought your sister was called Elisa." "That's right," said Elisabeth thoughtfully, "almost like me". The therapist was startled at the child's suddenly intense relationship to her dead sister, whom she knew only from her parents' stories. At the same time, she noted that Elisabeth initially used her mother's name— Luise—for this dead sister. What did this mean? Was she currently experiencing her mother as absent, or had she in her early development experienced her mother sometimes as "dead", because she was so unapproachable and unattainable in her depressive numbness and in the unresolved mourning for her firstborn daughter? Elisabeth took up the game again abruptly. She added "Papa Johann" to Berta and the kitten and instructed the therapist to play the human figures.

Suddenly the kitten Linda exuberantly joined together with the dog and built a cave out of cardboard, which little by little was filled with the contents of the house—which actually belonged to the humans. The game became increasingly wild, with the animals being secretive about their strategies. When the therapist made the human figures peek curiously at what the animals were doing there, her toys were eaten up so brutally and relentlessly that a cold shudder ran down the therapist's back at this raw and unrelenting aggression.

The therapist noticed that a mother figure was lacking, and added one to Berta, the sister figure, and the father figure, and named it. Elisabeth was quite taken aback, and said, "No, Mama shouldn't play with us", whereupon she took the Mama figure and put her back in the attic of the house: "She'll only get sadder if she sees this here," The therapist was surprised again at the way that it appeared to be very significant to Elisabeth that her mother could not reasonably be expected to cope with all the wildness and destructiveness that existed in her psychic inner worlds. The therapist suspected that Elisabeth was afraid her rage would destroy her mother.

Little by little, the animals took possession of the contents of the doll's house, to build up their own kingdom. The animals raided the house until in the end the human figures were left with nothing. Their house was empty. They themselves were powerless and destitute. The therapist understood this looting of the house as the expression of early unconscious oral–sadistic attacks on the body of the disappointing, failing, and absent "bad" maternal body. She remembered the mother's narrative of withholding her breast from Elisabeth, who then probably perceived it as the "bad partial object" that was absent in early life (see Chapter Six, section headed "The significance of infantile sexuality in the therapeutic process", pp. 165–166).

(In this case, three sessions with the child took place before the focus was formulated. Although it was planned according to the manual's schedule, the parents were not able to attend the sixth session for parent work. Therefore, session 6 was an individual and not a parent session.)

In the next session (session 6) Elisabeth recounted, proudly and provocatively, that she only liked playing with boys at kindergarten, and instructed the therapist to play "the boys". She was to put them in the car and "the boys" were then to drive to the "birthday party". Elisabeth explained, "They want to drive there in the car, because the cat has had a little baby. They want to go to the birthday." The therapist was then relegated to an observer's perspective, and Elisabeth played "the animals have a birthday party". She stood all the animals—cows, sheep, and horses—in a semicircle, presenting each animal individually and giving it its own name. The scene reminded the therapist of the birth of the Baby Jesus, with the shepherd and the three kings reverently marvelling at the birth of their Messiah. Elisabeth said, "The cat Mimi has had a little kitten", and indicated that the others, the human children, should keep their distance and were not allowed to step forward to the baby. The therapist felt deeply moved by this scene. She attempted to take up the triadic position, and asked herself what this dramatic scene could signify. She thought this depicted the birth of a very special baby, the cat's, and Elisabeth apparently wanted this birth to be duly celebrated, as with the Baby Jesus, who received many visitors from far away. Everyone was supposed to wonder at the baby.

The therapist saw a link to Elisabeth's own birth, which had been overshadowed by the loss of her parents' first daughter, her sister Elisa.

The therapist also noticed that the toy figures in the game all had a particular name and were thus clearly distinguished from each other.

She interpreted this to Elisabeth: "You would like everyone to have different names and everyone who has a different name is a different person." Elisabeth looked at the therapist with big eyes and nodded.

The game proceeded rapidly. It looked as if the little mouse, who was called "Hans Bankrutt", was repeatedly taking revenge on the humans. The little mouse tricked the humans by pretending to be another little mouse, a "very good little mouse", and then suddenly ambushed the human figures.

The therapist announced the end of the session in good time and Elisabeth appeared disappointed that the session was over so soon.

Her play became wilder towards the end and she tried to dominate and provoke the therapist by ordering her to collect up things that Elisabeth was throwing about the room. She then threw her own shoes and shouted exuberantly to the therapist, "Fetch this, fetch that!"

The therapist set boundaries by saying that the session was over. Elisabeth then wanted the therapist to tie her shoelaces for her, although she had long been able to do this herself.

The therapist understood this as an anal power struggle, which Elisabeth enjoyed very much, but at the same time also as the expression of the regressive desire to be a baby again.

Theoretical considerations

After the session, the therapist thought how the little Elisabeth's access to her grief-absorbed mother must have been sealed off; how she now protected herself and her mother from her murderous impulses by turning away from the objects and withdrawing into her non-objectal, autistoid shelter and refusing to speak. In the sessions, she wanted the therapist to celebrate her birth, and not, as her mother had done previously, barely notice her arrival or presence through the veil of her grief. The therapist well understood why Elisabeth had locked up what was instinctive, so that she did not lose her sad mother by attacking her aggressively. In his work "The use of an object", Winnicott (1969, see Chapter Two, section headed "The object relations theory of Donald W. Winnicott", pp. 50–52) elaborated how important these aggressive impulses are for the development and contouring of the self. Only if the mother endures and survives the child's aggressive attacks does it become possible for the child to perceive its mother as a whole and not just as a bundle of its own projections. Only if the primary object survives the destructive attacks of the infant does the infant become able to experience it as separate from itself. Yet, at the same time, the infant increasingly experiences itself as being separate from the early object. The object is, thus, deprived of primary narcissistic omnipotent control, and can be experienced by the subject as having its own intrinsic, and not just projected, characteristics (Winnicott, 1969, see Chapter Two, section headed "The object relations theory of Donald W. Winnicott", pp. 50–52).

This process has crucial consequences for the differentiation of self–object boundaries, according to Winnicott: the child is able to use the object and not just to accommodate its projections (Winnicott, 1969, p. 713). Through this more differentiated perception of the other, the child is also able to reach a more integrated self-perception. Winnicott argued that aggressive impulses and the experiencing of motoric actions that the object resists and yet does not respond to with counteraggression, or by breaking off contact, are essential for the child's subject development (Winnicott, 1969). This is what the therapist thought that Elisabeth was catching up on in her wild play. In contrast to Klein, Winnicott did not focus solely on the world of the inner object, but accorded particular significance to the reaction of the real object. In play with Elisabeth, the therapist noticed a rapid alternation between libidinal transference positions, in which Elisabeth came close to her, and aggressive transference elements, in which Elisabeth wanted to persecute and fight her. The therapist understood this, with Klein (see Chapter Two, section headed "The object relations theory of

Melanie Klein", pp. 47–49), as an alternation of libidinal and aggressive impulses, directed against the therapist in the transference. During this oscillation between paranoid–schizoid and developing depressive positions (e.g., the mouse "Hans Bankrutt" *vs.* the bashful kitten), Elisabeth had to control the therapist by keeping her in check, and exerting the primary narcissistic omnipotent control over her and their shared play.

Focus formulation

In the therapist's emotional resonance, which developed over the first sessions, she most clearly noticed the irritation she felt when she realised that Elisabeth's name contained the name of the dead sister: Elisa. The therapist was very surprised by this, and asked herself whether the mother had been denying the first child's death by giving her second child a similar name. She suspected that the mother perhaps unconsciously felt guilty for the death of the first child, and was reproaching herself for being unable to prevent it. She also wondered whether the mother felt guilty that she had not accepted Elisabeth after her birth, because the dead child's shadow lay over Elisabeth and darkened the early mother–child interaction. Possibly she knew that something between mother and child had been lost forever, and believed that she could never again make good this loss. Presumably, it was these feelings of guilt for her own early unconscious destructive feelings towards Elisabeth that now stopped her setting Elisabeth age-appropriate boundaries, for example, sleeping in her own bed.

The therapist noticed two conflict topics in Elisabeth's play, which she integrated into a transgenerational focus.

Elisabeth was concerned with the topic of her own self and of identity. This was associated with another topic, that of dealing with aggressive impulses. It appeared to be very important to her to build up her "own empire", of the animals, and thus to have something to which no one else had access. Elisabeth had been born to a mother who was preoccupied with mourning her first child. Elisabeth even had to bear the name of dead sister, "Elisa", for ever. The dead child was omnipresent. The mother, caught in the unresolved grief for this first child, found it difficult to become an object that could stand up to Elisabeth's aggressive impulses. She may have been so burdened by her grief for the lost child that she was unable to take up, in "reverie" (Bion 1962, p. 36, see Chapter Two, section headed "The container–contained model of Wilfred R. Bion", pp. 53–57), the child's projective identifications, to digest all the destructive elements and to contain what the infant externalised. Presumably, she was then unable to help the child develop by integrating its archaic destructive impulses and symbolising them. For fear of destroying her depressive mother, Elisabeth turned these aggressive impulses—which in early childhood development are directed towards the mother's body—against herself. At the age of 1½ years, this expressed itself in autoaggressive behaviour. At the age of five, these destructive feelings and fantasies could only be defended against, with the symptom of nightly bedwetting. In this way, Elisabeth regularly soiled her parents' "nest". This satisfied both the early unconscious desire to destroy the body of her mother through her urethral power, and the oedipal desire to have her father for herself and to prevent the union of her parents, which excluded herself.

During the day, Elisabeth gave the impression of being cut off from the world, lifeless and unreachable like the "dead child in heaven", as if Elisabeth were identifying with her dead sister, Elisa. In play, the aggressive impulses against her mother expressed themselves in the persistent, pleasurable raiding of the house, which could be seen as a symbol for the maternal body. Feelings of guilt arose when these destructive contents penetrated into consciousness. In play, the mother figure had to be saved from even seeing this aggressive action.

At a transgenerational level, it also became clear that Elisabeth's mother did not herself have adequate opportunities for expressing aggression in the relationship with her own mother. The therapist concluded that Elisabeth's mother was also unable to symbolise the destructive parts of the personality adequately, and, in order to protect the object, probably had to defend very strongly against these aggressive impulses by turning them against herself.

Focus for Elisabeth

The transgenerational focus can be expressed in the following way.

If Elisabeth gave in to the aggressive impulses towards her weak and grieving mother, she was afraid they would destroy her. Therefore, she preferred to be weak and anxious herself, and libidinally turned away from objects, to ensure her mother's love. In her own world, away from people, she found a compromise: in turning away from the objects through emotional numbness, she retained her own identity and did not confront her mother openly with her aggressive impulses. At the same time, this formed a defence against "survivor guilt" for being alive instead of her dead sister, in that Elisabeth identified with the dead sister and became dead and unapproachable to her parents. As Elisabeth did not speak, was libidinally "frozen" and unavailable for the objects, the objects endured and were not destroyed by the child's pressing aggressive impulses.

Focus formulation towards Elisabeth

"You're afraid that Mama won't like you any more if she notices how angry you are sometimes. So you build a fence around yourself, like the animals in the barn. You mostly play on your own and you don't talk because you're frightened that you could hurt Mama and Papa if your feelings of rage come out."

Treatment planning for the therapist–child sessions

The therapeutic work with Elisabeth was to consist of work on her fears of aggression towards the object. The transference relationship played a decisive role here. Because Elisabeth experienced in the therapist an object that survived her destructive impulses, she was increasingly able to experience aggressive impulses as belonging to herself, and over the course of treatment, to integrate them into her personality. At the same time, this was also intended to promote a sense of identity, through enabling her to experience different feelings and impulses as belonging to herself. Relationships acquired a more differentiated quality. We were, thus, also able to promote the differentiation of self–object boundaries.

Focus formulation to the mother

"Elisabeth has been unable to integrate aggressive impulses into the picture of herself for fear that you, her mother, does not want the 'bad' Elisabeth, but rather the 'good' Elisa, who, sadly, is dead. Elisabeth, therefore, has increasingly withdrawn behind a lifeless protective shield so that she does not display lack of control or stubbornness in an age-appropriate way. Elisabeth actually wants sometimes to behave wildly with you, and to be able to fight with you."

Focus formulation to the father

"You sense that it is important to treat Elisabeth in an age-appropriate way, and sometimes set boundaries for her. You also notice that it is not helpful for Elisabeth's development always to avoid conflicts. But you also shy away from conflict with your wife, and so you don't dare to say that the marital bed is territory for the two of you, and that the child should sleep in her own bed. For Elisabeth's development it is important for her to know that she will not be rejected if she sometimes plays wildly and turbulently, or is obstinate."

Treatment plan for the parent sessions

In the work with the parents, particularly with the mother, the focus was directed towards the inhibition of aggressive impulses and also the denial of these impulses in her daughter. We intended to process carefully with the mother how much the unresolved grief for her first-born daughter had hindered the free development of Elisabeth as the second child in her own right.

The therapist aimed to encourage the father to follow his spontaneous, healthy impulse to set limits for his daughter in an age-appropriate way. She also encouraged him to pay attention to fulfilling his needs towards his wife, and keep the shared marital bed for themselves, instead of always withdrawing in disappointment. This strengthened the father in his parental function, and he was, thus, available for Elisabeth in the triangulation. Elisabeth found the aggression associated with turning away from her mother increasingly tolerable, and was able to integrate it into her personality development.

Course of treatment
Initial phase

The next session was the first after Elisabeth had started school. She was very proud to be a schoolchild now. Elisabeth started to play immediately, turbulently and wildly. She said, "For me everything's about boys", mentioned various names, and instructed the therapist to write them down. She was very coquettish and recounted everything she had already learnt at school.

She behaved spontaneously, but was also invasive and wanted to write on the therapist's notes of the session. Elisabeth wrote, "Mia", "Mimi", "Nini" skilfully and neatly. She behaved boyishly and then said exuberantly, almost screaming, "Boys, more boys, I need boys."

Then she stood the Lego-Duplo toy figures in a row and instructed the therapist to remember the names that she gave them. The therapist was supposed to write them down, so that she did not forget. Elisabeth gave them the names Alex, Paul, Flori, Anton, Peter, Oskar. It was not clear whether she had made up the names, or whether they were boys whom she knew from school. The speed of play was very fast; the therapist could hardly keep up with it, and experienced this tempo as an "attack" on her thought processes. She had difficulty preserving an inner space in which she could reach and mobilise her own thoughts. The therapist realised that Elisabeth was trying to keep her in check, so that her interpretations could not become threatening.

Then suddenly a mouse was introduced into the game, a tiny mouse. Elisabeth called it "Hans Bankrutt". This name made the therapist think of "bankrupt", standing empty and without means, but was unable to pursue this line of thought as Elisabeth went wild and scuttled around like a spider. She wanted the therapist to crawl around like her, and sought body contact by crawling under the therapist.

In play it became obvious that although the little mouse "Hans Bankrutt" was tiny, it also carried the greatest aggressive potential and only cared about disrupting the actions of the other toys. It attacked and bit them all. The game obviously gave Elisabeth great pleasure.

Middle phase

One session later (session no. 11, as no. 10 was a parent session), Elisabeth stormed into the treatment room, threw her jacket down boisterously, and impetuously asked the therapist, "Guess where Thomas lives! Thomas is my boyfriend." Then she threw herself on the rug and played "today it's raining ice cream". The therapist said, "Today everything can fly, your jacket can fly, ice cream flies out of the sky". Elisabeth said, "Yes, I can fly too, sometimes I dream that I can fly," thus communicating to the therapist how omnipotent she was. The therapist was happy at this sign of openness and lively fantasies of omnipotence, but the tide quickly turned.

All at once, Elisabeth "bit" the therapist with a toy rat, which was in turn swallowed by a frog. Elisabeth was pleased, and showed the therapist that the frog hat eaten the rat. Then she suddenly noticed that another child, who had been for a session since her last visit, had rebuilt the Lego-Duplo house. It now looked quite different from before. She asked accusingly, "Where is the house; who has rebuilt it?" and returned to building her own house again. The therapist thought Elisabeth wanted to reconstruct the house as it had been before, and understood this as the expression of her fear that she might have destroyed the object (symbolised by the house) with her primary narcissistic, paranoid–schizoid attacks. However, the therapist noticed that Elisabeth's new construction had a completely different style from before.

But this construction appeared to reveal that Elisabeth was overwhelmed with the new task, because the floors and walls, or the doors and windows, failed to fit together. However, Elisabeth was energetic and determined. She had got it into her head to build her own house, and so she tried out all variations that she liked. She asked the therapist for help, but was in charge of what to do. The therapist gave this interpretation: "Elisabeth, you would like to build your own house, and not like it was before, you want your very own house." Elisabeth nodded and said, "Yes, just like I want it."

Then they succeeded in building a roof. Suddenly Elisabeth said, "I'm putting a candle up here on the roof, so that if the people up on the terrace want to be sexy, they at least have a candle." She laughed as she said it, and at the same time seemed to be testing out how the therapist would react. The therapist interpreted, "The candle is to make it light so that you can see how they are being 'sexy'." Elisabeth laughed in embarrassment but also with pleasure, and evaded the comment by suddenly starting a singing game, in which she slapped her thighs and asked the therapist to sing along. The song sound like "We will, we will rock you". This was effectively a displacement activity, a defence against the previous oedipal topic of watching parental intimacy, "being sexy". In her countertransference, the therapist experienced herself as pleasurably amused by the meaning of "rock you!" and thought of the meaning of shaking the early objects in the transference awake, which Elisabeth presumably wanted to wake out of depressive torpor. At the same time she was startled that Elisabeth had unconsciously communicated this meaning of "we will rock you" even though she did not yet have command of the English language.

Suddenly, Elisabeth took up the topic of sex again, and said, "The vacuum cleaner wants to have sex with the chimney", and told the therapist to put the vacuum cleaner on the roof. Then she took hold of it and pantomimed a "sexy" gesture. She said, "Down there in the house, those two want to have sex with the Tic, they want to be sexy with the Tic." And then she said, "Today everything is about sexy", and "I want to have sex." The therapist thought that the previously sealed-off drive had now been set free in the joint space of the therapeutic situation, and was now moving there unimpeded and tumultuously. The therapist interpreted, "You're very interested in what Mama and Papa do, and that's why you always want to sleep with them at night, because you don't want Mama to be alone with Papa, because you want to have Papa all for yourself!"

At this point Elisabeth left the play carpet and moved into the area of the room that she knew was not intended for playing. It was the "taboo adult area", with writing desk, computer, and couch. Elisabeth boldly sat on the couch on which the therapist treated her adult patients. There she took up the hand puppets and instructed the therapist to play with the big doll and she the little one. Suddenly, Elisabeth asked the therapist, through the doll, "Shall we have sex, come on, let's be sexy." Then the dolls kissed each other and then she said, "That's what they're doing, hu hu hu," singing along very loudly. She wanted the therapist to sing very loudly as well and go "hu hu hu". Despite the obviously oedipal topics in the transference, the therapist understood this as a marked desire for closeness to the maternal object. She wanted to be physically very close to her and to try out whether this was possible despite the oedipal competition for the father.

The therapist announced to Elisabeth the approaching end of the session, and this again turned into a drama, as it had in the previous sessions. Elisabeth was very disappointed and said, "Oh, I'd much rather play all day with you." The therapist replied, "You would like to decide for yourself when our game is over, wouldn't you? It annoys you that it's already over." Elisabeth nodded. Suddenly she said, "Ah,

I'm supposed to bake cakes for tomorrow with Mama. Then I'll come along with her," and the therapist said, "Ah, you're pleased that you can bake cakes together with Mama afterwards, so it's not so bad that you have to leave. It's very important to you to be close to Mama, even though here you enjoy playing freely."

Instantly, Elisabeth tried to test out the therapist's boundaries, by romping uncontrollably about the room, and would not put her shoes on as the therapist had asked her. She had to be asked several times, and sought body contact with the therapist while continuing her wild play. The therapist, however, was firm, so Elisabeth again asked for help with tying her shoelaces. The therapist gave her interpretation: "You sometimes want to be a little baby here, and have me care for this tiny baby." Elisabeth nodded. Then, on leaving the treatment room, she turned around again after a few steps and sneaked a look at the therapist as if to reassure herself that she was still there, despite Elisabeth's destructive "attacks" against her and despite the libidinal desires.

A couple of minutes later, there was a knock at the door, and the grandmother appeared, asking for a new appointment. The therapist was surprised and felt this was a pretext of the grandmother's, as in fact the next appointment was always fixed. The grandmother asked, "Did Elisabeth behave herself today?" In context, this question seemed to the therapist to come from almost another world, with no relevance to the boisterous, wild goings-on of the session. The therapist referred politely to the next parent session and said goodbye.

The therapist remembered that Elisabeth had been brought to her with the initial diagnosis of mutism, and had shown barely any object-related interest, preferring to play alone or at home with the animals. Suddenly, there had arisen not only the question of personal boundaries, of variations of identity in the relationship to the object, but also her interest in what she called "being sexy", what her parents got up to with one another when she was shut out, especially at night. She wanted to do it too, and showed her interest in "boys" aggressively to the therapist. There were no female competitors in this, only herself and the boys. She did not have to share "the boys" in her pretend play with anyone, and had them for herself alone. Having to rein herself in and in this way protect her mother from her own aggression thus confronted her again, mediated this time through themes of oedipality and phallicity. In the therapist, she had a counterpart who did more than just mourn the loss of the sister. She was now able to entrust this counterpart with the instincts themselves.

However, she could not allow herself to become too close to the therapist. That made Elisabeth afraid of losing her own boundedness, and sparked fears of losing her self- and object-boundaries. She obviously also used uncontrolled play to defend contraphobically against the desires of a pre-oedipal closeness to the object. By involving the therapist in the rapid flow of play, through her wild, harried, breathless behaviour, Elisabeth also ensured that the therapist was unable to reflect, to feel or interpret. Thus, she kept her "in check" and at a distance, so that she could not come to close to Elisabeth. Possibly Elisabeth was also defending against her own intense desires to merge with the therapist in the transference.

Before the thirteenth session, the therapist fetched Elisabeth from the waiting room. The grandmother provided brief information that everything was going very well, except for the fact that Elisabeth was sometimes a "little bit aggressive towards her little sister"—"but that's what we want," she added.

Elisabeth stormed into the treatment room and held the door closed from inside, so that the therapist could not get in. Aha, she thought, so Elisabeth is angry today; she wants to take over my position. The therapist thought that by attempting to block the door, Elisabeth was trying not to allow her in the transference into her inner, psychic space. The therapist understood this as identification with the subject pole in the transference, and thought that Elisabeth was unconsciously placing her own feelings of not being able to get to the early object in the therapist, using projective identification. She wanted the therapist to feel as she had done when she had not had access to her postnatally depressed mother. At this point, Elisabeth allowed the therapist in, and wanted first to play "good and bad fairy" with two toy figures. Did she want to see how the therapist reacted if she was "bad" for once? Whether the therapist was able to withstand the "bad" in her? The therapist gave her this interpretation: "You want to see if I still like you if you're nasty to me sometimes!" Elisabeth nodded slightly and then immediately turned away from the therapist and towards the room.

Then she briefly took up a Lego-Duplo plant and said, "Come on, let's play Sleeping Beauty." The session was very dynamic. Everything happened very fast. Elisabeth apparently had a lot of energy and a tremendous urge to move. The therapist said, "You have a lot of energy today, you have to keep moving, because you want to wake me up like Sleeping Beauty, because you're afraid that otherwise I won't want to be lively and play with you." Elisabeth suggested she should play a "spider" again, a "yoga exercise" in which she also wanted the therapist to move. She, however, did not do what Elisabeth wanted, to "entangle" and "enmesh" with her, and said, "If we get tangled up together like this you won't be able to tell any more what's you and what's me." "That's right," said Elisabeth, "that's not good, but it is a lot of fun!" The therapist said, "You want to be very close to me, but it also makes you scared that you won't know who I am and who you are. It's always important for you that everyone is an individual and has their own name." Elisabeth nodded seriously at this.

Elisabeth then played uncontrollably again, leaping around the room. She briefly turned to the toy figures and when the therapist tried to join in the game, Elisabeth rounded on her harshly: "I said we aren't playing Sleeping Beauty after all." Her wildness had something exuberantly pleasurable about it, and the therapist also had the impression that she wanted to test out how much the therapist could bear, and whether she was allowed to be like this in her relationship to the therapist.

Suddenly, she interrupted her play with the abrupt statement: "Now I want breasts. Look at your black bottom, there are breasts in it," she said, and laughed exuberantly. Then she romped about the room and said, "Breasts, breasts, big fat breasts, I want breasts." Her play acquired an impetuous quality. She lifted up her sweater and said, "Here is my breast, I want it to be as big as Mama's!" She approached the therapist, seemed to want to "crawl into" her, asking, "Where are your breasts?" and feeling the therapist's back, trying to get under her sweater. The therapist was relieved that Elisabeth was unable to reach her breast. She experienced Elisabeth's behaviour as transgressive in a way which made her uncomfortable, and she tried to set limits, saying, "You're very interested in where my breast is, but I'd like to ask you to stop now because it hurts me when you're so wild with me." The therapist tried not to be too limiting, but also not too permissive. Elisabeth accepted the limitation and the explanation, and carried on playing. The oscillation between the desire to incorporate the good object and the desire to expel the bad object tipped over again into a paranoid–schizoid position. The absence of the good objects, or the presence of the frustrating object, was then answered by Elisabeth with an "attack".

Elisabeth took the big stuffed crocodile and said, "Now the prey is going to be savaged!" and lay on the crocodile. She crawled across the room, lying on the crocodile. She was playing at being "a wild animal, savaging its prey", and bit repeatedly and wildly into the crocodile, attempting to subdue it, and always keeping the upper hand. It became clear that this was a form of pleasurable closeness; that Elisabeth really enjoyed hunting and fighting like this.

In the midst of her play, she stopped abruptly, fetched drawing paper from the shelf and asked, "Shall we draw playing?" She lay the paper and the pens down on the table, but then returned to her wild game with the "ball and the crocodile". This was as if she wanted to be the sweet, devoted kitten for the therapist once again. The therapist did not accept the dominant role that Elisabeth assigned her in the transference, whereupon Elisabeth abandoned the suggestion of drawing, and took up her game again. It occurred to the therapist that Elisabeth's mother had told her, in Elisabeth's presence, how pleased she was when Elisabeth drew "so beautifully" but that, unfortunately, she didn't do this often. Did Elisabeth want the therapist to like her in this way, like her mother, because she assumed in the transference that the therapist would also be pleased if she "drew beautifully"?

As the session went on, the therapist was again relegated to the role of audience. When she said: "But Elisabeth really wants to fight today", the previously spirited atmosphere tipped and Elisabeth again wanted to be "a sweet kitten". Naming it obviously made her own behaviour appear so threatening that she wanted to hide it from the therapist. So she abruptly slipped into the opposite role again, playing a "sweet little kitten", meowed and looked at the therapist with big, helpless eyes. The therapist thought this sweet, adoring kitten was the mute Elisabeth, who had locked up the bad kitten in herself so as not to hurt her mother. Next she played "Fetch", showing the therapist that she wanted to be very good. She brought the therapist a ball, wanting it to be thrown repeatedly so she could fetch it like a dog and lay it at her feet.

Initially, playing "good dog" and "fetch", she made herself submissive. The therapist was supposed to decide what to do. Gradually, however, the good kitten became more cheeky, would not give up the ball, and fought to keep it. Elisabeth then told the therapist that the crocodile should take the ball away from the kitten. The therapist was supposed to keep trying, with the crocodile, to take the ball away from her, that is, from the kitten. Elisabeth herself defended the ball passionately, repeatedly attacking the crocodile.

The game carried on like this for a while. Elisabeth crawled across the room with the crocodile, and the therapist was supposed to attack over and over again, Elisabeth would defend herself and win, defeating the crocodile. Elisabeth looked as though she was interwoven with the crocodile.

When the session was over and Elisabeth had already tied her shoelaces, she asked the therapist in an accusing tone, "Why didn't we do any drawing?" pointing to the blank paper on the table. The therapist answered, "Because you wanted to play the other game, with the ball and the crocodile." Elisabeth said to the therapist, "You could have put the ball away." The therapist understood that Elisabeth was trying to shift the responsibility for the wildness of the session on to the therapist. She placed her own aggressive impulses projectively in the therapist, so that they were not part of her self. Through this projective defence manoeuvre, it was now the therapist who was supposed to have played this wild and aggressive game, so that Elisabeth no longer embodied "the bad". The therapist again named the focus, by saying to Elisabeth, "You're afraid that I don't like you any more if you play so wildly. Like you're afraid that Mama doesn't like you any more if you have angry feelings." Elisabeth listened attentively and nodded.

In the parent sessions, the therapist worked with the parents on a shared understanding of why Elisabeth sealed herself off within the family and also in other social contexts. The mother had had the impression, from right after Elisabeth's birth, of a kind of vicious circle. She now understood more clearly that Elisabeth remained a stranger to her, precisely because mother and daughter "protected" each other from their aggressive impulses and did not express the normal conflicts and frustrations with each other. As Elisabeth (and also her mother) increasingly dared to expect more aggression to be tolerated in her interaction with someone else, the mother experienced Elisabeth as increasingly "graspable", not so alien, but, rather, part of her own world, and was better able to empathise with her. Over the course of PaCT, the mother could also increasingly see parallels with herself as a child.

In the parent sessions, the therapist learnt that Elisabeth was developing very well. At school she was more confident and had become friends with some boys in the group. She enjoyed playing the flute, and had even insisted that she play something "of her own" at the school's Advent concert.

Concluding phase

A few sessions before the end of the treatment, the therapist noticed that it was apparently important for Elisabeth that—even though there was always an alternation between aggressive and libidinal transference elements in the sessions—she and the therapist always parted amicably. The therapist thought that even if Elisabeth attacked her wildly in play, she always reassured herself at the end of the session that these attacks had been survived and that the therapist had been preserved as an object.

Elisabeth constructed the final session particularly impressively. In the run-up to saying goodbye, which was apparently very important to her, she asked the therapist repeatedly what she "would like to play", or what sweets or biscuits she liked to eat. Some sessions previously, she had announced that she wanted to do something special with the therapist to say goodbye. The therapist understood this as meaning that, just as Elisabeth wanted her first encounter with the object after her birth to be a special act, which had been symbolised in her play through the ritual of the "birth of the kitten", it was also important to her to construct the letting go and separation from the object as an important psychic act. Elisabeth showed the therapist that this important psychic act of separation from the object required particular attention and an appropriate ritual. Separation from the object is a painful process and requires gradual preparation. The therapist thought that Elisabeth did not want to have to deal with her separation from the object with no preparation, as when, at the age of seven months, she had had to go to day-care, with no period of acclimatisation. She no longer accepted the separation from the object as something that happened insidiously, but actively marked what she had been unable to at the age of seven months when she had been abruptly entrusted to day-care, in a move her parents had viewed as "unobtrusive".

Elisabeth brought twelve little "pony figures" along to the final session (no. 25); they all had names, and the therapist was supposed to say goodbye to each of them. To do this, she first had laboriously to learn all twelve of their names off by heart! Elisabeth also brought muffins that she had baked herself, to eat together with the therapist. The therapist understood that Elisabeth wanted them both to take something into themselves to be preserved in her inner psychic space even after she had said goodbye. Something must remain, a "good internal object". The therapist saw very clearly that it was important to Elisabeth that they parted amicably, despite her attacks on the therapist and despite the battles that Elisabeth had fought with her in the transference; and it was also important that both of them had survived these battles. Elisabeth appeared to have achieved a better integration of good and bad self and object parts through treatment with PaCT, despite its short duration, and was now able to expect the object to be able to deal with her instinctual sides as well.

At the time of the follow-up, her mother reported that Elisabeth had "developed wonderfully". She now played the violin and even enjoyed playing in public, and she was now good friends with two other little girls.

NOTES

1. In this book, we use the female form for the therapist in order to enhance the readability. Of course, PaCT can also be administered by male therapists. Likewise, we use the male form for the child in order to improve readability.
2. Freud (1933a) describes a differently organised Oedipus complex for girls, in which he stresses above all the girl's pre-oedipal bond to her mother.
3. The names of the children in the case studies of this book have been changed, as have details of their families.

REFERENCES

AACAP (2012). Official action. Practice parameter for psychodynamic psychotherapy with children. *Journal of the American Academy of Child and Adolescent Psychiatry, 51*(5): 541–557.

Abelin, E. (1971). The role of the father in the separation-individuation process. In: J. B. McDevitt & C. F. Settlage (Eds.), *Separation–Individuation* (pp. 229–252). New York: International Universities Press.

Abelin, E. (1975). Some further observations and comments on the earliest role of the father. *International Journal of Psycho-Analysis, 56*, 293–302.

Abraham, K. (1924). *Versuch einer Entwicklungsgeschichte der Libido auf Grund der Psychoanalyse seelischer Störungen.* Leipzig: Internationaler Psychoanalytischer Verlag.

Achenbach, T. M. (1991). *Manual for the Child Behavior Checklist/4–18 and 1991 Profile.* Burlington: University of Vermont Department of Psychiatry.

Ainsworth, M., Blehar, M., Waters, E., & Wall, S. (1978). *Patterns of Attachment: A Psychological Study of the Strange Situation.* Hillsdale, NJ: Lawrence Erlbaum Associates.

Alonso, J., Angermeyer, M. C., Bernert, S., Bruffaerts, R., Brugha, I. S., Bryson, H., de Girolamo, G., de Graaf, R., Demyttenaere, K., Haro, J. M., Katz, S. J., Kessler, R. C., Kovess, V., Lepine, J. R., Ormel, J.,

Polidori, G., Russo, L. J., Vilagut, G., Almansa, J., Arbabzadeh-Bouchez, S., Autonell, J., Bernal, M., Buist-Bouwman, M. A., Codony, M., Domingo-Salvany, A., Ferrer, M., Joo, S. S., Martinez-Alonso, M., Matschinger, H., Mazzi, F., Morgan, Z., Morosini, R., Palacin, C., Romera, B., Taub, N., & Vollebergh, W. A. M. (2004). Prevalence of mental disorders in Europe: results from the European Study of the Epidemiology of Mental Disorders (ESEMeD) project. *Acta Psychiatrica Scandinavica, 109*: 21–27.

Alsaker, F., & Gutzwiller-Helfenfinger, E. (2009). Social behavior and peer relationships of victims, bully-victims, and bullies in kindergarten. In: S. R. Jimerson, S. M. Swearer, & D. L. Espelage (Eds.), *The International Handbook of School Bullying* (pp. 87–100). New York: Routledge.

American Psychiatric Association (2000). *Diagnostic and Statistical Manual of Mental Disorders (DSM-IV-TR)*. Lanham, VA: American Psychiatric Association.

Angold, A., & Costello, E. J. (2000). The Child and Adolescent Psychiatric Assessment (CAPA). *Journal of the American Academy of Child & Adolescent Psychiatry, 39*: 39–48.

Arbeitskreis OPD-KJ (2007). OPD-KJ – *Operationalisierte Psychodynamische Diagnostik im Kindes- und Jugendalter. Grundlagen und Manual.* Bern: Verlag Hans Huber.

Argelander, H. (1983). *Das Erstinterview in der Psychotherapie.* Darmstadt: Wissenschaftliche Buchgesellschaft.

Astington, J., & Jenkins, J. M. (1995). Theory of mind development and social understanding. *Cognition and Emotion, 9*: 151–165.

Baldwin, M. W. (1992). Relational schemas and the processing of social information. *Psychological Bulletin, 112*(3): 461–484.

Barber, J. P., Crits-Christoph, P., & Luborsky, L. (1996). Effects of therapist adherence and competence on patient outcome in brief dynamic therapy. *Journal of Consulting and Clinical Psychology, 64*(3): 619–622.

Baron-Cohen, S. (1995). *Mindblindness: An Essay on Autism and Theory of Mind.* Cambridge, MA: Bradford, MIT Press.

Baron-Cohen, S., Tager-Flusberg, H., & Cohen, D. J. (1993). *Understanding Other Minds: Perspectives from Autism.* Oxford: Oxford University Press.

Baron-Cohen, S., Wheelwright, S., Hill, J., Raste, Y., & Plumb, I. (2001). The "Reading the mind in the eyes" test revised version: a study with normal adults, and adults with Asperger Syndrome or high-functioning autism. *Journal of Child Psychology and Psychiatry, 42*: 241–251

Bateman, A. W., & Fonagy, P. (2006). Mentalizing and borderline personality disorder. In: J. G. Allen & P. Fonagy (Eds.), *Handbook of Mentalization Based Treatment* (pp. 185–200). Chichester: John Wiley.

Bauriedl, T. (1980). *Beziehungsanalyse: Das dialektisch-emanzipatorische Prinzip der Psychoananlyse und seine Konsequenzen für die psychoanalytische Familientherapie*. Frankfurt a. M.: Suhrkamp.

Bayer, J. K., Sanson, A. V., & Hemphill, S. A. (2006). Children's moods, fears, and worries: development of an early childhood parent questionnaire. *Journal of Emotional and Behavioral Disorders, 14*(1): 41–49.

Beebe, B., Jaffe, J., & Lachmann, F. M. (1992). A dyadic systems view of communication. In: N. Skolnick & S. Warshaw (Eds.), *Relational Perspectives in Psychoanalysis* (pp. 61–82). Hillsdale NJ: Analytic Press.

Beelmann, A., Stemmler, M., Losel, F., & Jaursch, S. (2007). The development of externalizing behavior problems in the transition from pre- to elementary school age: Risk effects of maternal and paternal parenting. *Kindheit und Entwicklung, 16*(4): 229–239.

Belsky, J., Bakermans-Kranenburg, M. J., & van IJzendoorn, M. H. (2007). For better and for worse: differential susceptibility to environmental influences. *Current Directions in Psychological Science, 16*: 300–304.

Bettes, B. A. (1988). Maternal depression and motherese: temporal and intentional features. *Child Development, 59*: 1089–1096.

Beyer, T., & Furniss, T. (2007). Child psychiatric symptoms in primary school. *Social Psychiatry and Psychiatric Epidemiology, 42*(9): 753–758.

Bick, E. (1968). The experience of the skin in early object relations. *International Journal of Psychoanalysis, 45*: 484–486.

Bion, W. R. (1962). *Learning from Experience*. London: Karnac, 1992.

Bion, W. R. (1963). *Elements of Psycho-Analysis*. London: Heinemann.

Birmaher, B., Ryan, N. D., Williamson, D. E., Brent, D. A., Kaufman, J., Dahl, R. E., Perel, J., & Nelson, B. (1996). Childhood and adolescent depression: A review of the past 10 years. *Journal of the American Academy of Child and Adolescent Psychiatry, 35*(11): 1427–1439.

Blanz, B., Schmidt, M. H., & Esser, G. (1991). Familial adversities and child psychiatric disorders. *Journal of Child Psychology and Psychiatry, 32*(6): 939–950.

Blatt, S. J. (1995). Representational structures in psychopathology. SE: Rochester symposium on developmental psychopathology. In: D. Cicchetti & S. L. Toth (Eds.), *Emotion, Cognition, and Representation* (pp. 1–33). Rochester, NY: University of Rochester Press.

Blatt, S. J., & Shahar, G. (2004). Psychoanalysis: with whom, for what, and how? Comparisons with psychotherapy. *Journal of the American Psychoanalytic Association, 52*: 393–447.

Blatt, S. J., Luyten, P., & Corveleyn, J. (2005). Zur Entwicklung eines dynamischen Interaktionsmodells der Depression. *Psyche – Zeitschrift für Psychoanalyse und ihre Anwendungen, 59*(9 / 10): 864–891.

Bohlin, G., Bengtsgard, K., & Andersson, K. (2000). Social inhibition and overfriendliness as related to socioemotional functioning in 7- and 8-year-old children. *Journal of Clinical Child Psychology*, 29(3): 414–423.

Boothe, B. (1992). The unavailable relationship, the capacity to be alone and the female Oedipal development. *International Forum of Psychoanalysis*, 1: 104–109.

Boothe, B., & Heigl-Evers, A. (1996). *Psychoanalyse der frühen weiblichen Entwicklung*. München: Ernst Reinhard Verlag.

Borens, R. (1993). "... Vater sein dagegen sehr". *Zeitschrift für Psychoanalytische Theorie und Praxis*, 8(1): 19–31.

Bosquet, M., & Egeland, B. (2006). The development and maintenance of anxiety symptoms from infancy through adolescence in a longitudinal sample. *Development and Psychopathology*, 18(2): 517–550.

Bowlby, J. (1969). *Attachment and Loss. I: Attachment*. New York: Basic Books.

Bramesfeld, A., & Stoppe, G. (2006). Einführung. In: G. Stoppe, A. Bramesfeld & F.-W. Schwartz (Eds.), *Volkskrankheit Depression? Bestandsaufnahme und Perspektiven* (pp. 1–12). Berlin: Springer.

Bretherton, I. (1985). Attachment theory: retrospect and prospect. *Monographs of the Society for Research in Child Development*, 50(1–2): 3–35.

Bretherton, I., & Oppenheim, D. (2003). The MacArthur Story Stem Battery: development, administration, reliability, validity, and reflections about meaning. In: R. N. Emde, D. P. Wolf, & D. Oppenheim (Eds.), *Revealing the Inner Worlds of Young Children. The MacArthur Story Stem Battery and Parent–Child Narratives* (pp. 55–80). New York: Oxford University Press.

Bretherton, I., Rodrigues, L. M., & Cassidy, J. (1990). Assessing internal working models of the attachment relationship: an attachment story completion task for 3-year-olds. In: M. T. Greenberg, D. Cicchetti, & E. M. Cummings (Eds.), *Attachment in Preschool Years. Theory, Research and Intervention*. Chicago, IL: University of Chicago Press.

Breton, J. J., Bergeron, L., Valla, J.-P., Berthiaume, C., Gaudet, N., Lambert, J., St-Georges, M., Houde, L., & Lépine, S. (1999). Quebec Child Mental Health Survey: Prevalence of DSM-III-R mental health disorders. *Journal of Child Psychology and Psychiatry*, 40(3): 375–384.

Brickman, H. R. (1993). Between the Devil and the deep blue sea: the dyad and the triad in psychoanalytic thought. *International Journal of Psychoanalysis*, 74(5): 905–915.

Buchholz, M. (1990). Die Rotation der Triade. *Forum der Psychoanalyse*, 6: 116–134.

Buchsbaum, H. K., & Emde, R. N. (1990). Play narratives in 36-month-old children: early moral development and family relationships. *Psychoanalytic Study of the Child*, 45: 129–155.

Caldji, C., Diorio, J., & Meaney, M. J. (2003). Variations in maternal care alter GABA(A) receptor subunit expression in brain regions associated with fear. *Neuropsychopharmacology Review*, 28: 1950–1959.

Carlson, J. G., & Hartfield, E. (1992). *Psychology and Emotion*. Fort Worth: Harcourt Brace Jovanovich.

Cartwright-Hatton, S., McNicol, K., & Doubleday, E. (2006). Anxiety in a neglected population: prevalence of anxiety disorders in pre-adolescent children. *Clinical Psychology Review*, 26: 817–833.

Caspi, A., Sugden, K., Moffitt, T. E., Taylor, A., Craig, I. W., Harrington, H., McClay, J., Mill, J., Martin, J., Braithwaite, A., & Poulton, R. (2003). Influence of life stress on depression: moderation by a polymorphism in the 5-HTT gene. *Science*, 301(5631): 386–389.

Chethik, M. (1989). *Techniques of Child Therapy. Psychodynamic Strategies*. New York: Guilford Press.

Cierpka, M. (1987). *Familiendiagnostik*. Heidelberg, Berlin, New York: Springer.

Cohn, J. F., Matias, R., Tronick, E. Z., Conell, D., & Lyons-Ruth, K. (1986). Face to face interactions of depressed mothers and their infants. In: E. Z. Tronick & T. Field (Eds.), *Maternal Depression and Infant Disturbance* (pp. 31–45). San Francisco, CA: Jossey-Bass.

Costello, E. J., Angold, A., Burns, B. J., Stangl, D. K., Tweed, D. L., Erkanli, A., & Worthman, L. M. (1996). The Great Smoky Mountains Study of youth: goals, designs, methods, and the prevalence of DSM-III-R disorders. *Archives of General Psychiatry*, 53(12): 1129–1136.

Costello, E. J., Mustillo, S., Erkanli, A., Keeler, G., & Angold, A. (2003). Prevalence and development of psychiatric disorders in childhood and adolescence. *Archives of General Psychiatry*, 60(8): 837–844.

Crits-Christoph, P., Crits-Christoph, K., Wolf-Palacio, D., Fichter, M., & Rudick, D. (1995). Brief supportive-expressive psychodynamic therapy for generalized anxiety disorder. In: P. Jacques & P. Crits-Christoph (Eds.), *Dynamic Therapies for Psychiatric Disorders (Axis I)* (pp. 43–83). New York: Basic Books.

Dammasch, F., & Metzger, H. G. (1999). Die Suche nach der Differenz – Zur Bedeutung des Vaters in der familialen Triade. *Zeitschrift für psychoanalytische Theorie und Praxis*, 14: 284–307.

De M'Uzan, M. (1994). *La bouche de l'inconscient*. Mayenne: Edition Gallimard.

Deater-Deckard, K. (2001). Annotation: recent research examining the role of peer relationships in the development of psychopathology. *Journal of Child Psychology and Psychiatry and Allied Disciplines, 42*(5): 565–579.

Deater-Deckard, K., Dodge, K. A., Bates, J. E., & Pettit, G. S. (1998). Multiple risk factors in the development of externalizing behavior problems: group and individual differences. *Development and Psychopathology, 10*(3): 469–493.

Deutsch, H. (1925). *Psychoanalyse der weiblichen Sexualfunktionen.* Wien: Psychoanalytischer Verlag.

Dunn, J., Brown, J., Slomkowski, C., Telsa, C., & Youngblade, L. (1991). Young children's understanding of other people's feelings and beliefs: individual differences and their antecedents. *Child Development, 62:* 1352–1366.

Dunn, V., & Goodyer, I. M. (2006). Longitudinal investigation into childhood- and adolescence-onset depression: psychiatric outcome in early adulthood. *British Journal of Psychiatry, 188:* 216–222.

Egger, H. L., & Angold, A. (2004). The Preschool Age Psychiatric Assessment (PAPA): A structured parent interview for diagnosing psychiatric disorders in preschool children. In: R. DelCarmen-Wiggins & A. Carter (Eds.), *Handbook of Infant, Toddler, and Preschool Mental Health Assessment* (pp. 223–243). New York: Oxford University Press.

Egger, H. L., Ascher, B. H., & Angold, A. (2004). *The Preschool Age Psychiatric Assessment (PAPA).* Durham, NC: Center for Developmental Epidemiology, Department of Psychiatry and Behavioral Sciences, Duke University Medical Center.

Ellis, B. J., Boyce, W. T., Belsky, J., Bakermans-Kranenburg, M. J., & van IJzendoorn, M. H. (2011). Differential susceptibility to the environment: an evolutionary neurodevelopmental theory. *Development and Psychopathology, 23:* 7–28.

Emanuel, L. (2011). Beobachtung, Reflexion, Containement: Psychoanalytisches Arbeiten mit Kinder unter 5 Jahren. *Kinderanalyse, 19*(3): 215–240.

Emde, R. N. (2009). From ego to "we-go": neurobiology and questions for psychoanalysis. Commentary on papers by Threvarthen, Gallese, Ammaniti & Trentini. *Psychoanalytic Dialogues, 19:* 556–564.

Emde, R. N. (2011). Regeneration und Neuanfänge. Perspektiven einer entwicklungsbezogenen Ausrichtung der Psychoanalyse. *Psyche-Zeitschrift für Psychoanalyse und ihre Anwendungen, 65:* 778–807.

Emde, R. N., Wolf, D., & Oppenheim, D. (2003). *Revealing the Inner Worlds of Young Children. The MacArthur Story Stem Battery and Parent–Child Narratives.* New York: Oxford University Press.

Eron, L. D., & Huesman, L. R. (1984). The relation of prosocial behavior to the development of aggression and psychopathology. *Aggressive Behavior, 10*(3): 201–211.

Esser, G., Schmidt, M. H., & Woerner, W. (1990). Epidemiology and course of psychiatric disorders in school-age children: results of a longitudinal study. *Journal of Child Psychology and Psychiatry, 31*(2): 243–263.

Field, T. (1998). Maternal depression effects on infants and early interventions. *Preventive Medicine, 27*(2): 200–203.

Fivaz-Depeursinge, E., & Corboz-Warnery, A. (1999). *The Primary Triangle*. New York: Basic Books.

Fivaz-Depeursinge, E., Lavanchy-Scaiola, C., & Favez, N. (2010). The young infant's triangular communication in the family: access to threesome intersubjectivity? conceptual considerations and case illustrations. *Psychoanalytic Dialogues, 20*(2): 125–140.

Fleming, J. E., & Offord, D. R. (1990). Epidemiology of childhood depressive-disorders—a critical review. *Journal of the American Academy of Child and Adolescent Psychiatry, 29*(4): 571–580.

Flinn, M. V., & England, B. G. (1995). Childhood stress and family environment. *Current Anthropology, 36*(5): 854–866.

Fonagy, P. (1995). Playing with reality: the development of psychic reality and its malfunction in borderline personalities. *International Journal of Psychoanalysis, 76*: 39–44.

Fonagy, P. (2000). Psychoanalysis and developmental psychopathology: From attachment to borderline personality disorder. *International Journal of Psychology, 35*(3–4): 96.

Fonagy, P. (2006). The mentalization-focused approach to social development. In: P. Fonagy & J. G. Allen (Eds.), *Handbook of Mentalization-based Treatment* (pp. 53–100). Chichester: John Wiley.

Fonagy, P. (2008). The mentalization-focused approach to social development. In: F. N. Bush (Ed.), *Mentalization. Theoretical Considerations, Research Findings, and Clinical Implications* (pp. 3–56). New York: Analytic Press.

Fonagy, P., & Target, M. (1994). The efficacy of psychoanalysis for children with disruptive disorders. *Journal of the American Academy of Child and Adolescent Psychiatry, 33*(1): 45–55.

Fonagy, P., & Target, M. (1997). Attachment and refelective function: their role in self-organization. *Development and Psychopathology, 9*: 679–700.

Fonagy, P., & Target, M. (2000). Mentalisation and the changing aims of child psychoanalysis. In: K. von Klitzing, P. Tyson, & D. Bürgin (Eds.), *Psychoanalysis in Childhood and Adolescence* (pp. 129–139). Basel: Karger.

Fonagy, P., Gergely, G., Jurist, E., & Target, M. (2004). *Affect Regulation, Mentalization and the Development of the Self*. London: Karnac.

Fonagy, P., Steele, M., Steele, H., Moran, G., & Higitt, A. (1991). The capacity for understanding mental states: the reflective self in parent and child and its significance for security of attachment. *Infant Mental Health Journal, 12*: 201–217.

Fonagy, P., Target, M., Steele, H., & Steele, M. (1998). *Reflective-Functioning Manual, Version 5.0, for Application to Adult Attachment Interviews*. London: University College London.

Frascarolo, F., Favez, N., Carneiro, C., & Fivaz-Depeursinge, E. (2004). Hierarchy of interactive functions in father–mother–baby three-way games. *Infant and Child Development, 13*(4): 301–322.

Freud, A. (1936). *The Ego and the Mechanisms of Defense*. In: *The Writings of Anna Freud* (Vol. II). New York: International Universities Press.

Freud, A. (1945). Indications for child analysis. *Psychoanalytic Study of the Child, 1*: 127–149.

Freud, A. (1965). *Normality and Pathology in Childhood: Assessments of Development*. London: Hogarth Press.

Freud, A. (1968). Indications and contraindications for child analysis. *Psychoanalytic Study of the Child, 23*: 37–46.

Freud, A. (1980). Transference. In: J. Sandler, H. Kennedy, H., & H. Tyson (Eds.), *The Technique of Child Analysis. Discussions with Anna Freud* (pp. 78–104). Cambridge, MA: Harvard University Press.

Freud, S. (1900a). *The Interpretation of Dreams*. S.E., 4. London: Hogarth.

Freud, S. (1905d). *Three Essays on the Theory of Sexuality*. S.E., 7: 125–245. London: Hogarth.

Freud, S. (1910d). The future prospects of psycho-analytic therapy. S.E., 11: 139–152. London: Hogarth.

Freud, S. (1911b). Formulations on the two principles of mental functioning. S.E., 12: 213–226. London: Hogarth.

Freud, S. (1912b). The dynamics of transference. S.E., 12: 97–108. London: Hogarth.

Freud, S. (1914c). On narcissism: an introduction. S.E., 14: 67–102. London: Hogarth.

Freud, S. (1915d). Repression. S.E., 14: 143–158. London: Hogarth.

Freud, S. (1915e). The unconscious. S.E. 14: 161–215. London: Hogarth.

Freud, S. (1917e). Mourning and melancholia. S.E., 14: 239–258. London: Hogarth.

Freud, S. (1920g). *Beyond the Pleasure Principle*. S.E., 18: 7–64. London: Hogarth.

Freud, S. (1921c). *Group Psychology and the Analysis of the Ego*. *S.E.*, *18*: 67–143. London: Hogarth.

Freud, S. (1923a). Two encyclopaedia articles. *Beyond the Pleasure Principle and Group Psychology and Other Works*. *S.E.*, *18*: 233–260.

Freud, S. (1923b). *The Ego and the Id*. *S.E.*, *19*: 3–66. London: Hogarth.

Freud, S. (1924d). The dissolution of the Oedipus complex. *S.E.*, *19*: 173–182. London: Hogarth.

Freud, S. (1933a). *New Introductory Lectures on Psycho-Analysis*. *S.E.*, *22*: 1–182. London: Hogarth.

Freud, S. (1950[1895]). Project for a scientific psychology. *S.E.*, *1*: 281–391.

Fuchs, S., Klein, A. M., Otto, Y., & von Klitzing, K. (2013). Prevalence of emotional and behavioural symptoms and their impact on daily life activities in a community sample of 3 to 5-year old children. *Child Psychiatry and Human Development*, *44*(4): 493–503.

Gast, L. (1996). Himmel und Hölle, Paradies und Schreckenskammer. Die Idee der Subjektgenese im phantasmatischen Raum bei Freud und Klein. *Luzifer-Amor*, *17*(9): 167–187.

Gergely, G., & Watson, J. S. (1996). The social biofeedback theory of parental affect mirroring: the development of social biofeedback theory emotional self-awareness and self-control in infancy. *International Journal of Psychoanalysis*, *77*: 1181–1212.

Gjerde, P., & Block, J. (1991). Preadolescent antecedents of depressive symptomatology at age 18. A prospective study. *Journal of Youth and Adolescence*, *20*: 217–232.

Goodman, R. (2001). Psychometric properties of the strengths and difficulties questionnaire. *Journal of the American Academy of Child and Adolescent Psychiatry*, *40*(11): 1337–1345.

Gopnik, A. (1993). How we know our minds: the illusion of 1st-person knowledge of intentionality. *Behavioral and Brain Sciences*, *16*(1): 1–14.

Gopnik, A., & Meltzoff, A. (1993). Imitation, cultural learning and the origins of theory of mind. *Behavioral and Brain Sciences*, *16*(3): 521–523.

Göttken, T., White, L. O., Klein, A. M., & von Klitzing, K. (under review). Short-term Psychoanalytic Child Therapy for anxiety disorders in young children: a pilot study in a clinical setting.

Gottman, J. M. (1981). *Time-Series Analysis: A Comprehensive Introduction for Social Scientists*. Cambridge: University Press.

Granger, D. A., Weisz, J. R., McCracken, J. T., Ikeda, S. C., & Douglas, P. (1996). Reciprocal influences among adrenocortical activation, psychosocial processes, and the behavioral adjustment of clinic-referred children. *Child Development*, *67*(6): 3250–3262.

Green, A. (2004). *Die tote Mutter. Psychoanalytische Studien zu Lebens-narzissmus und Tobesnarzissmus*. Gießen: Psychosozial-Verlag.

Günter, M. (2007). *Playing the Unconscious. Psychoanalytic Interviews with Children using Winnicott's Squiggle Technique*. London: Karnac.

Hahlweg, K., Heinrichs, N., Bertram, H., Kuschel, A., & Widdecke, N. (2008). Corporal punishment: prevalence and impact on psychological development of preschool children. *Kindheit und Entwicklung, 17*(1): 46–56.

Hariri, A. R., Mattay, V. S., & Tessitore, A. (2002). Serotonin transporter genetic variation and the response of the human amygdale. *Science, 297*: 400–403.

Hartmann, M., Kronmüller, K. T., Horn, H., Reck, C., Backenstraß, M., Neumann, K., Victor, D., & Winkelmann, K. (2000). Wirkfaktoren in der analytischen Kurzzeittherapie bei Kindern und Jugendlichen. *Analytische Kinder- und Jugendlichenpsychotherapie, 31*: 123–152.

Harvey, S. T., & Pun, P. P. K. (2007). Analysis of positive Edinburgh depression scale referrals to a consultation liaison psychiatry service in a two-year period. *International Journal of Mental Health Nursing, 16*: 161–167.

Hastings, P. D., Sullivan, C., McShane, K. E., Utendale, W. T., Coplan, R. J., & Vyncke, J. D. (2008). Parental socialization, vagal regulation, and preschoolers' anxious difficulties: direct mothers and moderated fathers. *Child Development, 79*(1): 45–64.

Hastings, P. D., Zahn-Waxler, C., Robinson, J., Usher, B., & Bridges, D. (2000). The development of concern for others in children with behavioral problems. *Developmental Psychology, 36*: 531–546.

Hatzinger, M., Brand, S., Perren, S., von Wyl, A., von Klitzing, K., & Holsboer-Trachsler, E. (2007). Hypothalamic-pituitary-adrenocortical (HPA) activity in kindergarten children: Importance of gender and associations with behavioral/emotional difficulties. *Journal of Psychiatric Research, 41*(10): 861–870.

Hay, D. F., & Pawlby, S. (2003). Prosocial development in relation to children's and mothers' psychological problems. *Child Development, 74*(5): 1314–1327.

Hay, D. F., Payne, A., & Chadwick, A. (2004). Peer relations in childhood. *Journal of Child Psychology and Psychiatry, 45*(1): 84–108.

Heimann, P. (1950). On counter-transference. *International Journal of Psychoanalysis, 31*: 81–84.

Hofstra, M. B., van der Ende, J., & Verhulst, F. C. (2002). Child and adolescent problems predict DSM-IV disorders in adulthood: a 14-year follow-up of a Dutch epidemiological sample. *Journal of the American Academy of Child and Adolescent Psychiatry, 41*(2): 182–189.

Holsboer, F., Lauer, C. J., Schreiber, W., & Krieg, J. C. (1995). Altered hypothalamic-pituitary-adrenocortical regulation in healthy subjects at high familial risk for affective disorders *Neuroendocrinology*, *62*: 340–347.

Horney, K. (1926). The flight from womanhood: the masculinity-complex in women as viewed by men and by women. *International Journal of Psycho-Analysis*, *7*: 324–339.

Hudson, J. L., & Rapee, R. M. (2000). Parent–child interactions and anxiety disorders: an observational study. *Behaviour Research and Therapy*, *39*(12): 1411–1427

Ialongo, N. S., Edelsohn, G., & Kellam, S. G. (2001). A further look at the prognostic power of young children's reports of depressed mood and feelings. *Child Development*, *72*(3): 736–747.

Ialongo, N., Edelsohn, G., Werthamer-Larsson, L., Crockett, L., & Kellam, S. (1995). The significance of self-reported anxious symptoms in first-grade children: prediction to anxious symptoms and adaptive functioning in 5th grade. *Journal of Child Psychology and Psychiatry and Allied Disciplines*, *36*(3): 427–437.

Ihle, W., Esser, G., Schmidt, M. H., & Blanz, B. (2000). Prävalenz, Komorbidität und Geschlechtsunterschiede psychischer Störungen vom Grundschul- bis ins frühe Erwachsenenalter. *Zeitschrift für Klinische Psychologie und Psychotherapie*, *29*(4): 263–275.

Isaacs, S. (1948). The nature and function of phantasy. *International Journal of Psychoanalysis*, *29*: 73–97.

Izard, C. E. (1994). *Die Emotionen des Menschen*. Weinheim: Psychologie Verlags Union.

Jacobs, B. L., van Praag, H., & Gage, F. (2000). Depression and the birth and death of brain cells. *American Scientist*, *88*: 240–345.

Jaffe, J., Beebe, B., Feldstein, S., Crown, C., & Jasnow, M. (2001). Rhythms of dialogue in infancy. *Monographs of the Society for Research in Child Development*, *66*(2): 1–153.

Jakobson, E. (1971). *Depression*. Frankfurt: Suhrkamp.

Jessop, D. S., & Turner-Cobb, J. M. (2008). Measurement and meaning of salivary cortisol: a focus on health and disease in children. *Stress — The International Journal on the Biology of Stress*, *11*: 1–14.

Jones, E. (1935). Early female sexuality. *International Journal of Psychoanalysis*, *16*: 263–273.

Jongbloed-Schurig, U. (2001). Die Fokalkonferenz. *Analytische Kinder- und Jugendlichenpsychotherapie*, *32*: 209–332.

Kaufman, J., Yang, B. Z., Douglas-Palumberi, H., Houshyar, S., Lipschitz, D., Krystal, J. H., & Gelernter, J. (2004). Social supports and serotonin transporter gene moderate depression in maltreated children. *Proceedings of the National Academy of Sciences of the United States of America*, 101(49): 17316–17321.

Kernberg, O. F. (1975). *Borderline Conditions and Pathological Narcissism*. Lanham, MD: Jason Aronson.

Kernberg, O. F. (1976). *Object Relations Theory and Clinical Psychoanalysis*. New York: Jason Aronson.

Kernberg, O. F. (1984). *Severe Personality Disorders: Psychotherapeutic Strategies*. Cambridge, MA: Yale University Press.

Kim-Cohen, J., Caspi, A., Moffitt, T. E., Harrington, H., Milne, B. J., & Poulton, R. (2003). Prior juvenile diagnoses in adults with mental disorder: developmental follow-back of a prospective-longitudinal cohort. *Archives of General Psychiatry*, 60(7): 709–717.

Klein, A. M., Otto, Y., Fuchs, S., Zenger, M. & von Klitzing, K. (2012). Psychometric properties of the parent-rated SDQ in preschoolers. *European Journal of Psychological Assessment*, doi: 10.1027/1015–5759/a000129.

Klein, M. (1928). Early stages of Oedipus conflict. *International Journal of Psycho-Analysis*, 9: 167–180.

Klein, M. (1940). Mourning and its relation to manic-depressive states. *International Journal of Psychoanalysis*, 21: 125–153.

Klein, M. (1946). Notes on some schizoid mechanisms. *International Journal of Psychoanalysis*, 27: 99–110.

Klüwer, R. (1983). Agieren und Mitagieren. *Psyche- Zeitschrift für Psychoanalyse und ihre Anwendungen*, 37: 828–840.

Klüwer, R. (2005). *Erweiterte Studien zur Fokaltherapie*. Gießen: Psychosozial-Verlag.

Kroes, M., Kalff, A. C., Steyaert, J., Kessels, A. G. H., Feron, F. J. M., Hendriksen, J. G. M., van Zeben, T., Troost, J., Jolles, J., & Vles, J. (2002). A longitudinal community study: do psychosocial risk factors and child behavior checklist scores at 5 years of age predict psychiatric diagnoses at a later age? *Journal of the American Academy of Child and Adolescent Psychiatry*, 41(8): 955–963.

Lacan, J. (1953). The function and field of speech and language in psychoanalysis. In: *Écrits. The First Complete Edition in English*, B. Fink (Trans.). New York/London: W. W. Norton & Company, 2006.

Lacan, J. (1993). *The Seminar, Book III. The Psychoses*, R. Grigg (Trans.), J.-A. Miller (Ed.). New York: W. W. Norton.

Lahey, B. B., Schwab-Stone, M., Goodman, S. H., Waldman, I. D., Canino, G., Rathouz, P. J., Miller, T., Dennis K. D., Bird, H., & Jensen, P. S. (2000). Age and gender differences in oppositional behavior and conduct problems: a cross-sectional household study of middle child-hood and adolescence. *Journal of Abnormal Psychology, 109*(3): 488–503.

Laplanche, J., & Pontalis, J.-B. (1973). *The Language of Psychoanalysis*. London: Hogarth [reprinted London: Karnac, 1988].

Lavigne, J. V., Arend, R., Rosenbaum, D., Binns, H. J., Christoffel, K. K., & Gibbons, R. D. (1998a). Psychiatric disorders with onset in the preschool years: I. Stability of diagnoses. *Journal of the American Academy of Child and Adolescent Psychiatry, 37*(12): 1246–1254.

Lavigne, J. V., Arend, R., Rosenbaum, D., Binns, H. J., Christoffel, K. K., & Gibbons, R. D. (1998b). Psychiatric disorders with onset in the preschool years: II. Correlates and predictors of stable case status. *Journal of the American Academy of Child and Adolescent Psychiatry, 37*(12): 1255–1261.

LeDoux, J. (1996). *The Emotional Brain*. New York: Touchstone.

Lesch, K. P., Bengel, D., & Heils, A. (1996). Association of anxiety-related traits with a polymorphism in the serotonin transporter gene regulatory region. *Science, 274*: 1527–1531.

Leuzinger-Bohleber, M. (2010). Depression und Neuroplastizität: Psycho-analytische Klinik und Forschung. Eine Einführung. In: M. Leuzinger-Bohleber, K. Röcherath, & L. V. Strauss (Eds.), *Depression und Neuroplastizität. Psychoanalytische Klinik und Forschung* (pp. 7–30). Frankfurt: Brandes & Apsel.

Leve, L. D., Kim, H. K., & Pears, K. C. (2005). Childhood temperament and family environment as predictors of internalizing and externalizing trajectories from ages 5 to 17. *Journal of Abnormal Child Psychology, 33*(5): 505–520.

Leverich, G. S., Post, R. M., Keck, P. E., Altshuler, L. L., Frye, M. A., Kupka, R. W., Nolen, W., Suppes, T., McElroy, S. L., Grunze, H., Denicoff, K., Moravec, M. K., & Luckenbaugh, D. (2007). The poor prognosis of childhood-onset bipolar disorder. *Journal of Pediatrics, 150*(5): 485–490.

Lewinsohn, P. M., Rohde, P., & Seeley, J. R. (1998). Major depressive disorder in older adolescents: Prevalence, risk factors, and clinical implications. *Clinical Psychology Review, 18*(7): 765–794.

Liu, D., Diorio, J., Day, J. C., Francis, D. D., & Meaney, M. J. (2000). Maternal care, hippocampal synaptogenesis and cognitive development in rats. *Nature Neuroscience, 3*(8): 799–806.

Lorenzer, A. (1970). *Sprachzerstörung und Rekonstruktion. Vorarbeiten zu einer Metatheorie der Psychoanalyse*. Frankfurt: Suhrkamp.

Luborsky, L., Popp, C., Luborsky, E., & Mark, D. (1994). The core conflictual relationship theme. *Psychotherapy Research, 4*(3&4): 172–183.

Luby, J., Belden, A., C., & Spitznagel, E. (2006). Risk factors for preschool depression: the mediating role of early stressful life events. *Journal of Child Psychology and Psychiatry, 47*(12): 1292–1298.

Luby, J., Heffelfinger, A. K., Mrakotsky, C., Hessler, M. J., Brown, K. M., & Hildebrand, T. (2002). Preschool Major Depressive Disorder: preliminary validation for developmentally modified DSM-IV criteria. *Journal of American Academy of Child and Adolescence Psychiatry, 41*(8): 928–937.

Lucia, V. C., & Breslau, N. (2006). Family cohesion and children's behavior problems: a longitudinal investigation. *Psychiatry Research, 141*(2): 141–149.

Lyons, J. S., Uziel-Miller, N. D., Reyes, F., & Sokol, P. T. (2000). Strengths of children and adolescents in residential settings: Prevalence and associations with psychopathology and discharge placement. *Journal of the American Academy of Child and Adolescent Psychiatry, 39*(2): 176–181.

Mahler, M., & Gosliner, B. (1955). On symbiotic child psychosis: genetic, dynamic, and restitutive aspects. *Psychoanalytic Study of the Child, 10*: 195–214.

Mahler, M. S., Pine, F., & Bergmann, A. (1975). *The Psychological Birth of the Human Infant.* New York: Basic Books.

Main, M., Kaplan, N., & Cassidy, J. (1985). Security in infancy, childhood and adulthood: a move to the level of representation. In: I. Bretherton & E. Waters (Eds.), *Growing Points of Attachment Theory and Research* (pp. 1–29). Chicago, IL: University of Chicago Press for the Society of Research in Child Development.

Malan, D. (1963). *A Study of Brief Psychotherapy.* London: Tavistock.

Malatesta, C. Z., Culver, C., Tesman, J. R., & Shepard, B. (1989). The development of emotion expression during the first two years of life. *Monographs of the Society for Research in Child Development, 54*: 1–104.

McArdle, P., Prosser, J., & Kolvin, I. (2004). Prevalence of psychiatric disorder: with and without psychosocial impairment. *European Child and Adolescent Psychiatry, 13*(6): 347–353.

McBurnett, K., Lahey, B. B., Rathouz, P. J., & Loeber, R. (2000). Low salivary cortisol and persistent aggression in boys referred for disruptive behavior. *Archives of General Psychiatry, 57*(1): 38–43.

McDonnell, M. A., & Glod, C. (2003). Prevalence of psychopathology in preschool-age children. *Journal of Child and Adolescent Psychiatric Nursing, 16*(4): 141–152.

McEwen, B. S. (2002). Protective and damaging effects of stress mediators: the good and bad sides of the response to stress. *Metabolism, 51*(6): 2–4.

McHale, J. P., & Rasmussen, J. L. (1998). Coparental and family group-level dynamics during infancy: early family precursors of child and family functioning during preschool. *Development and Psychopathology,* 10: 39–59.

Meltzer, H., Gatward, R., Goodman, R., & Ford, T. (2003). Mental health of children and adolescents in Great Britain (reprinted from 2000). *International Review of Psychiatry,* 15(1–2): 185–187.

Meltzoff, A. N. (2002). Imitation as a mechanism of social cognition: origins of empathy, theory of mind, and the representation of action. In: U. Goswami (Ed.), *Handbook of Childhood Cognitive Development* (pp. 6–25). Oxford: Blackwell.

Menninger, K. A., & Holzmann, P. S. (1958). *Theorie der psychoanalytischen Technik.* Stuttgart: Klett-Cotta.

Mentzos, S. (2006). *Depression und Manie. Psychodynamik und Therapie affektiver Störungen.* Göttingen: Vandenhoeck & Ruprecht.

Mesman, J., Bongers, I. L., & Koot, H. M. (2001). Preschool developmental pathways to preadolescent internalizing and externalizing problems. *Journal of Child Psychology and Psychiatry,* 42(5): 679–689.

Mondimore, F. M., Zandi, P. P., MacKinnon, D. F., McInnis, M. G., Miller, E. B., Crowe, R. P., Scheffner, W. A., Marta, D. H., Weissman, M. M., Levinson, D. F., Murphy-Ebenez, K., DePaulo, J. R., & Potash, J. B. (2006). Familial aggregation of illness chronicity in recurrent, early-onset major depression pedigrees. *American Journal of Psychiatry,* 163(9): 1554–1560.

Morton, J., & Frith, U. (1995). Causal modeling: a structural approach to developmental psychology. In: D. Cicchetti & D. J. Cohen (Eds.), *Developmental Psychopathology. Vol. 1. Theory and Methods* (pp. 357–390). New York: John Wiley.

Moss, H. B., Vanyukov, M. M., & Marti, C. S. (1995). Salivary cortisol responses and the risk for substance abuse in prepubertal boys. *Biological Psychiatry,* 38: 547–555.

Mun, E. Y., Fitzgerald, H. E., Von Eye, A., Puttler, L. I., & Zucker, R. A. (2001). Temperamental characteristics as predictors of externalizing and internalizing child behavior problems in the contexts of high and low parental psychopathology. *Infant Mental Health Journal,* 22(3): 393–415.

Muris, P., Meesters, C., Merckelbach, H., & Hulsenbeck, P. (2000). Worry in children is related to perceived parental rearing and attachment. *Behaviour Research and Therapy,* 38(5): 487–497.

Murray, L., & Trevarthen, C. (1986). The infant's role in mother–infant communications. *Journal of Child Language,* 13: 15–29.

Novick, K. K., & Novick, J. (2005). *Working with Parents Makes Therapy Work*. Lanham, MD: Jason Aronson.

Offord, D. R., Boyle, M. H., Racine, Y. A., & Fleming, J. E. (1992). Outcome, prognosis, and risk in a longitudinal follow-up study. *Journal of the American Academy of Child and Adolescent Psychiatry, 31*(5): 916–923.

Ogden, T. H. (1987). The transitional oedipal relationship in female development. *International Journal of Psychoanalysis, 68*: 485–498.

Olino, T. M., Pettit, J. W., Klein, D. N., Allen, N. B., Seeley, J. R., & Lewinsohn, P. M. (2008). Influence of parental and grandparental major depressive disorder on behavior problems in early childhood: a three-generation study. *Journal of the American Academy of Child and Adolescent Psychiatry, 47*(1): 53–60.

Oppenheim, D., Emde, R. N., & Warren, S. L. (1997). Children's narrative representations of mothers: their development and associations with child and mother adaptation. *Child Development, 68*(1): 127–138.

Papousek, H., & Papousek, M. (1983). Biological basis of social interactions: implications of research for understanding of behavioural deviance. *Journal of Child Psychology and Psychiatry and Allied Disciplines, 24*: 117–129.

Papousek, M. (1989). Frühe Phasen der Eltern-Kind Beziehungen. *Ergebnisse der entwicklungspsychobiologischen Forschung, 34*: 109–122.

Perner, J., Leekam, S. R., & Wimmer, H. (1987). Three-year-olds' difficulty with false belief: a case for a conceptual deficit. *British Journal of Developmental Psychology, 5*(2): 125–137.

Perren, S., Groeben, M., Stadelmann, S., & von Klitzing, K. (2008). Selbst- und fremdbezogene soziale Kompetenzen: Auswirkungen auf das emotionale Befinden. In: T. Malti & S. Perren (Eds.), *Soziale Kompetenz bei Kindern und Jugendlichen: Entwicklungsprozesse und Förderungsmöglichkeiten* (pp. 89–106). Stuttgart: Kohlhammer.

Perren, S., Stadelmann, S., von Wyl, A., & von Klitzing, K. (2007). Pathways of behavioural and emotional symptoms in kindergarten children: what is the role of pro-social behaviour? *European Child & Adolescent Psychiatry, 16*(4): 209–214.

Premack, D. G., & Woodruff, G. (1978). Does the chimpanzee have a theory of mind? *Behavioral and Brain Sciences, 1*: 515–526.

Racker, H. (1953). A contribution on the problem of counter-transference. *International Journal of Psychoanalysis, 34*: 313–324.

Racker, H. (1970). *Übertragung und Gegenübertragung*. Munich: Ernst Reinhardt.

Radó, S. (1928). The problem of melancholia. *International Journal of Psychoanalysis, 9*: 420–438.

Ravens-Sieberer, U., Wille, N., Bettge, S., & Erhart, M. (2007). Mental health of children and adolescents in Germany. Results from the BELLA study within the German Health Interview and Examination Survey for Children and Adolescents (KiGGS). *Bundesgesundheitsblatt-Gesundheitsforschung-Gesundheitsschutz, 50*(5–6): 871–878.

Richman, N., Stevenson, J., & Graham, G. P. (1982). *Preschool to School: A Behavioral Study.* London: Academic Press.

Rothbaum, F., & Weisz, J. R. (1994). Parental caregiving and child externalizing behavior in a nonclinical sample—a metaanalysis. *Psychological Bulletin, 116*(1): 55–74.

Rudolf, G. (2009). *Strukturbezogene Psychotherapie: Leitfaden zur psychodynamischen Therapie struktureller Störungen.* Stuttgart: Schattauer.

Rudolf, G., Cierpka, M., & Clement, U. (2007). *Psychotherapeutische Medizin und Psychosomatik.* Stuttgart: Thieme.

Rudolph, K. D., Hammen, C., & Burge, D. (1995). Cognitive representations of self, family, and peers in school-age-children—links with social competence and sociometric status. *Child Development, 66*(5): 1385–1402.

Rupprecht-Schampera, U. (1995). The concept of 'early triangulation' as a key to a unified model of hysteria. *International Journal of Psychoanalysis, 76*: 457–473.

Rutter, M. (1989). Isle of Wight revisited: twenty-five years of child psychiatric epidemiology. *Journal of the American Academy of Child and Adolescent Psychiatry, 28*: 633–653.

Rutter, M. (2008). Genes, behaviour, and the social environment: moving beyond the nature–nurture debate. *Journal of Child Psychology and Psychiatry, 49*(3): 353–354.

Rutter, M., & Quinton, D. (1984). Parental psychiatric disorder: effects on children. *Psychological Medicine, 14*(4): 853–880.

Scheithauer, H., & Petermann, F. (1999). Handbook of antisocial behavior. *Zeitschrift für Klinische Psychologie, Psychiatrie und Psychotherapie, 47*(2): 226–231.

Scheithauer, H., Mehren, F., & Petermann, F. (2003). Developmental prevention of antisocial behavior and substance abuse. *Kindheit und Entwicklung, 12*(2): 84–99.

Schmidt, L. A., Fox, N. A., Rubin, K. H., Sternberg, E. M., Gold, P. W., Smith, C. C., & Schulkin, J. (1997). Behavioral and neuroendocrine responses in shy children. *Developmental Psychobiology, 30*(2): 127–140.

Seligman, M. E. P. (1975). *Helplessness: On Depression, Development, and Death.* San Francisco, CA: Freeman.

Shoal, G. D., Giancola, P. R., & Kirillova, G. P. (2003). Salivary cortisol, personality, and aggressive behavior in adolescent boys: a 5-year longitudinal study. *Journal of the American Academy of Child and Adolescent Psychiatry, 42*(9): 1101–1107.

Slade, A., Grienenberger, J., Bernbach, E., Levy, D., & Locker, A. (2005). Maternal reflective functioning, attachment, and the transmission gap: a preliminary study. *Attachment & Human Development, 7*(3): 283–298.

Soulé, M. (1982). L'enfant dans la tête – l'enfant imaginaire. In: T. B. Brazelton (Ed.), *La dynamique du nourrisson* (pp. 135–175). Paris: Les Éditions ESF.

Spitz, R. A. (1957). *No and Yes. On the Genesis of Human Communication.* New York: International Universities Press.

Spitz, R. A. (1963). Life and the dialogue. In: R. Emde (Ed.), *René Spitz: Dialogues from Infancy* (pp. 147–160). New York: International Universities Press.

Spitz, R. A., & Wolf, K. M. (1946). Anaclitic depression: an inquiry into the genesis of psychiatric conditions in early childhood. *Psychoanalytic Study of the Child, 24*: 313–342.

Stadelmann, S., Perren, S., von Wyl, A., & von Klitzing, K. (2007). Associations between family relationships and symptoms/strengths at kindergarten age: what is the role of children's parental representations? *Journal of Child Psychology and Psychiatry, 48*(10): 996–1004.

Steinhausen, H. C., Metzke, C. W., Meier, M., & Kannenberg, R. (1998). Prevalence of child and adolescent psychiatric disorders: the Zurich Epidemiological Study. *Acta Psychiatrica Scandinavica, 98*(4): 262–271.

Sterba, S., Egger, H. L., & Angold, A. (2007). Diagnostic specificity and nonspecificity in the dimensions of preschool psychopathology. *Journal of Child Psychology and Psychiatry, 48*(10): 1005–1013.

Stern, D. (1985). *The Interpersonal World of the Infant. A View from Psychoanalysis and Developmental Psychology.* New York: Basic Books.

Stern, D. (1994). One way to build a clinically relevant baby. *Infant Mental Health Journal, 15*: 9–25.

Target, M., & Fonagy, P. (1994). The efficacy of psychoanalysis for children: prediction of outcome in a developmental context. *Journal of the American Academy of Child and Adolescent Psychiatry, 33*(8): 1134–1144.

Taylor, D. (2005). Klinische Probleme chronischer, refraktärer oder "behandlungsresistenter" Depression. *Psyche-Zeitschrift für Psychoanalyse und ihre Anwendungen, 59*(9–10): 843–863.

Taylor, D. (2010). Das Tavistock-Manual der psychoanalytischen Psychotherapie – unter besonderer Berücksichtigung der chronischen

Depression. *Psyche – Zeitschrift für Psychoanalyse und ihre Anwendungen*, 64(9/10): 833–862.

Tronick, E., & Cohn, J. F. (1989). Infant–mother face-to-face interaction. Age and gender differences in coordination and the occurence of miscoordination. *Child Development*, 60: 85–92.

Tronick, E., & Reck, C. (2009). Infants of depressed mothers. *Harvard Review of Psychiatry*, 17(2): 147–156.

Tronick, E., Als, H., Adamson, L., Wise, S., & Brazelton, B. (1978). The infant's response to entrapment between contradictory messages in face-to-face interaction. *Journal of the American Academy of Child Psychiatry*, 17(1): 1–13.

Tronick, E., Cohn, J., & Shea, E. (1986). The transfer of affect between mothers and infants. In: B. Brazelton & M. Yogman (Eds.), *Affective Development in Infancy* (pp. 11–26). New York: Norwood, Ablex.

Trowell, J., & Etchegoyen, A. (Eds.) (2002). *The Importance of Fathers: A Psychoanalytic Re-evaluation*. Hove: Brunner-Routledge.

Uher, R., & McGuffin, P. (2008). The moderation by the serotonin transporter gene of environmental adversity in the aetiology of mental illness: review and methodological analysis. *Molecular Psychiatry*, 13(2): 131–146.

Verheugt-Pleiter, A. J. E., Zevalkink, J., & Schmeets, M. G. J. (2008). *Mentalizing in Child Therapy. Guidelines for Clinical Practitioners*. London: Karnac.

Von Klitzing, K. (2005). Rivalen oder Bündnispartner? Die Rolle der Eltern bei der analytischen Arbeit mit Kindern *Kinderanalyse*, 13(2): 113–122.

Von Klitzing, K. (2007). Affektive Störungen im Kindes- und Jugendalter (Affective disorders in childhood and adolescence). *Kinderanalyse*, 15(4): 287–304.

Von Klitzing, K. (2008). Depressionen im Kindes- und Jugendalter. *Kinder- und Jugendmedizin*, 8: 18–23.

Von Klitzing, K., & Bürgin, D. (2005). Parental capacities for triadic relationships during pregnancy: early predictors of children's behavioral and representational functioning at preschool age. *Infant Mental Health Journal*, 26(1): 19–39.

Von Klitzing, K., & Stadelmann, S. (2011). Das Kind in der triadischen Beziehungswelt. *Psyche*, 65(9–10): 953–972.

Von Klitzing, K., Kelsay, K., Emde, R. N., Robinson, J., & Schmitz, S. (2000). Gender-specific characteristics of 5-year-olds' play narratives and associations with behavior ratings. *Journal of the American Academy of Child and Adolescent Psychiatry*, 39(8): 1017–1023.

Von Klitzing, K., Perren, S., Klein, A. M., Stadelmann, S., White, L. O., Groeben, M., Holsboer-Trachsler, E., Brand, S., & Hatzinger, M. (2012). The interaction of social risk factors and HPA axis dysregulation in predicting emotional symptoms of five- and six-year-old children. *Journal of Psychiatric Research, 46*: 290–297.

Von Klitzing, K., Simoni, H., & Bürgin, D. (1999). Child development and early triadic relationships. *International Journal of Psychoanalysis, 80*(1): 71–89.

Von Klitzing, K., Simoni, H., Amsler, F., & Bürgin, D. (1999). The role of the father in early family interactions. *Infant Mental Health Journal, 20*: 222–237.

Vreeburg, S. A., Witte, J. G., Hoogendijk, M. D., van Pelt, J., DeRijk, R. H., Verhagen, J. C. M., van Dyck, R., Smit, J. H., Zitman, F. G., & Phennix, B. J. H. (2009). Major depressive disorder and hypothalamic–pituitary–adrenal axis activity: results from a large cohort study. *Archives of General Psychiatry, 66*(6): 617–626.

Weaver, I. C. G., Cervoni, N., Champagne, F. A., D'Alessio, A. C., Sharma, S., Seckl, J. R., Dymov, S., Szyf, M., & Meaney, M. J. (2004). Epigenetic programming by maternal behavior. *Nature Neuroscience, 7*(8): 847–854.

Whaley, S. E., Pinto, A., & Sigman, M. (1999). Characterizing interactions between anxious mothers and their children. *Journal of Consulting and Clinical Psychology, 67*(6): 826–836.

Wiefel, A., Titze, K., Kuntze, L., Winter, M., Seither, C., Witte, B., Lenz, K., Grüters, A., & Lehmkuhl, U. (2007). Diagnostic classification of mental disorders in infants and toddlers age 0 to 5. *Praxis der Kinderpsychologie und Kinderpsychiatrie, 56*(1): 59–81.

Wiegand-Grefe, S., Geers, P., Petermann, F., & Plass, A. (2011). Children of mentally ill parents: the impact of parental psychiatric diagnosis, comorbidity, severity and chronicity on the well-being of children. *Fortschritte in Neurologie, Psychiatrie, 79*(1): 32–40.

Wiegand-Grefe, S., Halverscheid, S., & Plaß-Christl, A. (2011). *Kinder und ihre psychisch kranken Eltern. Familienorientierte Prävention – Der CHIMPs-Beratungsansatz.* Stuttgart: Hogrefe.

Windaus, E. (2006). Psychoanalytische Kurz- und Fokaltherapie bei Kindern, Jugendlichen und ihren Eltern. *Kinderanalyse, 14*(4): 335–365.

Windaus, E. (2007). Psychoanalytische Kurz- und Fokaltherapie bei Kindern, Jugendlichen und ihren Eltern. In: H. Hopf & E. Windaus (Eds.), *Psychoanalytische und tiefenpsychologisch fundierte Kinder- und Jugendlichenpsychotherapie* (pp. 535–551). Munich: Cip-Medien-Verlag.

Winnicott, D. W. (1949). Hate in the counter-transference. *International Journal of Psychoanalysis, 30*: 69–74.

Winnicott, D. W. (1960). Ego distortion in terms of true and false self. In: *The Maturational Processes and the Facilitating Environment* (pp. 140–152). New York: International Universities Press, 1965.

Winnicott, D. W. (1964). What about father? In: *The Child, the Family, and the Outside World* (pp. 113–118). Reading: Addison-Wesley, 1987.

Winnicott, D. W. (1965). *The Family and Individual Development*. London: Tavistock.

Winnicott, D. W. (1967). Mirror-role of mother and family in child development. In: *Playing and Reality* (pp. 111–118). London: Tavistock, 1971.

Winnicott, D. W. (1969). The use of an object. *International Journal of Psychoanalysis, 50*: 711–716.

Winnicott, D. W. (1971a). *Playing and Reality*. London: Tavistock.

Winnicott, D. W. (1971b). *Therapeutic Consultations in Child Psychiatry*. International Psycho-Analytic Library, 87. London: Hogarth Press and the Institute of Psychoanalysis.

Winnicott, D. W. (1980). *The Piggle: An Account of the Psychoanalytic Treatment of a Little Girl*. The International Psychoanalytic Library, 107. London: Hogarth Press and the Institute of Psychoanalysis.

Wittchen, H. U., Kessler, R. C., Pfister, H., & Lieb, M. (2000). Why do people with anxiety disorders become depressed? A prospective-longitudinal community study. *Acta Psychiatrica Scandinavica, 102*: 14–23.

Wood, J. J., McLeod, B. D., Sigman, M., Hwang, W. C., & Chu, B. C. (2003). Parenting and childhood anxiety: theory, empirical findings, and future directions. *Journal of Child Psychology and Psychiatry and Allied Disciplines, 44*(1): 134–151.

Youngblade, L., & Dunn, J. (1995). Individual differences in young children's pretend play with mother and sibling: links to relationships and understanding of other people's feelings and beliefs. *Child Development, 66*: 1472–1492.

Zahn-Waxler, C., Klimes-Dougan, B., & Slattery, M. J. (2000). Internalizing problems of childhood and adolescence: prospects, pitfalls, and progress in understanding the development of anxiety and depression. *Development and Psychopathology, 12*(3): 443–466.

INDEX

For Product Safety Concerns and Information please contact our EU
representative GPSR@taylorandfrancis.com
Taylor & Francis Verlag GmbH, Kaufingerstraße 24, 80331 München, Germany